Celebrating Holy Week
in a Post-Holocaust World

Celebrating Holy Week
in a Post-Holocaust World

HENRY F. KNIGHT

WESTMINSTER
JOHN KNOX PRESS
LOUISVILLE · KENTUCKY

Book design by Sharon Adams
Cover design by designpointinc.com

First edition
Published by Westminster John Knox Press
Louisville, Kentucky

This book is printed on acid-free paper that meets the American National Standards Institute Z39.48 standard. ♾

PRINTED IN THE UNITED STATES OF AMERICA

05 06 07 08 09 10 11 12 13 14 — 10 9 8 7 6 5 4 3 2 1

Library of Congress Cataloging-in-Publication Data

Knight, Henry F.
  Celebrating Holy Week in a post-Holocaust world / Henry F. Knight.— 1st ed.
    p. cm.
  Includes bibliographical references (p.) and index.
  ISBN 0-664-22902-6 (alk. paper)
    1. Holy Week. 2. Holocaust (Christian theology) 3. Jerusalem in Christianity. I. Title.

BV90.K58 2005
263'.925—dc22

2004054989

Contents

Foreword

*E*ncountering Hank Knight has changed me. Reflecting on this change means recalling a critical process of changing consciousness that preceded my engagement of his work. It began some years ago in Toronto. Friends had invited my marriage-partner Barbara and me to what looked like an ordinary dinner party. Of the eight persons present, only two were not known to us. We were introduced to Emil and Rose Fackenheim, and from then on for me personally things changed.

It was some months after the Six Day War in 1967. The change in attitude of the churches in Canada was becoming apparent. There had been admiration for the accomplishments of the state of Israel and the feeling that, being completely surrounded by manifestly hostile nations, Israel needed protection. Now there was an articulated antipathy for Israel, arising from what was said to be oppression of the Palestinian population in territories occupied by the Israeli Defense Forces. Of the people gathered around our friends' dinner table, only the Fackenheims were not associated with the United Church of Canada. The editor of that church's monthly magazine, *The United Church Observer,* had written several pieces, describing from interviews with Palestinian Christians whom he had visited in the Middle East, the treatment they, relatives, and friends had received at the hands of Israelis since 1948, after the establishment of the state of Israel, and since the end of the Six Day War. Dr. A. Forrest, the editor, reaped a controversy uncharacteristic in its furor for Canadians at that time. It preoccupied our conversation around the table that night. At one point, Emil Fackenheim said something I had not heard before: There is now a new God-given commandment: do not give a posthumous victory to Hitler. He did not imply that the United Church of Canada, through its declared support for the editorial freedom of its official publication, was giving Hitler such a victory. But for me, born in Germany during the reign of that dictator, those words of Fackenheim opened up a wholly new perspective on my then incipient engagement of the culture of the perpetrators and the consequent burden of shame and guilt that rests on Germany as a result of the Shoah.

Some time after that dinner party, Emil Fackenheim invited me to a public event in one of Toronto's prominent synagogues, a discussion between himself and Rabbi Richard Rubenstein. The latter had recently published his challenging work *After Auschwitz: Radical Theology and Contemporary Judaism*. To this day, it is difficult for me to describe the impact of their encounter on me. I agreed with so much that both men were saying, even though they themselves did not—perhaps even could not—agree on essential matters. Richard Rubenstein drew me irrevocably into the necessity of facing Christian theology and faith after the Shoah, while Emil Fackenheim bound me firmly to the resolve that no vindication and, therefore, no victory must be possible for Hitler. Any reconsideration of matters of faith and theology that would suggest an even remote opposite to that "new commandment" had to be rejected ipso facto as wrong. A third Jewish theologian, Rabbi Irving Greenberg, later gave me crystal clear contours of my own reconsideration of the church's theology and tradition when he said that no statement, theological or otherwise, ought to be made that would not be credible in the presence of the burning children.

It has been a long journey since those evenings in Toronto. It took me from congregational ministry and its task of preaching regularly from the texts of Holy Scripture to the lecture and seminar rooms of a university and, finally, to a school of theology. The "discipline" that occupied my work there was systematic theology or, as one in the Reformed tradition prefers to say, dogmatics. At first, the company of colleagues that committed themselves to examining Christian theology in the face of the Shoah was small, and the suggestion that there was a possible connection between what Christians believed, what they did in the name of the faith, and the Shoah, was taken to be somewhat of a curiosity. In my personal experience, it has been perceived as the idiosyncrasy of a German with an "Auschwitz complex," a syndrome to be addressed and "healed" with the aid of psychology. For years, the Annual Scholars Conference on the Holocaust and the Church Struggle (now the Holocaust and the Churches) was almost the only place in North America where critical discussion and exchange was possible, allowing for reexamination of one's conclusions, questions, and proposals and for developing a post-Holocaust biblical hermeneutics. The presence there and significant contributions of Jews—rabbis, theologians, writers, teachers and, of value beyond measure, Shoah survivors and descendants of survivors—have given the critical examination of Christian theology and faith, as well as the desire to remain "faithful" to the gospel, a creative and supportive impetus. And it has also raised the inevitable question: Is the New Testament anti-Judaistic and antisemitic?

For a number of years, this is where I personally experienced a profound, a very profound threat. On the one hand, I was rooted in the Protestant Reformation and its nonnegotiable principle of *sola scriptura*; on the other, I was moved by the power of resistance to the tyrants of this world derived from the biblical testimony as exemplified also during the Hitler era in several European countries. I could not concede that this question to and about the New Testament could be answered affirmatively. For such a concession would, as I saw it, provide a scriptural justification to the antisemitic program of Hitler and the anti-Judaism of the churches that had aligned themselves with him. It would, in other words, hand Hitler a posthumous vindication, the very victory prohibited by the "new" commandment Fackenheim speaks of. Yet those "terrible texts" are there in the New Testament. My Jewish colleagues, together with a sizable group of Jewish scholars whose exegetical work I know and respect, found unacceptable the arguments that those texts are not anti-Judaistic and antisemitic.

The way of interpreting biblical texts I had learned in the academy was within the boundaries of the scholarly methods of critical historical and literary studies. But the claim to objectivity and historicity made by these methods, without any reference to what is going on around those who work with them, leaves such approaches finally speechless in face of the Holocaust. Thus, the idea that factors like gender and race, poverty and social class, or—as in this present work—the Shoah have to become an essential factor in the work of biblical and theological scholarship had not occurred to me. The existential dilemma remained.

I was born in Nazi Germany, received my early education there, was baptized in and attended a Lutheran congregation whose leadership belonged to what is known as the Faith Movement of German Christians. My home was not overtly anti-Judaistic or antisemitic, nor did it overtly oppose the policies of Hitler. My father held a relatively high executive position with I. G. Farben, the significant industrial conglomerate. Between the family of the director of the Buna-Project at Auschwitz-Monowitz and our family, there existed a strong bond, and Father went at least once to that Auschwitz Three site. After my studies in Basel, Switzerland, with Karl Barth and especially as my friendship with Emil Fackenheim and Richard Rubenstein deepened, I began to ask Father about what he knew of the Holocaust. I heard repeatedly that he knew nothing. But the question of what is in me of those who gave me the values I live by became very heavy, touching my relation not only to Father and Mother but also to home, church, and faith itself.

It was at this time that I came to know Hank Knight. He was actually fulfilling what I had maintained was an inescapable condition for Christians
seeking to interpret the Bible after the Shoah: namely, work with Jews in the
task of exegesis. Knight, a Protestant, works with other Christians and Jews
in presentations on biblical texts at the Annual Scholars Conference on the
Holocaust and the Churches. During one of those presentations, I came to recognize that my conviction concerning Christian-Jewish cooperation in interpreting the Scriptures after the Shoah had to break through the safe walls of
scholarly or academic theory if it was to mitigate the impact. Observing the
cooperative work of Hank Knight with James Moore, Steve Jacobs, and Zev
Garber, three of his wide range of associates in the project of reading the
Scriptures today, I became aware of how utterly essential making room for
"the other" is in that task. Hank Knight speaks of "hospitality" here: "making
room for the other in one's life and in one's world of relation and significance."[1] According to my belief concerning the possibility of biblical interpretation, "the other" was the Jewish person, the very one whom Germany
had shown utter inhospitality: there was no room for Jews in Germany, with
the German people, in fact, on this earth. Thus, to make room for Jews in the
work of Christians with the Bible is not simply a friendly, collegial gesture,
not simply a matter of honoring a principle, but a frank admission of the
exclusivism—the technical term is "supersessionism"—practiced by Christianity and, hence, its complicity in the Shoah.

I have experienced friendship offered me by Jewish men and women. Their
making room in their lives for me and all they know of me has allowed me to
discover how true it is that, as Karl Marx puts it, shame can be a constructive
emotional power. Facing the shame of the inhospitality that was expressed in
the antisemitism and anti-Judaism of my country and church now also made
it possible for me personally and existentially to face up to the inhospitality
or contempt toward Jews first in my own identity and then in the received
identities of the people and faith community I belong to. All these identities
are, as Hank Knight puts it, "narrated in the stories we tell about ourselves in
scripture and tradition. We must recognize that there is contempt in our narrated identity directed toward otherness per se and the otherness of our significant others, Jews."[2] I believe now that such recognition of the culture of
the perpetrators, which is wider than the Nazis' policies of extermination, is
conditional on hospitality offered to Christians or, more cautiously and personally, to a Christian who is also German and quite likely the child of a per-
petrator in the Shoah.

It is insufficient for Christians to decide unilaterally that their biblical
studies require the presence of Jews in order to be an honest response to

what the Shoah represents. Only Jews can provide this hospitality and Christians can only receive it. If that happens, however, healing can happen, as my experience testifies. Indeed, I have also experienced that healing on both sides. Receiving the gift of hospitality from the very ones whom my upbringing ruled not only unworthy of hospitality, but also incapable of offering anything other than self-serving and mendacious relationships, set free the process of what the rich concept of *metanoia* comprises: a repentant coming to one's senses, entering into analysis free of limits and determining—with the help of those who offer hospitality—to change. Healing here, however, is not a restoration to wholeness but an enabling to recognize one's woundedness and to live creatively within it. In the work at hand, Hank Knight calls it "limping." In my context, "limping" signifies that I have to live and work within the realization that there are no "innocent" texts and no "innocent" biblical studies and that hermeneutics, too, is no "innocent" field of study and research. Post-Shoah hermeneutics has to approach texts of Scripture and Scripture scholarship in face of the history of the anti-Jewish violence that marks the history of the church itself and of Christian theology. And that requires methodologically that my own social location as an interpreter has to be part of the hermeneutical "landscape"—the who, when, where, and how my reading takes place.

When "limping" is applied metaphorically to the study and interpretation of the Scriptures, especially to the so-called "New Testament," the denial of the charge that it includes "dreadful texts"—antisemitic and anti-Judaistic ones, a denial that chiefly serves to protect one's perceived identity—can be left behind. And then, in recognition and acknowledgment of the woundedness that breeds inhospitality, one can take up what Emil Fackenheim calls the "destructive recovery of the Christian Scriptures, of Christian tradition, of the Christian faith."[3] In other words, the offer and gift of hospitality to one whose sense of identity as a follower of Jesus of Nazareth is threatened by the acknowledgment of dreadful antisemitic and anti-Judaistic texts in the Bible permits that recognition and acknowledgment not to be seen as giving Hitler victory posthumously.

In the following pages, Hank Knight shows how the practice of hospitality given and received by both Jews and Christians in interpreting biblical texts may heal the brokenness of the very inhospitality that the history of interpretation of the New Testament nurtured and codified. He focuses on the time in the Christian or church year known as Holy Week, the period that for centuries in Christian Europe was the most dangerous time for Jews: they feared for their very lives. Even when it was not threatening the physical existence of Jews elsewhere, it was the preaching on Holy Week texts that made

Jews feel derogated, diminished, excluded also in North America. Can those texts be reclaimed after the Shoah? Does what the Shoah has made so radically plain about the exclusivism and supersessionism of the triumphalism and contempt of Christian faith and life over all these centuries have the final word and leave Jews and Christians in unmitigated woundedness? Is it a woundedness beyond blessing? Hank Knight phrases the question at the end of this book in the terms used in the book of Ezekiel when it has God ask: "Can these bones [that is, these texts] live?" Whatever qualified the answer given by the ancient prophet— "You know, G-d!"—the answer Christians give today is qualified by their wounded limp, the injury dealt by their own participation and complicity in the culture of the perpetrators. Reading Hank Knight's work shows that a wounded faith, an injured theology, and a limping liturgy may yet also say: "You know, O G-d."

Martin Rumscheidt
Atlantic School of Theology
Easter 2004

NOTES

1. Henry F. Knight, "The Holy Ground of Hospitality: Good News for a Shoah-Tempered World," in Carol Rittner and John K. Roth, eds., *"Good News" after Auschwitz? Christian Faith within a Post-Holocaust World* (Macon, GA: Mercer University Press, 2001), 99.

2. Op. cit., 105–6.

3. Op. cit., 103.

Acknowledgments

As the reflections in this volume attest, I have had many conversation partners in the journey this book recounts. Some have been more direct than others; but all of them have left their mark on me and the resulting text. While I utilize the biblical metaphor of limping to describe the post-Holocaust walk of faith, I am reminded again and again that limping is a way of walking, often because of the support and companionship of colleagues and friends who share the journey with me. At the risk of failing to identify them more fully than they are due, I cannot risk stumbling in this regard. They have meant too much.

Foremost in this project is Martin Rumscheidt. His invitation to prepare a series of lectures for Atlantic School of Theology was the occasion that began this particular project. However, I owe him so much more. Martin and his wife Barbara welcomed me into their world in Nova Scotia and deepened an already important friendship in the process. They introduced me to their friends and colleagues at AST, where they both taught, and made a lecture visit an extensive series of conversations that have enriched me far beyond what this text can express. To Martin and his late wife, Barbara, I am profoundly grateful. Similarly, I wish to thank the students and faculty at Atlantic School of Theology for their hospitality—especially Gérald Caron. While they all welcomed me into their lives through the Nicholson Lectures and Aitken Workshops, Gérald in a special way welcomed me into the class he taught with Martin.

There are other friends who have walked this path with me as well. Early on, my colleagues in the Department of Philosophy and Religion at The University of Tulsa (Jane Ackerman, John Bowlin, Steve Gardner, Russ Hittinger, Jacob Howland, and Richard Lynn) heard the initial plan for the lectures and gave me important feedback during their composition. Partners in the Jewish-Christian Dialogue of the Tulsa National Conference for Community and

Justice offered counsel on many matters related to the lectures and the subsequent book. I am quite sure they are unaware of the scope of their impact on this project, but they have walked much of this journey with me and are mentioned toward the end of the text. In similar ways, members of the Goldner Holocaust Symposium have left their mark. Not only have they helped me think about many of the issues confronted in the text; they have participated in helping shape some of the liturgical offerings shared as case studies in the various chapters. Likewise the students who participate in University Worship at The University of Tulsa: they too have helped me think through how a community of faithful Christians can honor the views discussed in this book in the context of an ongoing worship community.

I owe many others my thanks: members of adult Sunday school classes at Boston Avenue United Methodist Church and members of the Serendipity Group at St. John's Episcopal Church in Tulsa, Oklahoma—Rita Bell, especially; Rebecca Damron from Oklahoma State University, who organized opportunities to test the midrashic strategies in local churches in Stillwater, Oklahoma; and Donald McKim, academic and reference editor at Westminster John Knox Press, who believed in this project and encouraged me in turning extended lectures into the current book. However, I am especially indebted to a post-Shoah midrash group with whom I have been engaged in intensive dialogue for the last decade. James F. Moore, Steven L. Jacobs, and Zev Garber have been partners in a unique project, and from them I have learned the power and grace of sharing the limp of walking in wounded faithfulness. They are companions on the articulated journey this book recounts and more.

Throughout the writing of this book I have been blessed by an understanding family that has encouraged my writing, including the distractions and preoccupations that come from a project like this. With them I have limped in much less articulate ways, often stumbling over my own limitations and oversights. Their grace and generosity have made it possible to continue the walking and, I hope, the progress this work is meant to signify. To them and for them—Pam, my wife; Laura and Paul, my children; and Brooke, my future daughter-in-law—I offer my deepest thanks and gratitude.

Introduction

Limping through Jerusalem

*T*he 2004 release of Mel Gibson's film, *The Passion of the Christ,* initiated widespread public conversation in the United States about the passion story—particularly the role of suffering in its narrative and its negative portrayal of Jews in the texture of that story. In addition, other issues were raised by that film such as questions of historical accuracy, the conflation of the various Gospel testimonies into a single witness, and an understanding of divinity that, in the light of the Holocaust, needs extensive rethinking. Many of those concerns are addressed in the following pages; however, the reflections contained in them are not dependent on, nor formulated in response to, the controversy generated by Gibson's movie. Begun long before, these reflections have grown out of sustained attention over the last two decades to confessionally-based problems raised by Christians who find themselves interrogated by what did and did not happen during the twelve-year darkness we call the Shoah or the Holocaust. Those questions demand more than a passing attempt to deal with a controversial film.

To put the matter boldly, Christian discipleship is a fallible enterprise. That insight may not be new, but in the sobering light of our post-Holocaust world, it speaks to the core of Christian faith and life in haunting ways. As Irving Greenberg has so poignantly put it, the Holocaust is a reorienting event. In its aftermath, thoughtful Christians and their leaders have been wrestling with the task of integrating their problematic relationship toward their Jewish siblings into a holistic sense of Christian history. This work has led to denominational statements and theological projects like Mary Boys's excellent text, *Has God Only One Blessing? Judaism as a Source of Christian Self-Understanding,* which calls for revised confessional narratives and appropriately mended liturgical practices. But rarely has post-Holocaust theological work made a self-conscious connection between reconfigured hermeneutical strategies and practical concerns about how Christians might worship when they gather for the key moments of their common life in our world. The reflections in this volume address the responsibility of guiding others in their liturgical and confessional return to Holy Week in the context of a post-Shoah age.

The chapters that follow began as the C. M. Nicholson Memorial Lectures and the C. D. Ed Aitken Memorial Workshop in Homiletics for the Atlantic School of Theology. The occasion was a week of continuing education for pastors and current seminarians midway through the spring academic year in 2002. I had been asked to address matters of pastoral leadership in preaching and worship for Holy Week, particularly with regard to questions raised by serious encounter with the Holocaust. Originally I delivered only four lectures, supplemented by two workshops and visits in several classes. Since that time I have reworked the lectures significantly, adding additional chapters and integrating the practical concerns originally addressed in the workshops. As a result, I have been able to focus on the full scope of Holy Week, from Palm/Passion Sunday to Easter Sunday morning, addressing a range of methodological and substantive issues that inform the approach I have undertaken in this project.

Because of the thoughtful work of faculty at Atlantic School of Theology, I was not asked to convince others of the importance of doing post-Holocaust theology. Instead, I was able to begin my comments with the understanding that the ecumenical Christian community I was addressing had confronted the need for this kind of work and, furthermore, was ready for the constructive task of searching out new ways to tell and embody the Christian story in preaching and liturgy. My task, therefore, was to extend that concern to the tangible issues experienced in the recurring experience of leading other Christians through the liturgical and homiletical encounter with Holy Week and its central message for Christian faith and life. I have proceeded with a similar assumption in extending those reflections in this volume.

Since my visit came during Lent, just a few weeks before Easter in the first year of the three-year cycle of lectionary readings, I initially chose to follow the liturgical format of Holy Week and the Gospel readings of Matthew, as designated for those occasions. But given the midrashic thrust of the project, letting Matthew be the primary guide for this act of liturgical return is hermeneutically fitting as well. As I hope I have demonstrated throughout the text, Matthew's narrative portrait of Jesus is thoroughly midrashic and self-consciously constructed according to the Hebrew Scriptures. Hence, following Matthew's lead makes methodological as well as liturgical sense, a point I have sought to make in the opening chapter. Indeed, chapter 1 is devoted to the question of how one returns to Holy Week in our post-Shoah circumstances. The matter is addressed confessionally as well as methodologically and concludes with thoughts about how a pastor and congregation might embody such an approach. The chapter describes the movement of post-Shoah confessional return to Jerusalem, building double and triple entendres on the notions of a *confessional return*. In addition, I introduce the midrashic voice I will be employing throughout the book as the narrative approach that will be guiding this particular return, according to the Scriptures. Although it will be described in some detail in the opening chapter, midrash is a way of interpreting present experience as well as specific texts of Scripture by relying on the full body of Scripture to focus that work. Therefore, those who use midrash read their experience and their texts "according to the Scriptures." Scripture becomes an interpretive lens to view the world much like a prism enables its users to see the manifold richness of light in its refracted bands of color. The goal of such a process is not so much to find a single and correct meaning, or understanding, of a particular circumstance or text, but to engage it faithfully, by being guided by the resources one finds within the narrated world of the biblical witness. In this way, Scripture is used to interpret itself as well as to shape the way one dwells in the world. At the same time, how one experiences the world informs the way one inhabits the covenantal universe of the biblical text. A more extensive explanation will follow in chapter 1.

Chapter 2 begins the combined liturgical and confessional work of return by focusing on the issues that are raised at the head of the week, as Jerusalem is entered with other pilgrims making their way to the Holy City. The chapter concludes with an offering not unlike offerings that would have concluded earlier pilgrimages to the Holy City—at least in their intention.

Chapter 3 examines the conflict Jesus generated in the temple courtyard, the ostensible cause of the arrest, trial, and crucifixion. In the process of pondering the shape of this conflict, I hope to connect it to the actions that Jesus undertook at the table in the so-called upper room, enlarging the shape of the conflict usually associated with Jesus and the temple authorities in Jerusalem. In this way I intend to show that post-Shoah, the followers of Jesus must be willing to let themselves be confounded by this one who takes his disciples back to center, daring them, and now us, to reconsider how we approach and shape the holy. As in the previous chapter and in the remainder of the book, the chapter concludes with another liturgical offering presented for critique and consideration, seeking in the process a small measure of form-content correspondence in the recursive movement through this week's story.

Chapter 4 explores Jesus' time of crisis by asking about the nature of the cup he faced during his night of anguish. That dilemma invites us to come to terms with what Jesus called the rule and realm of heaven and what I have attempted to describe using the metaphor of hospitality as a gestalt of generosity and grace. In this regard, the historic night of the Shoah becomes the multilayered context for examining the trials of Maundy or Holy Thursday as they were manifest in the Last Supper, the night watch in Gethsemane, and the interrogations before Caiaphas and Pilate.

Chapter 5 concentrates on Good Friday and Holy Saturday by examining how we make our confessional return to the crucifixion and its aftermath. In this chapter my goal is to face the consequences of the political and covenantal crises that led to the cross, trusting that the cross does not have the final word—yet willing to face the possibility that it does. That is, I have sought to incorporate the risk that marks the crucifixion as the crisis that it is.

Chapter 6 was not part of the original lectures. At that time, I identified a missing Easter lecture that qualified the way I approached the crucifixion, as it did each of the other moments I had previously addressed. Since that time, I have separated those concluding comments from that earlier presentation and expanded them, as I promised I would, into an additional set of reflections on the empty tomb and the experience of a resurrected Christ. I should be clear now, as I hope I was then. This added chapter on Easter is not offered to *complete* the book, since this project remains open for me. Rather, together with amended versions of the earlier lectures, this chapter is offered as a path forward that I hope remains confessionally responsible as it limps out of Jerusalem on its way to the promised land and the future. That path forward is signaled by the concluding chapter that points the way back to the garden of the text and its continuing nurture for the unfinished journey that distinguishes a midrashic approach. It is meant to keep the story open and invite others into its way—like a concluding Sabbath rest before the pilgrimage resumes.

The confessional shape of the book, like that of the lectures, remains at least fourfold. It demands that I come to terms with the biblical witness as authentically as I can, that I face up to Christian history vis-à-vis Jews and their identities before God and neighbor, that I deal honestly and forthrightly with the more recent history of Nazi atrocity preceding and during World War II, and that I do so in a manner that personally embodies the concerns for doing such theological reflection in a self-consciously more responsible way. In short, the work must be authentically faithful to historic Christian identity, thoroughly rooted in the biblical witness, unashamedly forthright about a shameful and violent history of Christian identity built from the negative significance of Jewish life, and responsible to the reality of others (Christians and Jews as well as others) in the present. Whether or not I have been able to maintain fidelity to this confessional agenda will be up to others to decide. However, to bear that responsibility has been my uppermost goal throughout.

The book now incorporates strategies developed in the workshops I led at Atlantic School of Theology and later refined with my students at The University of Tulsa as well as local congregations in Stillwater and Tulsa, Oklahoma. They are offered as case studies for limping into action. Like the journey described in the text, they remain unfinished and are certainly flawed. Still, it is my hope that they may serve as landmarks for others to use as they undertake their own limping return to Jerusalem. Let the journey begin.

Chapter 1

Approaching Jerusalem

A Wounded Return to the Promised Land

The Confessional Dilemma

Palm Sunday. New clothes. New shoes. Excitement. Those are the words I can retrieve from my earliest memories of Palm Sunday and Easter. Anticipating Easter, our family bought new clothes, dressed up, then took family photos to send to relatives for Easter. That was the family tradition in my 1950s childhood. Easter began early with the celebrations and preparations of Palm Sunday. Then, a week later, usually with a drive to my grandparents' home, we joined hundreds of others as we packed the church sanctuary for the big Easter fanfare.

Later, as a seminarian in the early 1970s, and then as a young pastor, I participated in my denomination's newly restructured liturgical format for Holy Week. The United Methodists, my denomination, had joined others and shifted gears in a movement of liturgical reform challenging the easy enthusiasm of Palm Sunday parades with the sobering story of Jesus' passion and crucifixion. Palm Sunday had become Palm/Passion Sunday. The cross was put back into the story as triumph was tempered by suffering. But triumph remained, even when cast in sacrificial garb.

Hosannas were delayed, to be sure; they were suspended until Easter. But they remained, nonetheless, in the silent background. "Blessed is the one who comes in the name of the Lord" was challenged by "Is it I, Lord?" and "Crucify him!" then "Why have you forsaken me?" and "Forgive them, for they know not what they do." Then, finally, "It is finished."

Liturgical reform brought a return to center—restoration of the passion as the heart of the Christian story. But the triumphalistic theology remained, cast in the guise of a victorious cross. I was prepared for this, or thought I was, by my seminary education, through recurring and sometimes rather strong critiques of the manifest and latent theologies of glory that hopscotched over the suffering of others. But I was unprepared for the silent cry I would learn to hear later.

It began for me with a small book by Franklin Littell, *The Crucifixion of the Jews,* which I read in dialogue with Elie Wiesel's *Night* and other early works of his. Immersing myself in this material, I eventually discerned a fearful curse that shadowed the shouts of victory and blessing that punctuate our celebrations of Holy Week. I was shocked and disillusioned by what I was learning to hear: "Cursed is the one who comes in the name of the Lord."

Now I have not actually heard these words spoken aloud. But I know they have been felt and directed at Christians like me. What else could the Jews of Trier in the western Rhine River valley have felt when approaching crusaders, bound for the Holy Land, began to slaughter them, their brothers and sisters, their sons and daughters, their mother and fathers—because they were the "infidels" at hand? What else could Jews summoned to disputation have felt when a representative of the Inquisition approached them, demanding they defend their faith before representatives of the church? What else could Jews in eastern Europe have felt when Christians stirred up by sermons and dramatic portrayals of their Master's suffering came looking for someone to punish for the death of their Savior? What else could Jews living in the shadows of their local church have felt when the Nazis came to transport them to the east and no one voiced their opposition? Now none of these things happened in every case. But they happened enough for their images to haunt their victims and for this testimony to have disturbing continuity.

An excerpt from Andre Schwarz-Bart's *Last of the Just* makes the point dramatically. In it, two lovers, Golda and Ernie, are speaking just prior to being deported to Auschwitz:

> "Oh, Ernie," Golda said, "You know them. Tell me, why, why do the Christians hate us the way they do? They seem so nice when I can look at them without my star."
>
> Ernie put his arm around her shoulders solemnly. "It's very mysterious," he murmured in Yiddish. They don't know exactly why themselves. I've been in their churches and I've read their gospel. Do you know who the Christ was? A simple Jew like your father. A kind of Hasid."
>
> Golda smiled gently. "You're kidding me."
>
> "No, no, believe me, and I'll bet they'd have got along fine, the two of them, because he was really a good Jew, you know, sort of like the Baal Shem Tov—a merciful man, and gentle. The Christians say they love him, but I think they hate him without knowing it. So, they take the cross by the other end and make a sword out of it and strike us with it! You understand, Golda," he cried suddenly, strangely excited, "they take the cross and they turn it around, they turn it around, my God . . . ."[1]

We can say that what Golda and Ernie describe is all an aberration. To be sure, it *is* aberrant. But it is more than that. James Carroll has grasped what is at stake and chosen to wrestle with it in his popular history, *Constantine's Sword*. One doesn't have to agree with all of his historical reconstructions to recognize the force of his argument either. The problems of anti-Judaism and later of antisemitism, as well as those of displacement theology and supersessionism, are not just aberrations of Christian identity; they are intimately tied to it, woven into its fabric. They form what Franklin Littell has called a "crisis of credibility," what Alan Egglestone calls a "cancer in the Body of Christ," what Kendall Soulen calls a "flaw in the heart of the crystal," what Rosemary Ruether calls "the left hand of Christology," and what Regina Schwartz calls an "identity born of scarcity and violence." The problem is not just one of behavior, as tragic as that is; it is also, and more importantly, a problem of identity.

Theologians who have focused on the Shoah as a reorienting moment in Jewish and Christian history have identified several important and interrelated dimensions of this problem. We can summarize them in the following manner, recognizing that they weave in and out of the fabric of Christian identity in subtle as well as overt ways:

1. The Shoah could not have happened without Christian complicity regarding widespread anti-Jewish attitudes and antisemitic beliefs about Jews. That is, the anti-Judaic sentiment and rhetoric of Christian identity vis-à-vis Jewish others built up the soil of anti-Jewish prejudice without which widespread antisemitism could not have taken root and grown in western Europe. It has served as compost, fertilizing the terrain with vitriol and, all too frequently, contempt.

2. Christian contempt for the Jewish other has been utilized in the building of Christian identity by way of a negative portrayal of a rival other whose identity Christians have taken over, as they understand it, in a more faithful form.

3. This sentiment is supported by a logic of displacement in the biblical story of a covenanting God. Called supersessionism, this logic builds on the notion that Christianity has surpassed and replaced Judaism as the people of God and is the rightful heir of the name Israel and Israel's identity as God's representative people.

4. The nature of the suffering in the Shoah, particularly that which stalked the one and a half million Jewish children slaughtered by the Nazis, exposes a flaw, perhaps the flaw, in covenantal theism's view of God and divine providence. This exposure echoes that of the Job story, where the limits of the conventional covenantal piety of the day failed to account for Job's situation and the victimization of Job's family. By extension, Job's

ten children become the 1.5 million children of the Shoah, symbolized by the burning children of Auschwitz, and they challenge even the most sophisticated views of covenantal theism. In the face of all this, how does one conceive of God? This question, however, stalks not only Christianity but Judaism as well.

These issues punctuate the form and content, the structure and substance of Christian identity in ways that demand a careful reexamination of how we approach the problem. As with Job, the task is how to face these problematic dimensions and integrate them into our daily lives and shared worlds while maintaining an integrity that in the process abandons neither the suffering children nor our faith. To be sure, also like Job, we may be changed in that same process as we take on this challenge.

The confessional nature of the problem is captured in two brief statements that for me form twin prayers that guide my work. The first is from Psalm 19: "Let the words of my mouth and the meditation of my heart be acceptable to you, O LORD, my rock and my redeemer." The second I learned from a brave and insightful Orthodox rabbi, Irving Greenberg: "No statement, theological or otherwise, should be uttered that would not be credible in the presence of the burning children."[2] These statements frame my work daily, whether I am in the classroom, working at my computer, or standing in the pulpit or behind the Lord's Table in my university's chapel. The first calls me to be faithful in my words and deeds to the witness of Scripture and to the Holy One whom Scripture mediates. The second calls me to be responsible with my words and deeds to those victims who perished in the fires of hatred, stoked and fueled by religious disdain and a long legacy of faith-based contempt, for which I continue to bear and confess responsibility. So I have learned to pray, "May the words of my mouth and the meditations of my heart be acceptable in your sight, O God, and may they be credible in the presence of the burning children."

By Way of the Jabbok—A Midrashic Approach

"How does one worship in such a context? How does one dare not?" Emil Fackenheim determined that the way forward had to be midrashic. He explains, in a brilliant little book called *God's Presence in History*, that Jewish tradition modifies and qualifies its relationship to its root experiences within a midrashic framework characterized by what he calls a dialectical form of narrative resistance.[3] Dwelling within the biblical story, those faithful to the narrated root experience (e.g., the gift of Torah at Sinai) raise probing questions generated in their own unfolding reality and pose them to the root events themselves, pushing and resisting the very story they trust. But those who pose their questions do so as participants in their story. At the same time, the story and its root experience resist the questions being posed to them by providing the framework and the vantage points for raising such questions. Fackenheim calls the result a narrative "stubbornness" that meets an equally "unyielding realism."[4] New understandings arise from and about the story as hitherto unperceived dimensions in the problematic experience are recognized and incorporated into an expanding tradition. In this way, the narrated tradition is used to challenge itself in a lively and dynamic manner.

For over ten years three colleagues and I have been engaged in precisely this kind of midrashic dialogue.[5] Working self-consciously as two Christians and two Jews, we have tried to hold our concerns together: to do theology together in dialogue as post-Shoah Jews and Christians and to do it midrashically, wrestling with each other's texts. Our first gathering began by facing a text that has described, for me, this effort ever since: Genesis 32:22–33. Again and again I have returned to the story of Jacob at the Jabbok, to clarify what I am doing and to remind myself of what is at stake in this enterprise. Indeed, I have discovered that Jacob's story of estrangement and attempted reconciliation continues to provide a guiding metaphor for my own efforts in this regard. The work of post-Shoah faithfulness is always flawed; one walks this path limping. Indeed, pre-Shoah faithfulness was also flawed; but the limping was overlooked and at best only myopically understood.

Moreover, in my encounter with my colleagues I learned the promise of midrashic discourse to hold and shape our struggles with this flawed faithfulness. The story of Jacob's encounter at the Jabbok mirrored both the larger legacy of Christian relations with Jewish siblings and my own attempt to face up to this problematic legacy in my own identity. Midrashic struggle gave me a way to come to terms with the violence embedded in my narrative identity and then to move forward without remaining trapped in the shame occasioned by my discovery of this negative component at the heart of my historic identity vis-à-vis Jews.

The story of Jacob's night struggle is familiar. After a twenty-year exile from his estranged brother, Jacob had set out on a journey home. As he approached the encounter with Esau and prepared to cross over the river that separated them, he sent all his family, animals, and possessions ahead and camped for the night. The next morning he would face Esau and all that Esau might bring to their encounter. That night, as the story puts it, Jacob wrestled with a mysterious, unnamed figure, an *ish* or man. Together they struggled through the night, with Jacob refusing to let go of his assailant until he secured a blessing and the assailant's name. Likewise, the assailant asked to know Jacob's identity before releasing Jacob from his grip. Jacob revealed himself; the *ish,* in return, blessed him and gave him his release and a new name, Israel, for he had striven with human beings and with God and not been overcome. He had prevailed, survived. In the process, however, the unknown figure did not reveal his identity to Jacob. Instead he asked Jacob why he wanted to know. The story simply concludes that Jacob, now Israel, emerged from that encounter limping, wounded by the wrestling or the *ish* or perhaps both. And when he departed, he named the place (not the *ish)* Peniel/Penuel, meaning "the face of God."

Jacob brought a mixed legacy of deceit and struggle to that night, including the history of his relationships with his father, his mother, and his brother and the accompanying shame and fear. Likewise he brought his relationships with his uncle and his wives. In short, Jacob brought an entire lifetime to that night. When I first joined my colleagues and entered that story and its dynamics with them, I found I was facing my own mixed legacy with estranged siblings, as I faced Jacob struggling with his. I was bringing an historic lifetime and its accompanying shame and fear. I too was facing a history of usurpation that marked my historic relationship to Jewish brothers and sisters over the centuries. Indeed, I was facing up to it; and I was doing so in the morning shadows of a distinctively tragic night. My questions of the text opened the text at the same time they opened my own history for new exploration:

- Who was the figure that Jacob faced?
- Why was that figure unnamed in the story?
- Could the figure be more than one significant other Jacob faced in his life?
- Why did the unnamed assailant ask Jacob his name but not give one in return?
- Why after the night of struggle did Jacob name the place as he did, but not his assailant?
- Why did Jacob, now Israel, limp?
- What does it lead us to ponder when we remember that Jacob emerges from this night with the reconfigured identity of Israel, but that in doing so he limps thereafter?

Working with questions like these and bringing them to bear on the text and on our own post-Shoah situations, my colleagues and I wrestled with the text just as Jacob wrestled with his other—facing manifold others at the river bank. Like Jacob, we held on, insisting that the text bless us by addressing (though perhaps not answering) our questions, as the text, in turn, asked questions of us. And like Jacob I was wounded and blessed in the process, moving from the Jabbok to the promised land beyond, walking with a limp. I will not presume to speak for my colleagues with regard to how they emerged from this encounter, but since then I have approached every text with the full awareness of the flawed and mixed legacy I bring to it. In other words, my approach to Torah and to the New Testament is wrapped in contrition and undertaken with the full awareness of past misreadings and supersessionary distortions. To put the matter figuratively, facing any text in its full, inquiring otherness means I face it limping. But such an approach is more than penitential, even if it limps. Approaching the biblical text by way of the Jabbok includes the other dynamics that distinguish this story as well.

In midrash, the text generates questions for the reader by means of the gaps or open spaces left in the story. Or to put the matter as Geoffrey Hartman has phrased it, the frictionality of the text is key.[6] Wherever the text doesn't fit neatly together, the text provides a doorway to penetrate more deeply into the dynamics being expressed in the text. In the case of Jacob at the Jabbok, the questions raised above are evoked by the oddities the reader notes when reading the text closely and attentively. The gaps become what the rabbis called the "white fire" or the open spaces between the words that generate intensive grappling with the text and its issues.

When I entered that first midrashic conversation with my three colleagues, I was taken by the text directly into the problematic history of estranged siblings—Jacob and Esau as well as ourselves. I was led deeper into the conflated nights of anguish to which we had committed our dialogue: the night described in our text, the nights of intense introspection vis-à-vis estranged relationships, the nights of faithful anguish regarding our mixed legacies, and the twelve-year night of devastation and destruction we call the Shoah. Since then my colleagues and I have met annually to discuss a number of different texts together, every time working with one from the Hebrew Scriptures and one from the Christian New Testament. In each case, I have returned again and again to the banks of the Jabbok—to face up to the dynamics of estranged siblings and to follow the example of Jacob—grasping hold of the texts before us as well as my dialogue partners and the history that has brought us to such a threshold, while wrestling with each of these significant others in my life until being blessed in the process. And as with Jacob, each struggle wounds as it heals.

Through the help of my colleagues I have discovered a text that mirrors the multifaceted circumstances of our post-Shoah dilemma. It describes a situation of estrangement between two of Abraham's descendants. That estrangement had lingered for twenty years, half a generation's time, without healing.

A similar estrangement between Abraham's descendants has lasted for two millennia, likewise without healing. As I enter into the dynamics of this historic narrative, I am struck by a strange reversal of roles, wherein Jacob/Israel's legacy has been usurped by those with whom I identify. Christianity has claimed the birthright and blessing of Israel in ways that deny Jacob his claim. And now, in using this very story to express that displacement, I even run the risk of theological theft once again, unless I enter its dynamics dialogically with Jewish conversation partners.

To put the matter boldly, we Christians begin with a long history of theological theft with regard to our Jewish siblings. We have read our texts with a logic that usurps their place in the covenantal story by displacing them from their rightful inheritance. Furthermore, we have moved via that displacement logic to a form of triumphalism that has fed historic attitudes of contempt and disdain toward our covenantal siblings. Facing up to the negative place we give this still-signifying other in our lives, brings us face-to-face with a shameful legacy that must give way to a new relationship. We enter that new relationship, as the story at the Jabbok suggests, with a reconfigured sense of ourselves and our relationship to this displaced other, wounded by our awareness of how we have built or narrated our identity at the expense of that other. In the case of Jacob, his new identity of Israel is that of one who walks with a limp. He walks, but always with the sign of this struggle modifying his way of walking. Indeed, this story suggests that the larger story of Israel's walk with God and others is always one that limps. That is, it is imperfect in its embodiment. We can view that larger story negatively, as many Christian readings of the Hebrew Scriptures have done, and see the communal story of Israel as that of a people who have failed in their fidelity to God. However, in the morning light of the Jabbok, the story of Israel's walk may be more authentically recounted as a confessional acknowledgment of the always-flawed nature of walking in God's ways.

In this way, Jacob's/Israel's story becomes a paradigm for walking with the other/Other in our lives. We limp. As western Christians return to this story after centuries of exile from it, we can learn, as Jacob did, a way of proceeding that requires acknowledgment and understanding of our own flaws. And that understanding must be integrated into the reconfigured identity that emerges from such a life-changing encounter. Hence, each time we encounter the other/Other, either in person or in a text, we do so with the awareness that we will limp. Or to return to the image that emerged for me, every encounter with the biblical text in our post-Shoah context is undertaken on the banks of the River Jabbok.[7] And I have come to this awareness midrashically, according to the Scriptures.

Midrashic Dialogue

Limping translates into a fundamental assumption for me now as I work with our biblical and theological texts post-Shoah. Past encounters, as well as present and future ones, are and will be flawed. So we need the help of others. In other words, dialogue is fundamental to this work, not just incidental. We do our wrestling with the text ever aware that we must listen closely to what others in the conversation have to show us about the texts and about ourselves, no matter how discomforting that might be. Consequently the goal of such conversation should not be to convince our conversation partners that our interpretations are right; we know they are unfinished and incomplete at best. Rather our task is to venture into the world of the text together, prepared to encounter ourselves, the troubling world within and around us, and the witness of the text in what may be reorienting ways.

In Jacob's encounter with the *ish,* the text emphasizes Jacob's tenacity in holding on to the other with whom he struggles. As the text reports, Jacob declares, "I will not let you go, unless you bless me." We must be equally insistent and learn not to let go of the other, whether a human partner in dialogue, the text, or both. In fidelity to the text we can take what it presents to us and wrestle with its otherness; yet we dare not relinquish the questions we bring to it, questions generated by the issues occasioned by the Shoah, or the flawed nature of our grappling. Rather, we proceed by way of a challenging and sometimes playful dialectic—walking, limping as it were, with others in the way of midrash.

Fackenheim concluded that the return to the Jewish Bible could occur only in a midrashic framework, whereby its "narrative stubbornness" would be held in tension with an "unyielding realism" that was committed to an honest encounter with human suffering. His comments express a similar sentiment by Douglas John Hall, perhaps the preeminent North American Christian theologian of the last fifty years. Drawing upon what he calls the Jerusalem tradition shared by Christians and Jews, Hall argues for a truly dialectical faith that lives and thrives in the tension between honest confrontation and wrestling with human suffering and the promise that death does not have the last word in creation. Adopting language similar to Dietrich Bonhoeffer's, he calls this "costly hope."[8] It shares with Fackenheim the tenacity of holding tight in the name of compassion to the humanity that we all share and to the God of creation, who intended and still intends an abundant life for all creation. That is, we do not let go of suffering victims in order to affirm what our theology tells us. Rather, suffering humans summon us to demand even more from our theological traditions.

Emmanuel Levinas articulates the same kind of tenacity in his essay "The Temptation of Temptation"; however, he begins with the givenness of the biblical text by which people of faith derive their identities. He points out that while we never let go of this source, in the name of responsibility to the other, we must never cease to challenge the text to come to terms with the other and the other's needs and concerns. Indeed, Levinas points out the creative quality that comes from this unceasing dialectic, explaining that often the text yields far more than its biblical authors may have intended; but this is the depth and richness of creation embodied in the text and the covenantal partnership in which the text is honored and served. The "temptation of temptation" is to collapse the tension and its accompanying ambiguity.

In this way, I have learned to walk the path that Emil Fackenheim says we must. However, as a Christian walking that path I have sought to incorporate J. B. Metz's admonition to Christian interpreters that we must make our return in solidarity with the victims.[9] They or their representatives must be included as partners in the interpretive enterprise. They are significant others with whom we must make our way as we undertake this journey. Whether that happens literally or through written dialogue, or in some combination, as it has for me, will depend upon individual circumstances.

With these strategies and fundamental commitments guiding the way, I have learned to move from the Jabbok to other texts and their stories. I have been helped most in this regard by working with the Gospel of Matthew, since Matthew seems to be constructed midrashically, according to the Scriptures—most especially in its use of the master story of exodus and its Mosaic traditions. To be sure, one may read Matthew as if it were written to show how its good news and portrait of Jesus were predicted in the Hebrew texts that were used by Matthew to tell his story. A midrashic approach suggests a different strategy: Matthew wrote from his own knowledge of the Hebrew Scriptures to convey his experiences with the figure named Jesus. It was the anchor in his knowing, even when he stretched its meaning beyond the accepted boundaries of interpretation to account for the life-changing encounter he had experienced with Jesus. While this point may sound minor or heavily nuanced, its impact is significant.

As Michael Polanyi has made clear, all our knowing is rooted knowing. All knowing, he argues, is situated; it has a *from-to* quality. We know from an already known or trusted reality that orients the knowing of our focal awareness. Polanyi called these paired aspects of our knowing the tacit and explicit, or subsidiary and focal dimensions of human knowing. We know from something to something else. Christians need only turn to the Gospel of Matthew to see this quality demonstrated with power and grace. Matthew (or whomever Matthew might have been) knew from his understandings of Torah to the new experiences he was integrating with regard to Jesus. He used his knowledge of Torah to make sense of his experiences with Jesus.

Importantly, Matthew was not presuming to fully understand Jesus and then seek typological verification in the Hebrew Bible. Rather, he was relying on the world he had been given by the Hebrew Bible to understand the significance and character of this one who was (still) transforming his life. We can put the matter figuratively, according to the Scriptures, in the following way:

> Matthew knows from Sinai to Jesus and in turn reflects back upon the Sinai material . . . .
>
> The stylistic rendering of the Jesus story we meet in *Matthew* utilizes the larger story of the Jewish people to tell his story of Jesus. It requires a thorough knowledge of the exodus tradition, the story of Moses and the midrashic style of relating to it. What is known and cherished by Matthew and his audience is used to illumine and clarify the identity of Jesus. Allusions to existing scripture, whether explicit or implicit, are at best unclear or arbitrary unless the larger narrative context of the Torah is used by the hearer/reader in orienting and understanding Matthew's task. When we try to learn this contexting story by way of the narrative embedded in the larger one, we reverse the hermeneutic employed by Matthew. To be sure, Matthew reads the Torah back from Jesus, as a fully interactive critique. But he begins knowing Torah first. His knowing is interactive, moving from Torah to Jesus and then back. Typically, Christians have read the Matthean tradition in the reverse manner, and more often than not, failing to retain the interactive quality of Matthew's way of knowing.[10]

After Auschwitz and as an expression of a reconfigured Christian identity, Christian readers of the Gospels must recover this forgotten dynamic if they are going to free themselves from the myopia of their displacement logic. The study of midrash and the incorporation of its way of knowing according to the Hebrew Scriptures offers an important way forward. But Christians must be careful when they choose this path, lest they overstep the boundaries that continue to separate Jewish and Christian ways of dwelling in the world and reading our texts. We must guard against any temptation to take over a Jewish hermeneutic whose tradition has developed in ways that remain other to us as Christians. Still we may work midrashically, seeking to recover the thoroughly Jewish dynamics that have been preserved in the biblical texts and that were most probably active in some form as these texts were taking shape. That is, we may approach our texts midrashically, keeping our work in constant dialogue with midrash proper, but never confused with the formal work of midrash itself. And when our study is enhanced by actual dialogue as well, it helps clarify our differences at the same time we discover common ground in the narrated worlds of each other's texts.

Reading Midrashically, Not Typologically

As we proceed along this path it will also be helpful to distinguish doing midrash from reading Scripture typologically. In the case of Christian hermeneutics, midrashic dialogue provides a way of moving beyond the displacement logic of triumphalisitic theologizing; typology does not. According to Sandra Schwartz, typology is a way of focusing the reading of a collection of texts in order to show their shared commitment to a uniform message or overarching meaning and truth. Typology is monolithic. She writes:

> There is little room for genuine innovation in typology, not because the canon is closed—typology promiscuously welcomes virtually all variations—but because all of these variations are reducible to one story. All events, biblical and postbiblical, all narratives, biblical and extrabiblical, are simply shadows of the real story, [for example,] the fall of man and his redemption by Christ. A procedure that looks proliferating is instead totalizing, cramming all memories into its vast interpretive maw.[11]

Midrash, on the other hand, is a way for keeping a "closed canon" open. Midrash acts as a hermeneutical wedge, resisting one meaning of a text by positing alternative readings, while relying on the text itself to do the resisting. Michael Fishbane has expressed it well:

> For the truth of midrash is not the truth of historical information or textual analysis. It is the truth of the power of scriptural words to draw a reader into an authentic relationship with the mystery of the world—a world constituted by speech and the face-to-face relations which *Gesprochenheit* [genuine spokenness] demands.[12]

In our post-Shoah context, this contrast provides a way of resisting what Schwartz calls a form of interpretive imperialism that breeds a logic of scarcity, which in turn feeds a displacing violence toward the religious other. While Schwartz does not explore the contrasting logic of midrash, it operates according to a logic of plenitude that fosters interpretive openness to an abundance of meanings.

Midrash seeks to reenter the text as a network of dynamic relations whose meanings depend upon and grow out of its own ecology of textual relationships. In fact, Michael Fishbane, seeking to recover the richness of midrashic discourse, compares the narrated world of the text to that of an orchard. He utilizes the medieval acronym *PaRDeS* (a Persian loanword meaning "orchard") as a prism to focus the interactive texture of this narrative garden of delight. He adapts the traditional four levels of the text represented by the acronym to stand for a more dynamic model of four interactive dimensions. According to the medieval model, the first level, *peshat,* corresponds to the plain meaning of the text. The second level, the allegorical meaning of the text, is its *remez.* The third level of the text, its *derash,* corresponds to the intrinsic meaning of the text; and the fourth level, its spiritual or secret meaning, is its *sod.* Fishbane has proposed viewing the plain meaning of the text, its *peshat,* as its givenness, which is never as simple as one might think, but always the limit for any interpretation, however elastic its *peshat* may turn out to be. The external meanings brought to the text by scholars regarding its social, cultural, and historical contexts, as well as traditional meanings associated with it, Fishbane identifies with the external character of allegory, the *remez* of the text. The derived meanings of the text that grow out of close and critical readings of the text and its immediate textual setting, he identifies with *derash.* The spiritual meanings that bring integration, insight, and wholeness for the reader or listener he links to the secret of the text, its *sod.* Together, these differentiated moments of interpretation form an abundant textual ecology of meaning, its *PaRDeS.*[13] That is, the narrated world of the text is a richly textured orchard of meaning. Incidentally, the Persian word *pardes* is the word from which we also derive the word *paradise.*

Importantly, *PaRDeS* is more than the narrative or even a metanarrative. It is a narrated world, to be sure, but it is not subsumed under a single narrative plot. Rather, it is a narrated world complexly punctuated by contrasting and sometimes fragmented stories and other internal ambiguities. As well, *PaRDeS* not only describes the partnership between God and Israel; it mediates it. That is, the partnership itself is conveyed along with the narrated renderings of it. In other words, *PaRDeS* is narrated, but it is more than narrative; it is also a world of covenanted partnership. The act of interpretation unfolds in and extends that partnership in the ongoing creation of its covenantal world.

Reading midrashically should also be distinguished from recovering midrash as a missing form or genre of biblical interpretation that we can restore as the "right" interpretation of a particular passage, as Bishop John Shelby Spong attempts to do. While much of Spong's work is bold and refreshing, he is nonetheless trapped in a view that looks for the text to have only one correct meaning and that sees the task of the interpreter as discerning the true or correct meaning of a text, which may or may not be an unending process. In Spong's case, he is not foreclosing the dialogue on the meaning of the text, but he is seeking the singularly correct meaning; when or as that meaning is determined, the interpreter's task is to help his reader or listener relate to that proper interpretation. Midrashic reading, however, does not search for the only or single meaning of a text but seeks to open the text to its several and, at times, many possible meanings. The task is not to find what the text means and then proceed with the correctly recovered truth, which exists on its own merit, but to return to the world of the text so that its richly textured orchard of meaning can bear fruit for the gardeners tending its orchard.

The Pastoral Task

What then is the goal of our preaching and liturgical leadership when we approach Jerusalem and Holy Week in this fashion? The pastoral task begins by cultivating a penitential walk that acknowledges the limp in our walking. A midrashic approach that begins at the Jabbok provides such a way. In a midrashic approach the goal is not to lead others to an overarching answer or metanarrative, subsuming any competing concerns and putting them in order. Rather, the task is to guide others to the narrated world mediated in and through the text, its *PaRDeS*. In providing such guidance we seek to unlock the text's logic of abundance and then to help those we guide to discover the promise of its orchard and to introduce them to its many fruits.[14] In this context, one may introduce others to overarching narratives, life-generating insights, and other fruits of the vineyard of covenant life. But the goal is to return to the narrated world of the text. It is not to share its singular message, its summarized truths, or the experience that lies behind or before it. Goals like these, when abstracted from the text, too easily become distinct realities that, in their turn, measure the text. They replace the narrated world of the text with a monolithic rendering of that world. The multifaceted richness of that world is reduced; its texture is lost. We replace the text with meaning we abstract from it.

Instead, in a midrashic approach we return to the text and its narrated world carefully, thoughtfully, limping as it were, aware of what we need to look for within it, but not to control it. Rather, we return to serve its narrated world and help others to be fed by it. Our objective is to care for and feed on the fruit of this orchard. But our limping reminds us that even here in the orchard we must be careful. The orchard is not Eden, even though it may provide a glimpse or taste of what that garden of delight might be.

When we limp through Jerusalem in the shadows of our own violence, our goal can be nothing less than complete honesty with regard to the violence that has been nurtured in the construction of our own identities. That is what the patriarch Jacob/Israel learned. That is what the people Israel learned and preserved in the core of their Scriptures. That is what we must learn as we return to Jerusalem, accompanied by Israel's children. And when we lead others into this narrated world, we must help them learn to bring every uncensored question they have into active dialogue, even resistance, with the texts of this scriptural vineyard, trusting the texts enough to insist that they bless us and honor those on whose behalf we engage the texts, even when we encounter violence narrated in those texts—especially then. We must not let go of the text, nor of our responsibility to confront and confess the violence in it.

Such confessional honesty leads us also to face the issue of covenantal wholeness. Indeed, our pastoral task turns on this matter. Our limping return to Jerusalem and Holy Week reminds us that our covenantal wholeness, our covenantal health, requires a positive significance for the Jewish other in our lives, irrespective of how he or she regards us. Indeed, the limping grows out of this awareness. Every step we take limps because of the restored wholeness that we have learned that we have violated. This point is important.

It is not the restored covenantal wholeness that wounds us. Still, it is because of the restored covenantal wholeness that we are wounded. We discover the pain we have caused others when we restore the others who have been wounded to positive significance in our covenantal world. Then, as we listen to their side of the stories and histories we share, we discover the shadows we have cast on these whom we have reclaimed as essential in positive ways to our identity. As we incorporate this increased sense of covenantal wholeness in our walk through Holy Week, we limp because the restored wholeness has caused us to face up to the violence that has distorted our walk all along. The limp comes from healing a brokenness that was our own doing. The subsequent wholeness enables us to see the violence we have done to others. But the wholeness is healing, because it restores the estranged other to positive relationship and the promise of shared life.

Consequently our pastoral task is not to wound those with whom we walk. Even though we limp, our task is not to cause others to limp. If we seek to bring about someone else's limping, then we have only taken more victims and hidden behind another triumphalistic disguise—the limping figure of

Israel. Our pastoral task must be to encourage covenantal wholeness, though we may be moved to wholeness by our own limping. This point is critical. Limping, we walk with others to encourage their wholeness, not their limping. Our task is to honor and serve the covenantal wholeness that has blessed and continues to bless our lives. Still, we can never forget that such wholeness has confronted us with the knowledge of how we have constructed our covenantal identity in the past to exclude and deny those in whose covenantal world we were included in the first place. That knowledge and the violence that it confronts are the realities that wound us.

In other words, even as we limp, our liturgical and homiletical approaches to Holy Week must first honor and serve the covenantal wholeness of our faith. That wholeness, when it is fully encountered and fully embraced, given our history with Jews, exposes us to being wounded. As we face our own lack of wholeness, the wounding can also bless and heal us as we find a way to walk, to move forward, limping along the way in processions and prayers, hymns and sermons, that while they too are wounded, seek the wholeness of those they serve.

Embodying the Task

Our pastoral task, however, is incomplete unless it is embodied in our work with others. In the case of the hermeneutical concerns articulated here, that task moves in two directions at the same time: facing the confessional dilemma and discerning a way of living into and out of the narrated world of the passion story in such a way that we remain faithful to who we are as Christians, yet responsive to those who have been wounded by how we have claimed our identity in the past. In this regard it should come as no surprise that I wish to commend intensive encounter with the story of Genesis 32 as a way to engage this dual concern. The task is to learn how to face the other, especially Christianity's significant others—the biblical text and our covenantal siblings—more responsibly.

One strategy available to pastors is to undertake an extended study of Christianity's relationship with Judaism while using the text of Genesis 32 as a frame for facing up to that history "according to the Scriptures." This can be done as part of a special Lenten adult study series, a series of sermons, or in extended workshops. Sunday school groups or worship planning teams could be presented the disturbing history of Jewish-Christian relations using Genesis 32 as a resource for facing this difficult history. Just as easily, a worship planning team could be asked to consider how they might help their pastor plan for the liturgical return to Christian holy ground that recurs every Holy Week. The wrinkle, of course, will be to undertake the biblical study in the light of what we learn about ourselves in facing the violence that dwells in the legacy of Jewish-Christian relations over the centuries. In this regard, the Genesis text could be used to frame the approach taken in the planning process in much the same way that the text is being used to frame the work undertaken in this book.

With regard to sharing the historical record, several media could be useful:

- videos like *Shadow on the Cross* (Landmark Films) or *The Cross and the Star* (First Run/Icarus Films)
- books like James Carroll, *Constantine's Sword*; Franklin Littell, *The Crucifixion of the Jews*; Mary Boys, *Has God Only One Blessing?*; Carol Rittner, Stephen D. Smith, Irena Steinfeldt, eds., *The Holocaust and the Christian World*; or Paul van Buren, *According to the Scriptures*
- lectures prepared by informed leaders

The important step in pursuing this task midrashically is learning to read and relate this history according to the Scriptures—in this case, using the language and dynamics of Jacob's paradigmatic struggle at the Jabbok.[15] The questions referenced earlier in this chapter should be helpful, but they must be posed in open-ended fashion, generating discussion and dialogue. They can be posed along with questions like

- What does it mean to take another person's birthright or rightful heritage?
- How does Jacob's encounter mirror our encounter with the significant other in our historic identity?
- Do the dynamics between Jacob and Esau change if the matter is more one of shame than one of guilt? [Be sure to clarify the relationship between shame and guilt, with shame rooted in how we see ourselves or hold our identities and guilt rooted in actions or deeds we have committed or should have undertaken but haven't.]
- How does Micah's question in Micah 6:8 ("What does the LORD require of you but to do justice, and to love kindness, and to walk humbly with your God?") take on new meaning in the light of Israel's limping walk of faith?

As the leader works with questions like these, care should be taken to keep the responses open. The goal in working with this text is to draw the discussants into the narrated world of the text, asking questions that generate a variety of responses that engage the narrative information supplied by the biblical text and that invite the conversation to wrestle with such matters responsibly.

Throughout, the goal should be to face the text as closely as possible. At the same time, the conversation seeks to face up to the problematic history of Jewish-Christian relations by facing the violence in that story with as much specificity as possible. The wordplay is important here and is rooted in the text of Genesis 32 itself. To speak of facing the text implies that we incorporate the need to deal with the characters and issues in the biblical text, as well as in our own history, in ways that restore the human faces that are hidden in them. In doing so, the leader of the discussion works by moving back and forth between the historical record and the text while keeping the conversation focused on the faces looking back at us as partners in the conversation. How that is done will depend on the method of telling the story of what happened between Jews and Christians. If a video or film is used, it can be viewed before undertaking the close reading of the Genesis text. Or the Genesis text can be read and discussed prior to an encounter with the historical record. Then the text can be discussed again to draw the insights and connections that grow out of reading the historical record through the lens of the text. Either way, as the dynamic of the text is articulated, the discussion can move to questions that explore how Jacob's struggle embodies the issues and dynamics of people like us who are trying to come to terms with our relationships with significant others whose legacies or birthrights we have taken from them.

While a multileveled conversation like this applies to historic Christian relationships with Jews, it can also describe social structures that have displaced black Americans in Euro-American cultures as well as Native Americans in the expansion and development of the United States. For example, although individuals may not bear personal responsibility for the historic actions that predate their lives, they do bear responsibility for how their identity is shaped vis-à-vis these "significant others" in the narrative identities they share with so many others. In this regard, the distinction between shame and guilt may be helpful. But it should not be forced. It can provide for the recognition that our identities participate in the violence done to others by virtue of the "stories" our shared identities rely upon to locate ourselves in our social worlds. As a child of the American South, my being able to relate to others about ways in which my identity is tied to racism, without my having to view myself as one who exhibits specific racist behavior (explicitly prejudicial actions), often opens the door for healthy and constructive discussion. That is, I am one who participates in racism without feeling or even acting prejudicial toward others.

How this process unfolds depends, of course, upon each group's familiarity with the problematic legacy of triumphalism and the embeddedness of replacement thinking on the part of Christians with regard to their covenantal siblings, their Jewish brothers and sisters. Still, when we utilize the strength and integrity of working from Scripture to make sense of this problematic legacy, we demonstrate a way of facing aspects of ourselves and of our histories that would be too painful to face otherwise. The framework of Scripture, when used midrashically to critique itself, provides an open-ended way to face up to the shame of our violence while remaining faithful to the biblical identities we are seeking to embody more responsibly.

As I indicated earlier in the chapter, I have participated in several interfaith groups, local and national, that have undertaken such an integrated study. In each case, we have proceeded dialogically, wrestling with the Genesis text and asking how it might describe our present confessional dilemma. As we have probed and pondered our own situation, we have also been learning how to insist that the biblical text continue to bless us in the wrestling itself. Equally important, as Jews and Christians, our dialogue has been about our common ground as well as our differences—historic and theological—as we have faced our texts and faced up to the estrangement in our relationships. In other words, the interpretive process, as well as our interpersonal dialogue, has been essential. As far as possible, a process like this one will be strengthened if the leader is involved in some kind of dialogical relationship with those he or she is trying to represent in such a study. Study partners or dialogue groups work well. And if that option is not possible, reading and other forms of representative engagement with Jewish sources is vital.

Summarizing the Approach—Returning to Jerusalem

Clearly such work is always hermeneutical, but never only hermeneutical. It remains thoroughly confessional in every sense of the term. Accountable to our biblical identity, we are also accountable to the suffering children whose victimization is due in part not just to behavioral sins of past generations but to faithful expressions of flawed "confessional truths" as well. Consequently, this approach has been punctuated by the need for authenticity and relevance, responsible to the summons of our scripturally based identity at the same time it has been attentive to the cries of tortured children cruelly sacrificed on the altars of hatred and disdain for Jews and others deemed unworthy of life. Because our own identity has contributed to the contempt that has defined others as incomplete human beings, we have sought a way of coming to terms with that identity that both allows us to integrate this legacy of shame and provides us a way of moving forward, accountable to the claims of being God's people and the claims and cries of burning children. Midrash, or more accurately midrashic discourse, has offered us such a model, providing us with a way of remaining accountable to the biblical texts while able to ask of them important and critical questions about our world and ourselves. In midrashic fashion, we discovered a biblical model for facing up to the complicitous ways we have claimed our inheritance as beloved children of God by turning to the story of Jacob, who in facing his own legacy of shame became the limping figure of Israel. Furthermore, we have recognized that in the patriarch's singular story we glimpse a recurring story of the people Israel, one preserved with full, confessional integrity in the Hebrew Scriptures. Their walk, as a people, limps with their awareness of infidelity and failure to live up to the blessing of their inheritance and the responsibility of their identity as God's people. Nonetheless their walk continues with humility when it limps.

And so we return to Jerusalem empowered by their witness even now, limping with our awareness of our complicity. We too have failed to live up to the blessing of our inheritance as people included in Abraham's covenantal way. We recall Micah's summary challenge, offered to his people in the midst of this way: What does God require of us? To do justice, love steadfastly,[16] and to walk humbly (limping, as it were) with our God.

We proceed, therefore, empowered by the enduring presence of our covenantal siblings and their witness to covenant life. We proceed, by way of midrash, to the narrated world of the text, letting it provide as yet unperceived promise and richness for coming to terms with a world marked by the Shoah and an identity complicitous in the unfolding of that tragedy. We proceed, guided not by our answers but trusting the world of the text to be rich enough to handle unperceived intrusions into the texture of its world. We return to its orchard, knowing that east of Eden it is the garden in which we may know life and know it abundantly, provided we proceed responsibly.

NOTES

1. André Scharz-Bart, *The Last of the Just* (New York: Atheneum, 1960), 364–65, quoted in Robert W. Bullock, "After Auschwitz: Jews, Judaism, and Christian Worship," in Carol Rittner and John K. Roth, eds., *"Good News" after Auschwitz: Christian Faith within a Post-Holocaust World* (Macon, GA: Mercer University Press, 2001), 83.

2. Irving Greenberg, "Cloud of Smoke, Pillar of Fire: Judaism, Christianity, and Modernity after the Holocaust," in *Auschwitz: Beginning of a New Era?* ed. Eva Fleischner (New York: KTAV, 1977), 23.

3. Emil Fackenheim, *God's Presence in History: Jewish Affirmations and Philosophical Reflections* (New York: Harper Torchbooks, 1970), 20–31.

4. Ibid., 26.

5. See a representative sampling of this dialogue in James F. Moore, Henry Knight, Zev Garber, and Stephen L. Jacobs, *Post-Shoah Dialogues: Rethinking Our Texts Together* (Lanham, MD: University Press of America, 2004).

6. Geoffrey H. Hartman, "The Struggle for the Text," in *Midrash and Literature*, ed. Geoffrey H. Hartman and Sanford Budick (New Haven, CT: Yale University Press, 1986), 12.

7. This matter may be put another way as well: Beware of anyone who claims to bear the identity of God's people who does not limp!

8. Douglas John Hall, *Confessing the Faith: Christian Theology in a North American Context* (Minneapolis: Fortress Press, 1996), 466.

9. J. B. Metz, *The Emergent Church: The Future of Christianity in a Postbourgeois World* (New York: Crossroad, 1987), 19, 32.

10. Henry Knight, *Confessing Christ in a Post-Holocaust World: A Midrashic Experiment* (Westport, CT: Greenwood Press, 2000), 65.

11. Regina Schwartz, *The Curse of Cain: The Violent Legacy of Monotheism* (Chicago: University of Chicago Press, 1997), 167.

12. Michael Fishbane, *The Garments of Torah: Essays in Biblical Hermeneutics* (Bloomington, IN: Indiana University Press, 1989), 98.

13. Emannuel Levinas offers a similar spin on this hermeneutical strategy. His exegesis of the *PaRDeS* acronymn *remez* refers to allusive meanings, where Fishbane speaks of allegorical ones. Both, however, are locating the core of meaning externally from the text. Likewise, both Levinas and Fishbane see hermeneutical emphases on derived meaning intrinsically rooted in the text as the distinguishing feature of *derash*, a characteristic Levinas calls "solicited meaning." See his essay, "On the Jewish Reading of Scriptures," in Levinas, *Beyond the Verse: Talmudic Readings and Lectures*, trans. Gary D. Mole (Bloomington and Indianapolis: Indiana University Press, 1994), 101.

14. I agree with Walter Brueggemann that the urgent task before the church is the recovery of the biblical text. Indeed, I find much of his language descriptive of what I want to adopt. However, I fear the strong typological overtones that threaten to replace the rich world of the text with "the plot" (creation-covenant-consummation) driving Brueggemann's analysis. Indeed, the plot he describes is the one most attractive to the concerns I am raising here. But there are other typologies supported by the text, and his typology is an abstraction that stands apart from the text, however much it is rooted in it. See his article "A Text That Redescribes," *Theology Today* 58, no. 4 (January 2002): 526–40.

15. Readers may wish to consult my book *Confessing Christ in a Post-Holocaust World* (Greenwood Press), especially chapter 1, for an extended treatment of the midrashic implications of reading Genesis 32:22–33 in this fashion. In addition, my article "From Shame to Responsibility and Christian Identity," *Journal of Ecumenical Studies* 35, no. 1 (Winter 1998): 41–62, may be helpful for examining the ways in which the dynamics of shame and guilt interact in this encounter.

16. I have chosen to render the Hebrew word *"hesed"* with the English words "love steadfastly" instead of the NRSV translation of "love kindness." The NRSV is soft and does not convey the tenacity of faithful devotion that the Hebrew term conveys, especially when read in the light of the passage from Genesis 32.

Chapter 2

Limping into the City

Prophetic Return to Responsible Witness

A Wounded Approach

Our approach to Holy Week limps. In our time, thoughtful Christians will make their liturgical return to Jerusalem by way of the River Jabbok. While that may literally sound like strange geography to those who know the region, it is the way we must walk if we are going to follow Jesus into the Holy City and face his passion responsibly. The biblical path most typically moves from Jericho to Jerusalem, but our time, our situation, requires a detour that visits the banks of the River Jabbok. Consequently, when we return by way of the Jabbok, we approach Jerusalem limping. We walk to be sure, but our walking is flawed, wounded.

It is no accident that the word for law in Hebrew, *halakah*, is derived from the verb meaning "to go, to walk." To do God's will is to walk with God and responsibly with our neighbors. That is the covenantal summons of faith. Yet we stumble. Again and again, we stumble. If we keep going, we limp. Micah's prophetic insight, when paired with Jacob's emergence as Israel, helps us recognize an important quality of post-Shoah faithfulness. Ever a walk, the life of faith is active and filled with responsibility toward others; it is a way of doing. And the walking proceeds in humility, with the recognition that it is flawed or wounded by contending with others with whom we have wrestled and by what we have faced about ourselves.

Poised at the threshold of the Holy City, we are prepared to take up our journey of yearly liturgical return to its sacred precincts. However, we do so aware of the deep wounding that has occurred to our world and to our ways of walking in it. Therefore, we proceed limping—moving forward in the wounded walk of faith.

Companions on the Way

Limping and confessional detours are not enough, however. As essential as they are, we must make other adjustments as well. J. B. Metz has declared that after Auschwitz, any Christian theology that proceeds as if Auschwitz didn't happen and didn't implicate Christians and Christianity in its wake needs to be rethought.[1] That is, Christians who face Auschwitz and their complicities in it will limp. No less important, he added that responsible theology after Auschwitz must proceed with Jewish partners, either literally or figuratively.[2] For Christian identity, Jews are significant others. They signify the covenant that Christianity claims now includes them. For too long, that significance has been a negative one, with Christians viewing themselves as replacing their Jewish siblings. But if they are to follow in the footsteps of Jacob/Israel, they must seek a restored relationship with the sibling from whom they have usurped the blessing they claim belongs to them alone. Any post-Shoah return to Jerusalem must include a change in signification signaled by the presence, the abiding companionship, of Jews on the road that Christians walk. Covenantal wholeness can mean nothing less.

In other words, we approach Jerusalem limping, but not alone. We are to be accompanied by Jews, whether or not they are literally present, or virtually or figuratively so. Otherwise, the past has not been faced, and our identity vis-à-vis our signifying, covenantal other has not been reconfigured, moving from a negative relationship to a positive one. The return is a partnership, a covenantal affair, even when accompanying parties do not share the same covenant. This will not be easy, and it will occasionally lead to disagreement, even conflict, over the character of being in covenant with God and neighbor. But even essential conflict must not lead to mutual isolation and certainly not to the denial of the other's place in God's covenantal ways with creation.

We must also be clear about the companions we take for granted. We are not alone in this regard either. Many of us approach Jerusalem in our yearly liturgical return walking comfortably but indiscriminately with all four biblical evangelists. Limping, we have the opportunity, if not the need, to ask about the wisdom of such a naive approach. For some time, liturgical reformers and biblical scholars have called for more disciplined attention to which evangelist, which Gospel writer, we use in making our way into the city. Still, it is far too easy for us to confuse our entries and misperceive our biblical companions. For example, though we typically associate palm branches with each celebration of Jesus' entry into Jerusalem, palm branches are mentioned by name only in John. In Matthew, the people spread their cloaks on the ground with some persons cutting branches from trees to spread with the cloaks.

To help differentiate who our companions are along this way and to keep our story straight, we will follow the testimony of a single Gospel tradition, Matthew's. His testimony will guide our return to the city and how we make our way through the week that follows. In one sense, choosing to walk with Matthew is arbitrary. Any of the four canonical authors could be selected. However, Matthew offers a special opportunity, since his Gospel, more than the others, demonstrates a similar process of reading his Scriptures and then telling the story of his Jesus according to those Scriptures. In fact, the similarity between Matthew's interpretive style and the hermeneutical style of midrashic interpretation should work to improve our understanding of both Matthew and the midrashic strategies that guide our approach. However, as we approach the Holy City, we must include one more observation. There are yet others who accompany us on this journey; they have been there all along, hidden in the background of the text.

The center of Matthew's narrative was Jesus and his companions. As Matthew recounted Jesus' entry, he focused only on Jesus and what was happening with regard to him. Yet we should assume that there were others on the same road before Jesus entered and afterwards, making their way to Jerusalem for Passover. Similarly, we could even assume that there were others who were trying to make sense out of what was unfolding around them. They would have been present too. Perhaps some were unaware of anything around them and were exclusively focused on their own pilgrimage to the Holy City. Midrash teaches us to pay attention to the white spaces between the letters and the words of a text—the open spaces in what is being said. In this case, we recognize that there are missing persons whom we can restore without distorting Matthew's witness at all. In truth, we may be more faithful to his original testimony by putting them back into it. Matthew could presume their presence. We cannot.

Limping as we do enables us to look around and see these missing companions. We are not alone; indeed, we never have been. However, now in more careful review of others walking with us, we see that there are companions on the way whom we have failed to recognize before—Jews making *aliyah*—a ritual journey to the Holy City to express their faith and devotion. In fact, we may even be prepared to acknowledge that when Jesus made his historic approach to Jerusalem recounted by Matthew, he too was participating in this pilgrimage tradition, going up to Jerusalem in accord with the sacred liturgical practice of his time. Whatever distinction or even unique spin he put on his approach, it appears that Jesus joined others in making *aliyah*, or others joined him in doing so, or both.

As an act of *aliyah*, Jesus' approach to Jerusalem would have been a combined expression of thanksgiving and sacrifice, coordinated with one of the major festivals of the annual Jewish liturgical season. *Aliyah,* for most Jews of the Second Temple period, would have occurred during the celebration of one of three pilgrimage festivals and would have culminated in acts of sacrifice and thanksgiving at the temple. According to Matthew, Jesus' journey to Jerusalem coincided with the sacred pilgrimage festival of Passover and evoked the sacred meanings associated with its symbols of sacrifice and thanksgiving. Indeed, Jesus went immediately to the temple upon entry to the city. In itself, then, Jesus' journey to Jerusalem would not have been unique. He would have been joining other Jews in undertaking their pilgrimage, just as some would have been joining him. Furthermore, as an act of *aliyah*, we would expect Jesus, like the other disciples, to have understood that his ritual pilgrimage was not complete until he offered his sacrifice of thanksgiving as a symbol of the meaning and dedication his journey to Jerusalem embodied. Going up to Jerusalem in this way would have been a sacred obligation of rich symbolic significance for Jesus and for other Jews of Jesus' time.

Another Way

As we enter Jerusalem and reconnect to the significant others of this story and its city, we are challenged to reexamine our grasp of its historical context. Jerusalem was an occupied city. Its inhabitants were ruled by Rome in civil matters and guided in religious matters by the scribes and elders as well as by the priests, especially Caiaphas, the high priest. And while Jerusalem was responsible to Rome through its governor, Pontius Pilate, his seat was Caesarea on the coast. Consequently, Caiaphas and the high priests were often relied upon for civil order. For attentive readers, this dimension is present in the biblical texts, embedded in allusions and presumptions signaled within it. And from extra-biblical sources, particularly the work of Josephus, we discover more detail about these historical dimensions.

From the same extra-biblical sources we can restore another element missing from Matthew's story. There were two primary approaches to the city, one from the east and one from the west. Most pilgrims came from the east, moving along the fifteen-mile pathway from Jericho and then entering the city by way of the Mount of Olives. This, we may recall, is the path the messiah was supposed to follow as he entered Jerusalem. On the other hand, one could enter the city from the opposite side. Travelers from the coast would make their way and enter from the west. During Passover, Roman soldiers coming as reinforcements for the city during the festival would have made their approach from this side.

From the east, then, using the upward, winding road from Jericho, pilgrims would be making their way throughout the day for several days as they gathered in the city for Passover. It was this route that Jesus and his disciples followed and that is remembered in the Gospel texts. Matthew describes the entry sparsely, presuming enough familiarity with existing traditions for his hearers to catch the significance of his story. But the other route, known to Matthew's earliest readers but hidden from our view, requires our conscious attention to recognize its presence in the world narrated by the text. Indeed, restoring its presence as background to the narrative allows us to see more clearly the prophetic contrast embodied in Jesus' entry from the east, wrapped as it is in the imagery of Zechariah.

Before we turn our attention to a close and careful consideration of Matthew's use of Zechariah to recount his story, we need to be clear about this contrast. As Jesus and his various companions entered from the east, others were entering from the west, particularly the armed representatives of the empire of Rome. Each Passover a garrison of Roman soldiers was deployed to Jerusalem and housed at the fortress overlooking the Temple Mount. They were in Jerusalem in case of trouble. As they made their way from Caesarea Maritima, they were led by the ruling representative of Rome, Pontius Pilate, the prefect (governor) of the region. Pilate and his soldiers, representing the power of the empire, entered with pomp and ceremony from the west at or about the same time that Jesus entered from the east.[3] As we limp toward Jerusalem, we are challenged by this missing procession. In every public sense it was a "triumphal entry." In other words, the so-called triumphal entry of Jesus was a countermovement that challenged the notions of power and triumph that did characterize the entry of Pilate and the Roman soldiers. However, without that other entry being recalled, Jesus' entry too easily becomes its opposite, the story of triumphant power and conquest.

According to Matthew, Jesus was greeted not with the fanfare of empire but with the prophetic zeal of Israel's hopes. Whether Jesus manifested all or some of the features cited from Zechariah, or Matthew rendered them as midrashic signals to show the reader what was hidden in plain sight, the missing component that we must be sure to restore is the contrast with empire and its notions of power and honor. As we modern Christians recall this missing component and approach Jerusalem in the presence of Jews, as Metz says we should, we can imagine our companions including victims of Hitler's final solution. If we do, then we should also imagine goose-stepping soldiers saluting their Führer amidst the Roman guard as they enter the city in contrast to

Jesus. Then we get the post-Shoah implications of this scene and its relationship to the contrasting path of empire. The vulnerable entry on the east side by way of the Mount of Olives and in accord with its prophetic challenge is in direct contrast to the entry from the west by those who represent the power of empire and control. When we lose sight of that contrast, we distort the other features in Matthew's portrait and betray the way we think we have taken. It is no longer covenantally or prophetically whole. Of course, our limping return includes the awareness that for too long we have failed to see the other procession. In fact, too often and for too long a time, we have transposed the procession of pilgrims from the east, merging it with the entry of empire and power from the west. We have exchanged one for the other. After Auschwitz, we cannot overlook this matter. We limp with that awareness. Indeed, we are wounded by that knowledge.

Matthew, in using the language of Zechariah 9 to tell his story, sees Jesus through the image of a messianic king entering Jerusalem in an act that challenges the powers that be, subverting the ruling structures and establishing the hoped-for reality of harmony at every level in every dimension of created life—between nature and humanity, among human beings, and between nations. In other words, the royal messiah, as God's representative, ushers in God's rule and realm. Matthew, like Zechariah, sees this as triumph—but not the triumph of empire, not conquest. Matthew, writing after the leaders of Jerusalem and Rome reject Jesus, is forced by the circumstances of his time to rethink the promise of triumph, even when distinguished from the power structures and logic of empire.

Whatever else we must see, we must see that Matthew's testimony describes Jesus in protest against empire. A peasant who is crushed by the empire is declared to be the true ruler of God's realm, in spite of what has happened and in sharp contrast to the replacement logic of conquest. Writing at least a full generation after the events he describes, Matthew is declaring that a different kind of triumph may be seen in the failure of Jesus to bring what was hoped-for—in Jesus' refusing to participate in the life-denying game of empire and power. He did not yield his message or his person to the realities of empire or to those in collusion with empire. And the realities to which he did give his life prevailed. But that is getting ahead of the story.

Entering Midrashically

Recognizing the missing procession in Matthew's story helps us see in better light the procession he does describe. Wrapped in images from Zechariah,

Jesus enters the city in accord with the prophet's messianic expectations. Scholars debate whether or not Jesus actually understood himself in terms of these same images. Some, like Crossan and Borg, contend that we are dealing, at least in part if not in whole, with the creative work of Matthew or the early church. They explain that there are a number of options for relating history and prophetic discourse, from shaping history to fit prophetic expectation to shaping prophetic understanding to be fulfilled in history. Crossan calls the former history prophesized and the latter prophecy historicized.[4] Borg suggests alternative designations of history remembered and history metaphorized to underscore the rhetorical strategies involved.[5] Others, like N. T. Wright, contend that we are dealing with what actually happened.[6] Regardless, we are forced to deal with Matthew's strange rendering of the scene as he places Jesus atop two animals, a donkey and the foal of a donkey. Midrash suggests we take the anomaly seriously and view the text as a stylistic rendering that intentionally calls attention to itself, summoning forth interpretation.

There is more, to be sure, in this scholarly debate. However, we must be wary of hurrying on too quickly to engage it. Far too easily it can deflect us from the prophetic challenge that Matthew describes. Jesus has entered Jerusalem, according to the Scriptures, in a prophetic way and in sharp contrast to the posture of empire. Viewed through the prism of Zechariah's prophetic legacy and messianic hope, Jesus' entry unmasks the sociopolitical arrangements of his Jerusalem as being out of step with what God intends. That is, the emphasis is not on replacing one ruler for another but on challenging the structures of empire and collusion with empire—their logic, power, pretensions, and illusions. When we add the conflict he generates in the temple courtyard and then later focuses in his Passover meal with his disciples to the opposition he manifests to the ways of empire, the conflict becomes acute. But again, we are getting ahead of the story and need to confront the interpretive dilemma.

A close and careful reading of Matthew's text exposes the problem Crossan and Borg seek to resolve between history remembered and history metaphorized (Borg):

> This took place to fulfill what had been spoken through the prophet, saying, "Tell the daughter of Zion, Look, your king is coming to you, humble, and mounted on a donkey, and on a colt, the foal of a donkey." The disciples went and did as Jesus had directed them; they brought the donkey and the colt, and put their cloaks on them, and he sat on them. (Matt. 21:4–7)

As we examine the plain sense of the text, we see that Matthew not only cites Zechariah 9 but describes Jesus sitting on two animals as he enters the city.

Naturally we want to ask Matthew what he is doing. To account for Matthew's description, Crossan and Borg propose distinguishing how prophetic discourse relates to the recounting of history by positing a range of hermeneutical options to frame the dilemma. Crossan explains that at one end of a continuum, history can be rendered to fit the expectations of prophecy; at the other end, prophecy can be rendered to fit the occurrences of history. The question then becomes where on the continuum one should place a particular interpretation. Borg adopts a similar strategy as he attends to the figurative character of prophetic discourse, likewise positing a continuum of interpretive options. At one end he locates the possibility of history metaphorized; at the other, metaphor is historicized.

The temptation is to view these options as polar opposites expressive of an either-or logic. However, Borg and Crossan view the matter as a range of options with the either-or possibilities indicative of the far ends of the hermeneutical spectrum. Still, an either-or logic of scarcity[7] lingers in the temptation to look for a single correct interpretation to identify on their continuum. Approaching the narrative midrashically allows us to incorporate insights like theirs without having to opt for only one correct interpretation. Instead, we are encouraged to find multiple ways to enter the narrative at the same time we resist other problematic readings. That is, a midrashic interpretation does not stand outside the text and argue for one meaning; rather, midrash enters the text to open its world to another way of reading it. The additional perspective serves as one more vantage point from which to explore the world of the text. Hence, we can say that placing Jesus literally atop two animals renders the literal character of the text in absurd ways. When we read Matthew's text that way, we should resist such a reading. Instead, we may look for its literal character elsewhere in the sociopolitical dimensions that Zechariah is challenging.

Furthermore, we are not forced into a simplistic juxtaposition of the literal versus the figurative. Midrash encourages us to find the figures in the literal character of the text at the same time it avoids foreclosure of what the text *must* mean in order to make sense.[8] From the perspective of midrash we can envision Jesus approaching Jerusalem with an intentionality similar to Zechariah's without Jesus having to focus on himself as the one who fulfills the role Zechariah describes. That is, Jesus could have intended the prophetic reclamation of his Holy City without being preoccupied with his own identity as the one foreordained to bring this about. Jesus would still be focused on the prophetic action that calls into question the legitimacy of the present social order and its abuse of power. Just as easily, Crossan and Borg could be right with regard to Jesus not having Zechariah's prophetic testimony in mind. Or Jesus could self-consciously have been seeking to fulfill Zechariah's hope and critique. Regardless, by our focusing on the religious and social challenges in Jesus' entry, the perspective would shift from a triumphalistic declaration back to the prophetic dimensions Zechariah emphasized in his text. Moreover, such a move would be faithful to Jesus' own approach to the ways of empire, which he consistently undercut in parable and deed on his way to Jerusalem and during his last week in its domain.

In short, entering midrashically provides a way of returning to Jerusalem according to the Scriptures and alert to other avenues of approaching the Holy City. In addition, entering this way provides a means of returning that reflects important dynamics present in the biblical text as it renders its sacred story. Consequently, our goal focuses on finding gateways into the narrative and our liturgical celebrations of it that honor these dynamics and the witness they bear, while resisting problematic expressions of the same testimony. Importantly, our approach seeks to enter the narrated world of the text. It does not seek to find a correct rendering of that world or to abstract the most adequate meaning from it. The task is to enter Jerusalem as narrated by the text and celebrated in our individual communities of faith. Entering midrashically also means we do so drawing on clues provided by the texts themselves. Therefore we look for places in the text that invite our participation. According to the tradition of midrash, those openings are often encountered as gaps in the story, missing information, strange words or phrases, and points of friction or conflicts within the text. Consequently, the problem that surfaced in dealing with Matthew's use of Zechariah 9—Is Jesus riding two animals?—becomes instead an opportunity to enter the story midrashically and draw on insights from scholars who see Matthew's stylizing hand shaping his testimony. But we are not asked to abandon the plain sense of the text in the process—no matter how much we wrestle with what it might mean.

Making Our Way

As we follow Jesus and his disciples into the Holy City, I am struck by the way in which we are asked to confront a recurring duality in our tradition—word and deed. But in this case, the summons is not to avoid the dualism of separating words and deeds but to see how they are inevitably yoked together. That is, the hermeneutical task is also a summons to embodied pastoral leadership and action. Consequently these become our questions:

- If Jesus' entry was a prophetic challenge to the power of empire and its oppression and dehumanization, then how should we incorporate that feature into our established places of worship?
- If Jesus' entry generated conflict with ruling powers and with the religious establishment, how should we enter the sanctuary in our liturgical reconstructions?
- Furthermore, if we limp in our awareness of how we have misconstrued and abused this moment in the past, how might we incorporate this penitential humility in our wounded approach?

These are the questions we carry with us as we begin Holy Week and return to Jerusalem in the company of Jesus.

Clearly we must make our way cognizant of missing characters along the route and other paths that contrast with the one we follow. Similarly we must be acutely aware of the emotional power of the story that draws us forward, alert to the ways in which it can both heal and wound. And if we make our way midrashically, we seek to embody the very dynamics that drive this story and give it life. We do so by making its white fire visible, by providing timely invitations to enter into its dynamics, and by engaging the stylized character of the biblical narrative as a partner in shaping its testimony and bearing its witness. In other words, we enter the sanctuary as we have entered the critical issues we have discussed, according to the Scriptures. How then do we proceed? What do we say as we make our way?

In liturgically oriented churches, three elements often combine to focus the entrance rites of Palm/Passion Sunday: a procession with an accompanying hymn, an opening prayer, and a biblical reading proclaiming Jesus' entrance into Jerusalem. In some settings where only Palm Sunday is observed, the biblical reading for that day is often moved to later in the service. In settings where the combined celebration of Palm Sunday and Passion Sunday is observed, the entrance rite comprises a distinctive celebration in preparation for the rest of the service. After it concludes, the congregation is then prepared for a full encounter with the passion narrative. In this case, the passion of Jesus may be shared in several ways: in dramatic presentations, in an extended reading of the biblical narrative, or with selected readings from the passion that are expanded in preaching. Either way, we may think of this experience as an anticipatory encounter with the story that is to unfold over the course of Holy Week, knowing that many parishioners will hear the story only on this Sunday or in isolated parts over the course of the next several days.

However it is framed, the pastoral task at the head of Holy Week remains at least twofold: *how* to enter the remembrance and celebration of this core week and *how* to frame the anticipated story of Jesus' passion. Perhaps the best way to demonstrate that responsibility is to examine a worship service in which Palm Sunday and Passion Sunday converge. Just as first-century Jewish pilgrims concluded their going up to the Holy City with the presentation of a symbolic gift, so then do we, offering a representative service as a case study for analysis and critique. In the end, worship is the symbolic gift that embodies our entry into the city as well as our approach to the biblical text and the center of our sacred world. It also anticipates how we connect with and bear witness to the passion that calls us forward as disciples of Jesus Christ.

A Liturgical Offering

On the Sunday before Easter, the congregation I serve at my university begins our celebration with a formal entrance in which the entire congregation processes into the sanctuary. In an earlier form, when our service coincided with our Newman Center's Roman Catholic mass, we met at a common location at the center of campus and jointly held an opening ritual with the distribution of palms and readings for the day; then we split into two processing groups as we left for our separate locations while singing the same hymn. Now our congregation gathers as a separate community in the narthex of the university chapel to distribute palms, hear the Gospel reading for the entry into Jerusalem, and, following our opening prayer, process into the chapel singing an appropriate hymn. As the palms are distributed to participants, a brief orientation is offered, explaining the context for our actions and the twist that we have given it as we follow the leader of our procession pushing a shopping cart filled with palm fronds, some coats, and signs declaring, "Will work for food."

In seeking an appropriate way to enter in contrast to the processions of empire, we have drawn on the memory of the poor people's marches of the latter part of the civil rights movement. Mule-drawn wagons led thousands of people on foot into key U.S. cities to challenge their notions of power and justice. These processions were led by symbols of poverty, not power; and they were constituted by common folks who wanted to make a difference, not persons in uniform carrying weapons or bearing other symbols of power. In that light we have recalled an equally powerful event from our own worship community.

One Sunday several years ago, a man named Tom (not his real name) joined our campus community for the celebration of the Eucharist. He was a bit unkempt and older than our students. He had a reddish blond beard and longish hair, and his eyes searched out our intentions to welcome and include him in what we were doing, which we did enthusiastically. After the service was over, the community invited him to remain for lunch. At lunch he told us he was a graduate of our university from about twenty years earlier. He was reticent but obviously moved to be included in the simple meal we have together after we have shared Holy Communion. After everyone else had departed, Tom went to the stairwell where he had parked his shopping cart, out of sight. He said good-bye, then left to return to the streets.

Connecting these components—our unexpected visitor, the poor people's marches of the civil rights movement, and Jesus' prophetic approach to Jerusalem—we are provided with a contemporary image to contrast our entrance to the ways of empire and privilege: Jesus pushing a loaded shopping cart filled with all his belongings and entering our sanctuary in solidarity with the homeless. In this spirit we tell Tom's story and explain why we place at the head of our procession a shopping cart filled with coats and palm branches.

As we make our way into the sanctuary, our liturgy is punctuated by a second prayer to conclude the entrance rite and prepare for the liturgy of the Word that follows. It moves toward a climactic reading of the entire passion story, while also including the full scope of lectionary texts for the day. This portion resembles our regular Sunday order with readings from the Hebrew Scriptures, a psalm, an Epistle lesson, and then a reading from one of the Gospels. However, on this occasion, the Gospel lesson is extended to include the full passion narrative, read midrashically with another reader interrupting the narrative flow of the text to offer critical asides, commentary, and questions, while encouraging close and critical engagement with the story. The service of the Word is then followed by prayers of confession, prayers for others, an offering, a closing hymn, and benediction. As in other churches where this practice is honored, there is no standard sermon following the reading of the passion narrative. Instead, the emphasis is on a full hearing of the text. The goal is not to explain the narrative or provide a correct version of it but to invite thoughtful and respectful engagement with it, entering into its narrated world with appropriate information and questions for responsible engagement with its witness.

Given this liturgical structure, our service limps in two primary ways. First, in our planning as well as in our actual worship we proceed with care, ever alert to hidden contempt and the presence of supersessionary words and actions. In addition, we have asked, in the great procession with palms and readings that begin our service, how might we incorporate the presence of others on the road with us, or the contrasting presence of an imperial procession? How might we walk with a limp in the midst of our excitement and anticipation? So we begin by pushing a shopping cart and telling Tom's story.

Favorite hymns, cherished practices, solemn prayers, even root experiences are also challenged and frequently rewritten. If we are to follow Jesus responsibly, include missing companions, search out hidden contempt, and guard against subtle and overt forms of triumphalism, then that is how we must proceed. As a result we walk haltingly, examining our hymns, prayers, and gestures for contempt and disdain and for hidden and subtle forms of supersessionism. As we proceed, we seek to distinguish the vulnerable triumph we want to proclaim from the triumphalism that we more often express, as we look to the power of humility and hospitality to others to break the power of death, even in the face of a cross.

In anticipation of questions and concerns we will encounter as we move through the week, the passion story is presented using a prepared midrashic encounter with the text. The extended reading is, then, introduced by the worship leader with a brief explanation to orient the congregation to what they are about to hear. As the reading progresses, a second reader interrupts the lesson with occasional questions and commentary that seek to kindle the white fire in the narrative by articulating the gaps and anomalies in the text. The goal: to draw the congregation into the unfolding story. While this strategy is similar to a dramatic rendering of the story by utilizing more than one voice in the presentation, it clearly distinguishes the primary voice (or voices) of the narrative from the critical voices that interact with the text. As is the case with midrash, resolving the questions raised in such an exercise is not its purpose. Instead, the questions and cautions, comments and queries, are offered to open the narrative to thoughtful and active engagement.

Of course, the point of describing this experiment is not to say that this is what everyone should do. On the contrary, its story is offered as a case study for further analysis. It is simply an example of how one might invite a community into a dialogical encounter with the text—one that limps with a penitential awareness of the dangers of triumphalism and yet is fully attentive to its prophetic power. The intention is not to limit the text and its witness but to open its testimony at the same time we guard against its misuse or abuse. What follows is the full text of that service, including the script for rendering Matthew's passion narrative.* Even the hymns that we selected and revised for use by our congregation are included for inspection.

---

*Another strategy for encouraging close, critical engagement with the passion narrative, or any other text in the spirit of midrashic boldness, involves interactive reading with a class or community while the text is read slowly and thoughtfully aloud. In this case, the leader explains how midrashic reading or thoughtful engagement with the text requires paying attention to the details included in the text, especially those that don't make immediate sense, as well as to the

Palm/Passion Sunday

Order of Worship[9]

WELCOME

**GATHERING WITH PALMS

**CALL TO WORSHIP

> **Leader:** In the midst of pervasive despair and in the face of oppressive
> Power, Zechariah declared:
> Rejoice greatly, O daughter of Zion!
> **People: Shout aloud, O daughter of Jerusalem!**
> **Leader:** Lo, *your* king comes to you;
> Triumphant and victorious is he,
> **People: Humble and riding on a donkey,**
> **On a colt, the foal of a donkey.**

---

gaps in logic or the narrative flow that we find unsettling or fill in when we read them more routinely.

The reading begins by identifying the text to be read and briefly explaining the process. The leader explains that she (or he) will read the text and that each person in the room should speak aloud any questions they have about the text *as they occur*. For example, while reading the passage that places Jesus sitting on two animals someone might ask, "Was Jesus riding two animals?" The reading proceeds with listeners and other readers (the exercise works best with everyone having a copy of the text before them) following along looking for gaps, openings, points of friction, strange words or phrases, i.e., doorways in the text. Their job is to knock on those doors with their questions and interrupt the reading as they occur. For this strategy to work well, the leader should read the text slowly, but not ponderously, allowing for interruption as listeners participate in the experience by voicing their running, critical commentary. The goal is to encourage a close, interactive encounter with the text, not to answer questions generated in the process—at least not right away. Someone could be designated to take notes and record the questions for later discussion, or they can be recalled in a second stage of the exercise. But during the first stage, the reading should proceed without being sidetracked by the leader's desire to provide answers, though an occasional footnote, if carefully limited, will allow for the reading to be sustained.

A variation of this strategy, if time allows, would be to have the community of readers spend time with the text beforehand, indicating the places in the text they see a need for questions, either writing out their questions or inserting symbols (e.g., ∧) or brief marginal glosses on texts provided for the exercise. Then, as the narrative is read, the group could voice their questions using their notes.

**PRAYER

> **Eternal God, on this day Jesus Christ entered the Holy City of Jerusalem and was anointed by those who spread their garments and palm branches along his way. Let these branches be for us signs of his authority and symbols of his vulnerable way. Grant that we who carry them may follow him, even if we must risk suffering and a cross, so that dying and rising with him, we may dwell in your presence and walk in your way. In Jesus' name we pray. Amen.**

**PROCLAMATION OF THE ENTRANCE INTO JERUSALEM   Matthew 21:1–11

**GREAT PROCESSION   "All Glory, Laud, and Honor"

> **Leader:** Blessed is the one who comes in the name of the LORD.
> **People: Hosanna in the highest!**

ACT OF PRAISE   (anthem)

PRAYER FOR ILLUMINATION

> **Send the power of your Holy Spirit, O God, upon the reading, the preaching, the hearing, and the doing of your holy word. May it change our lives and help us grow into the likeness of the one in whose name we pray, Jesus Christ. Amen.**

> Or

> **May the words of our mouths and the meditations of our hearts be acceptable to you, O God, our rock and our redeemer; and may they be credible in the presence of suffering children. In Jesus' name we pray. Amen.**

FIRST LESSON   Isaiah 50:4–9a

PSALM   Psalm 31:9–16

SECOND LESSON   Philippians 2:5–11

**HYMN   "O Sacred Head, Now Wounded"

THE PASSION OF JESUS CHRIST   Matthew 26:14–27:66

CONFESSION AND PARDON

> **O God, we sing and praise you, happy of heart and strong of spirit, when we are among others who praise you too. But in times of stress,**

we seek scapegoats to be targets for anger. We betray those we love and
who have loved us; we turn against you, too busy to seek you, too self-
ish to obey you. Yet, your compassion is without bounds, O God, for you
forgive us again and again. Restore us, therefore, to a right spirit and
bring us together reconciled to you and one another. God of steadfast
love, teach us to be steadfast; through Jesus Christ, in whose name we
pray. Amen.

All pray in silence.

Hear the good news: Christ died for us while we were yet sinners. That is
our assurance of God's love for us.

Thanks be to God.

**PRAYERS FOR OTHERS

**LORD'S PRAYER

**Our Father in heaven, hallowed be your name, your kingdom come,
your will be done, on earth as in heaven. Give us today our daily bread.
Forgive us our sins as we forgive those who sin against us. Save us from
the time of trial and deliver us from evil. For the kingdom, the power,
and the glory are yours now and forever. Amen.**

**PEACE

OFFERING

    Offertory
    Presentation of Gifts

**DOXOLOGY

**Praise God, from whom all blessings flow;
Praise God, all creatures high and low;
Praise God, in Jesus fully known;
Creator, Word, and Spirit One. Amen.**

Words: Brian Wren
Music: Old 100th
Revised by Brian Wren
© 1989 Hope Publishing Co., Carol Stream, IL 60188
All rights reserved. Used by permission.

**HYMN   "Were You There?"

**ANNOUNCEMENTS

**BENEDICTION

**The congregation stands as they are able.

Matthew's Passion Story

Matthew 26:14–27:66

For two readers: first reader, italics and plain text; second reader, bold

The passion story in Matthew is marked by strong language, its own passion regarding Jesus and what happened to him. It was probably put in the form in which we now have it a generation after the destruction of Jerusalem, somewhere near the year 90 of the Common Era. The narrative carries in its language echoes of the fear and conflict of that time, and some of the finger-pointing and blame. As you hear the story, you will hear absolute statements like "all the crowd" and "the whole council" and "all the chief priests." Remember how our language will sometimes extend in too broad a compass when we are angry and upset. Remember too that Jesus and his disciples and others who followed him were almost always Jews, who lived in the midst of diverse interpretations of what it meant to be a Jew and to be faithful children of the covenant. After the revolt of 66–70 much of that diversity was lost, and those who followed Jesus were contending with others (mostly Pharisees) for the survival of Israel, as more and more Gentiles were incorporated into their movement. But enough introduction; let us hear the story as we enter Jerusalem, interrupted from time to time with commentary and questions meant to provide openings for our entering its narrated world in faith and prayer.

26   14 Then one of the twelve, who was called Judas Iscariot, went to the chief priests [15]and said, "What will you give me if I betray him to you?" They paid him thirty pieces of silver. [16]And from that moment he began to look for an opportunity to betray him.

17 On the first day of Unleavened Bread the disciples came to Jesus, saying, "Where do you want us to make the preparations for you to eat the Passover?" [18]He said, "Go into the city to a certain man, and say to him, 'The Teacher says, My time is near; I will keep the Passover at your house with my disciples.'" [19]So the disciples did as Jesus had directed them, and they prepared the Passover meal.

20 When it was evening, he took his place with the twelve; [21]and while they were eating, he said, "Truly I tell you, one of you will betray me." [22]And they became greatly distressed and began to say to him one after another, "Surely not I, Lord?" [23]He answered, "The one who has dipped his hand into the bowl with me will betray me. [24]The Son of Man goes as it is written of him, but woe to that one by whom the Son of Man is betrayed! It would have been better for that one not to have been born." [25]Judas, who betrayed him, said, "Surely not I, Rabbi?" He replied, "You have said so."

Notice the stylized way this portion is told. Is Matthew remembering that Jesus predicted the future or that he understood the fallibility of his disciples, all of them, from Judas to Peter?

26 While they were eating, Jesus took a loaf of bread, and after blessing it he broke it, gave it to the disciples, and said, "Take, eat; this is my body [my flesh]." [27]Then he took a cup, and after giving thanks he gave it to them, saying, "Drink from it, all of you; [28]for this is my blood of the covenant, which is poured out for many for the forgiveness of sins.

Jesus has used almost the exact words the priests in the temple would use when they offered their thank offerings, taking the flesh of the animal and presenting it to God, then presenting the animal's blood collected in a large bowl or cup and offered to God when poured on the altar. Was Jesus identifying his actions at the meal with these actions at the temple? Was Jesus offering bread and wine instead of a sacrificial animal and the animal's blood? Was he offering an alternative way of expressing one's devotion to God?

29 I tell you, I will never again drink of this fruit of the vine until that day when I drink it new with you in my Father's kingdom."

30 When they had sung the hymn, they went out to the Mount of Olives.

31 Then Jesus said to them, "You will all become deserters because of me this night; for it is written, 'I will strike the shepherd, and the sheep of the flock will be scattered.' [32]But after I am raised up, I will go ahead of you to Galilee."

Again we must ask, Is Jesus predicting the future, or is Matthew telling us Jesus' story "according to the Scriptures," as Paul turns the phrase?

33 Peter said to him, "Though all become deserters because of you, I will never desert you." [34]Jesus said to him, "Truly I tell you, this very night, before

the cock crows, you will deny me three times." 35Peter said to him, "Even though I must die with you, I will not deny you." And so said all the disciples.

36 Then Jesus went with them to a place called Gethsemane; and he said to his disciples, "Sit here while I go over there and pray."

As we hear these words and the invitation within them, we might ask, What would it mean for us to join Jesus in this garden? What might it mean for us to venture into the night of his anguish with him—especially now in the violent shadows of our time?

37 He took with him Peter and the two sons of Zebedee, and began to be grieved and agitated. 38Then he said to them, "I am deeply grieved, even to death; remain here, and stay awake with me." 39And going a little farther, he threw himself on the ground and prayed, "My Father, if it is possible, let this cup pass from me; yet not what I want but what you want." 40Then he came to the disciples and found them sleeping; and he said to Peter, "So, could you not stay awake with me one hour? 41Stay awake and pray that you may not come into the time of trial; the spirit indeed is willing, but the flesh is weak."

Was Jesus angry when he said this? Matthew doesn't tell us. Even those who want to stay awake often have difficulty.

42 Again he went away for the second time and prayed, "My Father, if this cannot pass unless I drink it, your will be done." 43Again he came and found them sleeping, for their eyes were heavy. 44So leaving them again, he went away and prayed for the third time, saying the same words. 45Then he came to the disciples and said to them, "Are you still sleeping and taking your rest? See, the hour is at hand, and the Son of Man is betrayed into the hands of sinners. 46Get up, let us be going. See, my betrayer is at hand."

If they were all sleeping, except for Jesus, how do you suppose Matthew knew all this? What is Matthew telling us here?

47 While he was still speaking, Judas, one of the twelve, arrived; with him was a large crowd with swords and clubs, from the chief priests and the elders of the people. 48Now the betrayer had given them a sign, saying, "The one I will kiss is the man; arrest him."

Again, how do you suppose they knew this? Perhaps Matthew only knew about the kiss, not the intention behind it . . .

49   At once he came up to Jesus and said, "Greetings, Rabbi!" and kissed him. [50]Jesus said to him, "Friend, do what you are here to do." Then they came and laid hands on Jesus and arrested him. [51]Suddenly, one of those with Jesus put his hand on his sword, drew it, and struck the slave of the high priest, cutting off his ear. [52]Then Jesus said to him, "Put your sword back into its place; for all who take the sword will perish by the sword. [53]Do you think that I cannot appeal to my Father, and he will at once send me more than twelve legions of angels? [54]But how then would the scriptures be fulfilled, which say it must happen in this way?"

Have these words been stylized to capture the grace with which Jesus confronted the violence and prevented something worse from happening?

55   At that hour Jesus said to the crowds, "Have you come out with swords and clubs to arrest me as though I were a bandit? Day after day I sat in the temple teaching, and you did not arrest me. [56]But all this has taken place, so that the scriptures of the prophets may be fulfilled." Then all the disciples deserted him and fled.

Why now? Why not earlier?

57   Those who had arrested Jesus took him to Caiaphas the high priest, in whose house the scribes and the elders had gathered. [58]But Peter was following him at a distance, as far as the courtyard of the high priest; and going inside, he sat with the guards in order to see how this would end. [59]Now the chief priests and the whole council were looking for false testimony against Jesus so that they might put him to death, [60]but they found none, though many false witnesses came forward. At last two came forward [61]and said, "This fellow said, 'I am able to destroy the temple of God and to build it in three days.'" [62]The high priest stood up and said, "Have you no answer? What is it that they testify against you?" [63]But Jesus was silent. Then the high priest said to him, "I put you under oath before the living God, tell us if you are the Messiah, the Son of God." [64]Jesus said to him, "You have said so. But I tell you, From now on you will see the Son of Man seated at the right hand of Power and coming on the clouds of heaven."

How did Matthew know what was said in the house of Caiaphas? Was Matthew reporting an actual conversation or telling us something else?

65   Then the high priest tore his clothes and said, "He has blasphemed! Why do we still need witnesses? You have now heard his blasphemy. [66]What is your verdict?" They answered, "He deserves death." [67]Then they spat in his

face and struck him; and some slapped him, [68]saying, "Prophesy to us, you Messiah! Who is it that struck you?"

There seems to be more here than meets the eye, or ear. Perhaps Matthew is telling us of more than one trial, all in a stylized way: first, Jesus in the garden, along with the disciples; now Caiaphas in his domain; next Pilate; then the crowds of bystanders, and indirectly all of us. Who, indeed, is on trial here?

69 Now Peter was sitting outside in the courtyard. A servant-girl came to him and said, "You also were with Jesus the Galilean." [70]But he denied it before all of them, saying, "I do not know what you are talking about." [71]When he went out to the porch, another servant-girl saw him, and she said to the bystanders, "This man was with Jesus of Nazareth." [72]Again he denied it with an oath, "I do not know the man." [73]After a little while the bystanders came up and said to Peter, "Certainly you are also one of them, for your accent betrays you." [74]Then he began to curse, and he swore an oath, "I do not know the man!" At that moment the cock crowed. [75]Then Peter remembered what Jesus had said: "Before the cock crows, you will deny me three times." And he went out and wept bitterly.

Peter's trial.

27   1 When morning came, all the chief priests and the elders of the people conferred together against Jesus in order to bring about his death. [2]They bound him, led him away, and handed him over to Pilate the governor.

3 When Judas, his betrayer, saw that Jesus was condemned, he repented and brought back the thirty pieces of silver to the chief priests and the elders. [4]He said, "I have sinned by betraying innocent blood." But they said, "What is that to us? See to it yourself."

Judas seems surprised, not expecting a death sentence. Perhaps we haven't understood him, or his role in this story after all.

5 Throwing down the pieces of silver in the temple, he departed; and he went and hanged himself. [6]But the chief priests, taking the pieces of silver, said, "It is not lawful to put them into the treasury, since they are blood money." [7]After conferring together, they used them to buy the potter's field as a place to bury foreigners. [8]For this reason that field has been called the Field of Blood to this day. [9]Then was fulfilled what had been spoken through the prophet Jeremiah, "And they took the thirty pieces of silver, the price of the one on whom a price

had been set, on whom some of the people of Israel had set a price, [10]and they gave them for the potter's field, as the Lord commanded me."

11 Now Jesus stood before the governor; and the governor asked him, "Are you the King of the Jews?" Jesus said, "You say so." [12]But when he was accused by the chief priests and elders, he did not answer. [13]Then Pilate said to him, "Do you not hear how many accusations they make against you?" [14]But he gave him no answer, not even to a single charge, so that the governor was greatly amazed.

15 Now at the festival the governor was accustomed to release a prisoner for the crowd, anyone whom they wanted. [16]At that time they had a notorious prisoner, called Jesus Barabbas. [17]So after they had gathered, Pilate said to them, "Whom do you want me to release for you, Jesus Barabbas or Jesus who is called the Messiah?"

There seems to be something else going on here. Barabbas is Aramaic and means "son of the father"—Bar-Abbas. Who is being cross-examined by whom?

18 For he realized that it was out of jealousy that they had handed him over. [19]While he was sitting on the judgment seat, his wife sent word to him, "Have nothing to do with that innocent man, for today I have suffered a great deal because of a dream about him." [20]Now the chief priests and the elders persuaded the crowds to ask for Barabbas and to have Jesus killed. [21]The governor again said to them, "Which of the two do you want me to release for you?" And they said, "Barabbas." [22]Pilate said to them, "Then what should I do with Jesus who is called the Messiah?" All of them said, "Let him be crucified!" [23]Then he asked, "Why, what evil has he done?" But they shouted all the more, "Let him be crucified!"

24 So when Pilate saw that he could do nothing, but rather that a riot was beginning, he took some water and washed his hands before the crowd, saying, "I am innocent of this man's blood; see to it yourselves." [25]Then the people as a whole answered, "His blood be on us and on our children!" [26]So he released Barabbas for them; and after flogging Jesus, he handed him over to be crucified.

Matthew has the crowd, like a dramatic chorus, using the language of King David in 2 Samuel. In effect, they are confessing, according to their Scriptures, that they have acted as Amalek, the feared adversary of Israel and the slayer of God's anointed. Matthew would be appalled at how

savagely this stylized, confessional language has been used out of context against the Jewish people through the centuries.

27 Then the soldiers of the governor took Jesus into the governor's head-quarters, and they gathered the whole cohort around him. [28]They stripped him and put a scarlet robe on him, [29]and after twisting some thorns into a crown, they put it on his head. They put a reed in his right hand and knelt before him and mocked him, saying, "Hail, King of the Jews!" [30]They spat on him, and took the reed and struck him on the head. [31]After mocking him, they stripped him of the robe and put his own clothes on him. Then they led him away to crucify him.

Humiliation. Degradation. It denies the humanity of the victim and shields the executioners from their own violence. It is but a prelude of the torture to come.

32 As they went out, they came upon a man from Cyrene named Simon; they compelled this man to carry his cross. [33]And when they came to a place called Golgotha (which means Place of a Skull), [34]they offered him wine to drink, mixed with gall; but when he tasted it, he would not drink it. [35]And when they had crucified him, they divided his clothes among themselves by casting lots; [36]then they sat down there and kept watch over him.

They didn't fall asleep.

37 Over his head they put the charge against him, which read, "This is Jesus, the King of the Jews."

Remember the disciples who earlier competed for who would sit on Jesus' right and who would have the privilege of being seated at his left? Look how the irony builds.

38 Then two bandits were crucified with him, one on his right and one on his left. [39]Those who passed by derided him, shaking their heads [40]and saying, "You who would destroy the temple and build it in three days, save yourself! If you are the Son of God, come down from the cross." [41]In the same way the chief priests also, along with the scribes and elders, were mocking him, saying, [42]"He saved others; he cannot save himself. He is the King of Israel; let him come down from the cross now, and we will believe in him. [43]He trusts in God; let God deliver him now, if he wants to; for he said, 'I am God's Son.'" [44]The bandits who were crucified with him also taunted him in the same way.

And the disciples were missing in action.

45 From noon on, darkness came over the whole land until three in the afternoon. [46]And about three o'clock Jesus cried with a loud voice, "Eli, Eli, lema sabachthani?" that is, "My God, my God, why have you forsaken me?" [47]When some of the bystanders heard it, they said, "This man is calling for Elijah."

Eliyahu [Eh-lee-yah-hu] in Hebrew.

48 At once one of them ran and got a sponge, filled it with sour wine, put it on a stick, and gave it to him to drink. [49]But the others said, "Wait, let us see whether Elijah will come to save him." [50]Then Jesus cried again with a loud voice and breathed his last. [51]At that moment the curtain of the temple was torn in two, from top to bottom. The earth shook, and the rocks were split. [52]The tombs also were opened, and many bodies of the saints who had fallen asleep were raised. [53]After his resurrection they came out of the tombs and entered the Holy City and appeared to many. [54]Now when the centurion and those with him, who were keeping watch over Jesus, saw the earthquake and what took place, they were terrified and said, "Truly this man was God's Son!"

Note well. Only the centurion and his cohorts seemed to observe the cataclysmic events Matthew has described. Perhaps he is once again telling the story using the language of Scripture, in this case Amos 8, to help us see what was hidden in plain sight as these events unfolded. The world was being shaken, but not in the way we usually think.

55 Many women were also there, looking on from a distance; they had followed Jesus from Galilee and had provided for him. [56]Among them were Mary Magdalene, and Mary the mother of James and Joseph, and the mother of the sons of Zebedee.

Mary, the mother of James and Joseph. Jesus' mother was named Mary and had four children according to Matthew: James and Joseph, Simon and Judas. Is *this* Mary also Jesus' mother? Perhaps Matthew is providing a veiled reference for those who know to make the right connections.

57 When it was evening, there came a rich man from Arimathea, named Joseph, who was also a disciple of Jesus. [58]He went to Pilate and asked for the body of Jesus; then Pilate ordered it to be given to him. [59]So Joseph took the body and wrapped it in a clean linen cloth [60]and laid it in his own new

tomb, which he had hewn in the rock. He then rolled a great stone to the door of the tomb and went away.

Is this a final irony? Even in death, Jesus depended upon the hospitality of another to receive his final resting place.

61   Mary Magdalene and the other Mary were there, sitting opposite the tomb. [62]The next day, that is, after the day of Preparation, the chief priests and the Pharisees gathered before Pilate [63]and said, "Sir, we remember what that impostor said while he was still alive, 'After three days I will rise again.' [64]Therefore command the tomb to be made secure until the third day; otherwise his disciples may go and steal him away, and tell the people, 'He has been raised from the dead,' and the last deception would be worse than the first." [65]Pilate said to them, "You have a guard of soldiers; go, make it as secure as you can." [66]So they went with the guard and made the tomb secure by sealing the stone.

Sealed. Secure. Jesus was buried. What else was buried with him and sealed up in that tomb? Surely more than a body.

Dear friends, this is the passion story of Jesus, as rendered by Matthew, interspersed with commentary along the way to help us wrestle with its text, so that we, like Jacob at the Jabbok, may be blessed in our wrestling. May the words of our mouths and the meditations of our hearts be acceptable in your sight, O Lord, our strength and our redeemer. Amen.

All Glory, Laud, and Honor

Refrain:
All glory, laud and honor,
To thee, Redeemer, sing,
To whom the lips of children
Made sweet hosannas ring.

Anointed one of Israel,
Thou David's royal Son,
Who in the Lord's name comest,
The longed-for, Blessèd One.
Refrain

The company of angels
Are praising thee on high,

And mortal folk and all things
Created make reply.

Refrain

Yes, people of Jerusalem
With palms before thee went;
Our prayer and praise and anthems
Before thee we present.

Refrain

To thee, before thy passion,
They sang their hymns of praise;
To thee, now high exalted,
Our melody we raise.

Refrain

Orig. Words: Theodulph of Orleans;
English Trans.: John M. Neale; revised: Henry F. Knight
Music: St. Theodulph

O Sacred Head Now Wounded

O sacred Head, now wounded, with grief and shame weighed down,
Now scornfully surrounded with thorns, thine only crown;
How pale thou art with anguish, with sore abuse and scorn!
How does that visage languish, which once was bright as morn!

What thou, my Lord, hast suffered, was all for sinners' gain;
Mine, mine was the transgression, but thine the deadly pain.
Lo, here I fall, my Savior! 'Tis I deserve thy place;
Look on me with thy favor, vouchsafe to me thy grace.

My burden in thy Passion, Lord, thou hast borne for me,
For it was my transgression which brought this woe on thee.
I cast me down before thee, wrath were my rightful lot;
Have mercy, I implore thee; Redeemer, spurn me not!

What language shall I borrow to thank thee, dearest friend,
For this thy dying sorrow, thy pity without end?
O make me thine forever, and should I fainting be,
Lord, let me never, never outlive my love to thee.

Latin words: Bernard of Clairvaux; German: Paul Gerhardt;
English trans.: James W. Alexander
Music: Hans L. Hassler; harmony: J. S. Bach

Were You There?

Were you there when they crucified my Lord?
Were you there when they crucified my Lord?
Oh! Sometimes it causes me to tremble, tremble, tremble.
Were you there when they crucified my Lord?

Were you there when they nailed him to the tree?
Were you there when they nailed him to the tree?
Oh! Sometimes it causes me to tremble, tremble, tremble.
Were you there when they nailed him to the tree?

Were you there when they laid him in the tomb?
Were you there when they laid him in the tomb?
Oh! Sometimes it causes me to tremble, tremble, tremble.
Were you there when they laid him in the tomb?

Words and music: African American Spiritual, trad.

NOTES

1. J. B. Metz, *The Emergent Church: The Future of Christianity in a Postbourgeois World* (New York: Crossroad, 1987), 19, 32.

2. Ibid.

3. Borg notes this irony in *The Meaning of Jesus: Two Visions*: "At approximately the same time, the Roman governor Pilate, with all the pomp and power of empire, would have been entering Jerusalem from the west at the head of a squadron of Roman Cavalry" (Marcus J. Borg and N. T. Wright, *The Meaning of Jesus: Two Visions* [San Francisco: HarperCollins, 1999], 83). Likewise Helen Bond explains, "On occasion, however, the governor did move to Jerusalem [from Caesarea]. This was especially important during festivals when the crowds and religious fervor generated could potentially lead to rioting. The presence of the governor with his troops helped to check such outbreak" (*Pontius Pilate in History and Interpretations* [Cambridge: University of Cambridge Press, 1998], 7–8).

4. John Dominic Crossan, *Who Killed Jesus? Exposing the Roots of Anti-Semitism in the Gospel Story of the Death of Jesus* (San Francisco: HarperCollins, 1995), 1–4.

5. Marcus J. Borg, *Reading the Bible Again for the First Time* (San Francisco: HarperCollins, 2001), 37–53.

6. Borg and Wright have provided a very helpful and accessible resource for dealing with these differences in their book *The Meaning of Jesus: Two Visions*. Their methodological and historical assumptions are explicitly contrasted and related to the distinctive portraits that they are able to develop with regard to Jesus, whom both view, though in different ways, as the Messiah. See pages 85–91 (Borg) and 97–100 (Wright).

7. The connection is subtle but important as Regina Schwartz has pointed out. The either-or logic of scarcity breeds the spirit of conquest. See Regina M. Schwartz, *The Curse of Cain: The Violent Legacy of Monotheism* (Chicago: University of Chicago Press, 1997), xi, 3–5, passim.

8. Crossan and Borg both make the point that we do not have direct access to Jesus' self-awareness in the witness of Scripture. But in doing so, they tend to rule out several options that midrash can retain as possibilities born by the text, namely, Jesus' intentions with regard to the

prophetic/messianic legacy of Zechariah. Borg and Crossan conclude that if Matthew is using the prophetic rhetoric of Zechariah, he is projecting it with little or no foundation in Jesus' own mindset. Of course, they are building their case from the inaccessibility of Jesus apart from confessional perspectives like Matthew's, as well as from other parts of the biblical record where Jesus resists such designations. But their approach may be too prone to arguing for one position or overly dependent on the larger text being more internally consistent with regard to its own logic and rhetoric.

9. Based on *From Ashes to Fire Supplemental Worship Resources 8* (Nashville: Abingdon Press, 1979), 50–53, quoted in Hoyt Hickman, Don E. Saliers, Laurence Hull Stookey, and James F. White, *The New Handbook of the Christian Year* (Nashville: Abingdon Press, 1986, 1992), 126–31.

10. The text of the doxology is adapted from Brian Wren's hymn, "Praise God, from whom all blessings flow," which he based on Thomas Ken's well-known doxology. See "Praise God, from whom all blessings flow," in *A New Hymnal for Colleges and Schools,* ed. Jeffrey Rowthorn and Russell Schulz-Widmar (New Haven, CT: Yale University Press, 1992), 330.

Chapter 3

Turning the Tables and Reconfiguring the Conflict

From the Temple to the Upper Room

The Dilemma of Return

Renewal and return are central concerns of Lenten piety and its confessional life. Annually, the church calendar guides Christians around the world on a journey of penitential return to the heart of their faith as followers of Jesus Christ. And that journey follows Jesus from his ministry in Galilee to the cross on Calvary. Through this return, the dedicated faithful prepare for the transformative good news of Easter—that death has not won, that the grave is empty, that Jesus has been raised from the dead.

This has been the liturgical and confessional pattern of return for Christians for centuries. After Auschwitz, however, we know that this pattern has told another, shadow story of violence to Jews. Embedded in its telling has been another pattern of disdain and contempt that has held Jewish identity hostage in Christian eyes to a negative significance on which Christian identity has built its central, confessional story. How do we face this dislocating realization? How do we not, now that we know what we do about its problematic configurations vis-à-vis Jews and suffering?

As we make our way to Jerusalem and once more encounter the differences that separate us as Christians from our Jewish siblings, we face a disturbing truth: the violent attitudes toward Jews are writ deep in the narratives of Christian identity, even in Scripture, and have been passed on to more than one generation in a legacy of dismissal and disdain. Now, when Christians go up to Jerusalem, prepared to follow their Messiah into the gates of its holy precincts, we limp in our awareness of shadow figures and ghosts of burning, tortured children. How do we proceed?

The matter is intensely focused for us as we follow Jesus to the temple precincts, where he confronts temple officials selling animals for sacrificial use to pilgrims who have come to Jerusalem for Passover. It is intensified further as he gathers his disciples for a last meal in the shadows of this prophetic act and in anticipation of the celebration of Passover. Even thoughtful and penitent Christians cannot avoid this conflict. What we must do is ask if it is fully understood and adequately configured in our ritual returns to the confessional heart of who we are as Jesus' disciples and guests in the house of Israel, included as we are by the actions that extend from him in the heart of Jerusalem. Let us take our place in the courtyard of the temple.

Problems with the Temple

Matthew's account is simple, at first glance. Having entered Jerusalem, Jesus' first stop was the temple, where he encountered temple officials who provided animals for sacrifice on the temple's altar. Jesus confronted their behavior in a symbolic action that many scholars link to his crucifixion later in the week. But such a reading of this act may need to be resisted, both because of questions with regard to the accuracy of what might have happened and because of our need to proceed more carefully and thoughtfully than in the past.

John Dominic Crossan contends that in this act Jesus was boldly confronting the temple and *all* that it represented.[1] Marcus Borg views the action as an intentional protest against the temple "as the center of a purity system that was also a system of economic and political oppression."[2] Hence his pairing, "a politics of compassion" versus a "politics of purity." Bruce Chilton offers a more nuanced, and to my mind more challenging, perspective. He explains that around the year 30 CE Caiaphas had removed the Sanhedrin from its location in the southern courtyard of the temple and replaced them with temple representatives who provided ritually pure animals to be used for sacrifices in the temple by traveling pilgrims. With this provision, they could purchase their animals without fear of their being blemished. The officials of the temple would take them immediately to be used in the sacrificial rites. In this way, the purity of the animals could be assured for anyone traveling to Jerusalem to make sacrifices during the festival pilgrimages. Chilton argues that Jesus would have been particularly concerned about the absence of a relationship between the sacrificial offerings and those coming to the temple to offer their sacrifices. Marcus Borg understands the confrontation similarly and concludes that the issue was a matter of inclusion more than it was a matter of purity. However, where Borg argues that Jesus was enacting a politics of compassion to challenge the existing politics of purity, Chilton highlights Jesus challenging the disconnection between the worshipper and his or her offering. In other words, instead of an offering of an animal that can be unquestionably certified as pure, Jesus seemed to be looking for an action that directly communicated the offering of oneself. When the animal was purchased for sacrifice but never possessed or even handled by the offerer, the connection between the sacrifice and the worshipper was lost. The focus has moved to the purity of the animal and away from the purity of the deed. According to Chilton, this shift lay at the heart of Jesus' act.

Of course, one need not choose between Borg or Chilton in order to see more clearly the conflict Jesus was generating at the temple. Either way, Jesus' actions in the temple courtyard did not provoke immediate action, either on the part of temple authorities or Roman ones. Instead, Jesus returned to the temple at least once more to teach, at some length, telling parables and offering strong observations about the temple and its limitations in contrast to the rule and realm of God. As Matthew recounts this extended story, these teachings include strong criticisms of the temple leaders, as well as direct challenges to its erstwhile reformers, the Pharisees. Any direct linkage with Jesus' initial act in the temple courtyard and his death must account for the interim period in which Jesus returns without being stopped by the temple leaders or arrested by the Roman authorities in the city. In my judgment Crossan does not provide this.

Between the Temple and the Upper Room

The narrative describing the time between the temple conflict and the last meal is full, but ambiguous. For Matthew, it is filled with sayings, parables and accompanying incidents. Matthew reports Jesus returning to the temple to teach there and in its shadows. As the days after his demonstration in the temple courtyard pass, he moves between Bethany and nearby Jerusalem, teaching about the rule and realm of God and challenging the ways of Jerusalem and its temple.

Several of the parables and sayings that Matthew places in the interim between the prophetic action at the temple and the upper room are recalled without reference to where they occurred. Their place is either assumed or unimportant. One possibility is that they are projected backwards into this empty space because they have been collected from oral memory without clarity regarding where or even when they were shared. Another possibility is that they occurred in transit between Bethany and the temple as Jesus made this walk on several occasions. Still another possibility is that some of these teachings happened over meals shared during this interim period. Midrash, of course, invites such speculation in order to deepen the texture of what

Matthew has shared. Indeed, he may have left the open spaces himself to encourage that. What midrash does not do is seek a singularly authoritative, historical reconstruction that would provide the definitive recovery of the missing data. Still, the reconstructions of scholars like Crossan and Chilton help us recognize the depth of what must have transpired in these openings left by the text.

As Crossan accounts for it, Jesus had adopted a sapiential eschatology, announcing "that God has given *all human beings* [italics in original text] the wisdom to discern how, here and now in this world, one can so live that God's power, rule, and dominion are evidently present to all observers."[3] In the interim between the action at the temple and his last meal, Jesus continued to relativize the sacrificial system of the temple. Using parables about fig trees and meals, he proclaimed the presence of God's rule and realm in the here and now of open eating and healing, as well as through the restoration of fractured community through forgiveness and other acts of radical hospitality.[4] He thereby challenged both the reform movement of the Pharisees and the reactionary concerns of the Sadducees.

Still, the conflict with the temple does not yet precipitate overt reaction. That does not occur until after his meal in the upper room. Of course, as Matthew tells this story, he points out occasions when the collusion began. But most scholars are in agreement that such narrative signals are the result of hindsight, not contemporaneous knowledge. In fact, some scholars view the time frame between Jesus' entry into the city and his subsequent death and resurrection as a collapsed period of time that actually spanned a much broader period. Regardless, the point is that the resistance to Jesus on the part of the religious and secular authorities grew in intensity after Jesus' encounter with the temple representatives in the courtyard. Their reaction, whatever it was, developed. Furthermore, the challenges Jesus brought to the sacrificial system and to its reformers likewise grew in intensity. As a result, we cannot collapse the conflict those encounters represent into a simple equation of Jesus against the temple or Jesus against the Pharisees, or Jesus against the Roman authorities. The conflict developed with increasing layers of intensity and meaning. When that conflict finally boiled over, it involved several groups and none in the same way.

Shaping the Conflict

Jesus clearly relativized the temple and its sacrificial system. Whether he wanted to do away with the temple or to reform it, we may not finally be able to determine. However, by following Chilton's observations and focusing on the sacrificial actions of the offerer and the act of offering, we can infer that Jesus did not want to obscure the importance of sacrifice properly undertaken. Rather, the important feature for Jesus appears to be the intentionality of the act offered on behalf of a restored covenantal reality. The point was to indicate the offerer's full expression of thanksgiving and commitment in response to the hospitality of inclusion and grace experienced as a participant in covenantal partnership with God.

Crossan argues that Jesus did not seek reform of the temple but destruction of the temple and its sacrificial system. But, as Chilton points out, this explanation cannot account for Jesus' reliance on the temple after his symbolic action in the courtyard or his disciples' later devotion to the temple after Jesus' crucifixion and resurrection. After all, the temple was the ritual as well as symbolic center of Jerusalem. The temple signaled the ever-present reality of Sinai and its claims on the people. It was not simply a place for sacrifice; it was the symbolic center of religious life and consequently the central location for teaching as well. While Jesus was challenging the sacrificial system of the temple and the authority of its priests, particularly Caiaphas, he was also presuming the power of its symbolic significance in choosing to teach there about the rule and realm of God. In this regard, Chilton's reconstruction can account for more of the details of the full passion story than Crossan's.

Raymond Brown, in his monumental study *The Death of the Messiah*, works from different presuppositions than Crossan, accepting the historical credibility of the narrative as it is presented in the text. He takes the biblical text as given. Yet according to Crossan, Brown has read the testimony of Matthew as history prophesized.[5] A midrashic approach, however, sees Brown's insistence on the canonical text in a different way, without forcing an either-or choice between Crossan and Brown. In midrash, the limits are stretched, pushed, even challenged. But they are not violated. The text cannot contradict itself, unless that is literally how the text reads. But the text can provide leverage to challenge and test itself by supplying other vantage points and different perspectives on the same matter. The interim activities and the gaps in the narrative provide such leverage in this case. Still the text remains what it is. Even so, we may discover, as we have here, that the plain meaning of the text may shift, depending on several factors. In this case, then, enlarging the scope of the text before us changes the shape of the conflict between Jesus and the temple authorities. In other words, the questions and concerns raised by Crossan do not depend upon the reconstruction he contends must lie behind the text. They arise from paying closer attention to the text and the boundaries by which we consider its plain meaning, its *peshat*.

Because Jesus was crucified, we must look for a crime in the eyes of Rome to explain this action. Crossan is right in this regard. Yet the shape of the conflict, as Chilton points out, does not fully account for the extreme actions that follow until we understand the way Jesus intensified the conflict initiated at the temple when he gathered his disciples at a table in the so-called upper room. With that goal in mind, let us move to the upper room.

Return to the Table

We take our place in the upper room looking over the shoulders of Matthew, who himself is looking in as an outside observer but over the shoulders of the disciples. The report he offers is again sparse, focusing on two primary moments in the meal: the prediction of betrayal and the words of institution. In each case, Matthew simply declares, "while they were eating" and then describes Jesus confronting the disciples about one of them at the table acting to betray him. Then with the same contexting statement ("while they were eating") he describes Jesus' words and actions with the loaf of bread and the cup of wine.

The scene is economically set. Earlier on the first day of Passover, after an inquiry as to where they should prepare for the evening Seder, Jesus tells his disciples to go into the city and to look for a certain man who would show them where to make their preparations. Evidently, arrangements had been made for Jesus and his disciples to gather in a room set aside for this purpose. In other words, preparations are made, without designating where or how, and the Passover meal takes place. In contrast, the Gospel of Mark describes this last meal with more specificity, locating it in the so-called "upper room" and identifying the unnamed man with an act of carrying a jar of water, suggesting that a specific arrangement had already been made with him. Still, the designated arrangement lies hidden in the background of the text. The Gospel of John, in contrast, describes the last meal differently, locating it on the evening before Passover begins, omitting any mention of words and actions associated with the offerings of bread and wine, instead describing Jesus washing his disciples feet in contrast to the betrayal of one of his disciples. As we return to Matthew, then, our focus is concentrated on the two moments of Jesus speaking to his disciples, first, confronting them about the infidelity present at the table and, second, identifying the bread and wine as his offerings of flesh/body and blood. Why?

If Chilton is right about his analysis of what happened at the temple, and his argument is quite convincing, then Jesus was concerned with the purity of the offering as an act, not the purity of the offering as an object, the animal. He contends that Jesus was not concerned with breaking the sacrificial system but with lifting up what was essential in it, revealed, as it were, in the failure to connect the person with the gift being offered. The lack of connection between worshipper and sacrifice, person and deed, leads to the recognition of what is either wrong with the act or missing from it. Furthermore, after Jesus turned the tables on the accommodations in the courtyard, he returned to the more familiar table shared with his disciples, now ritually intensified in the context of Passover. There, Jesus took bread and wine and identified them as his offerings in a covenantal act of sacrificial commitment to the covenantal fabric of life. "This bread," he declared, "is my flesh—my body; this wine is my blood." In effect, he was saying, "Not what was happening at the temple. These gifts of bread and wine are the sacrifice that I offer. This meal is the full embodiment of what was intended in the temple."[6]

Matthew remembers, albeit in an intensely stylized manner, that Jesus' final meal either provoked or evoked a crisis. Furthermore, the crisis he recounts affected not just one or two but all of the disciples. Moreover, as Matthew recalls the crisis (Matt. 26:14–56), he describes Jesus as fully aware of its scope and nature. We may read the text to mean that Jesus was able to predict the behavior of his disciples—or even that he knew of Judas's behavior and confronted him with it in the context of a meal, forcing him to face his own infidelity. We may equally read the story as the result of Matthew's weaving subsequent actions back into the actions at the table to characterize Jesus' understanding of his disciples' fallibility as they gathered there. Or we may interpret the crisis somewhere in the middle of this continuum. Regardless, Matthew's account of the crisis is highly stylized, guiding his readers and hearers to recognize that Jesus brought an intention to the meal to face the crisis of covenantal fidelity, however it was manifest there. Furthermore, Jesus embraced that covenantal crisis at the meal in a way that eventually transformed the growing rift he saw on the horizon.

Framing the Holy

If this reading of Jesus' actions at the upper room table is anywhere close to what happened, then Jesus reversed in powerful ways the relationship between the first offerings of Cain and Abel. But he did so by deepening the sacrificial dimension in the process by offering himself through the fruits of life (bread and wine)—not by offering an animal to be sacrificed, or any victim, for that matter. He effectively removed the violence implicit in the system.

Relationality, the key to Jesus' understanding of purity, stands in contrast to the more typical emphases of Pharisaic reform, which sought to extend the discipline of the temple to the household and embody in ordinary actions the purity necessary for serving in the temple. Jesus, on the other hand, saw the hidden dimensions of the holy in the relationality of the everyday, whenever one made room for the other with hospitality, respect, and compassion. The upper room *gestalt*[7] extends outward from forms of relation that are rooted in true hospitality for the other. In contrast, temple purity is rooted in the emptiness of the Holy of Holies and extends from there, with demands for purity required for each progressive movement toward the holy from the opposite direction on the part of the worshipper.[8] In each case, one made room for the holy in its "set-apartness." But in the case of the upper room, the space created for the holy was the space established for otherness in the actions of hospitality.

Post-Shoah, the importance of a relationally circumscribed sense of the holy cannot be overstated. The holy is honored and respected in acts of hospitality that establish, in relationships with others, room for the other to be other. And such acts also provide room for the holy, in its otherness, to be welcomed and embraced as well. Whatever else the Shoah was, it was an assault on hospitality to the other, most particularly the Jewish other and all that he or she represented to the gentile world.

During this week, the conflict that had been developing between Jesus and the Pharisees overflowed its boundaries, as Jesus came into direct conflict with the priestly authorities at the temple (high priests), and their conflict spilled over to the conflict with the civil authorities. Consequently, the nature of the conflict in Jerusalem was more complex than one might grasp in a first or second reading of the story. Its shape has to do with the shape of what is good and holy and the center of our lives—not with whom to blame in a zero-sum game of winning and losing, or even a dispute solely about what is clean and unclean. When we add to this the conflict between a later generation of Jesus' followers and the heirs of the Pharisaic tradition,[9] we have some sense of the complex character of the conflict that marks Jesus' encounters with Jerusalem as they punctuate the narrative of this week.

Interpretive Tasks

As we come to terms with the conflict that Jesus occasioned in the heart of Jerusalem, we discover that it extends farther and deeper than we realized. The *peshat*, the plain meaning of the text, is not as clear or fixed as we thought. As a result, the meaning and information we bring to the conflict is extended to reflect a more extensive text. Similarly, the immediate context and our historical understandings of it are resituated. With this enriched texture we may engage in close, critical reading and recognize hitherto unperceived connections that now appear almost obvious, except that it required the enlarged *peshat* to make that plain. This too is midrashic.

What then are the implications of this reconfigured encounter with the story for how we make our way through Holy Week liturgically, homiletically, and pastorally? As we move from the narrated world of Scripture to the liturgy and drama of Holy Week, as we let the larger conflict shape our understanding of what happened in the transition from the temple to the upper room, we must ask how it is expressed or repressed in the liturgical frame of the week. Restricting the conflict to the Temple Mount, and not including what happened at the upper room table, misconstrues the shape of the real conflict. Consequently, our first goal is to get the conflict right. There is conflict in the story, even as there is conflict between Jews and Christians as they meet post-Shoah. New sensitivities and spiritual humility do not erase our differences. But they do challenge us to reconfigure our conflicts more wisely.

Furthermore, Jesus was not unique or even the first in waging conflict with the temple authorities. Some among the Pharisees, most notably Hillel in his arguments with Shammai and his followers, challenged the shape of the temple's sacrificial system as it found expression under the leadership of the high priest Caiaphas. As well, familiarity with the biblical witness should remind Christian readers that Jesus is reported to have taught in the temple precincts following his confrontation with the "money changers," and that following Easter Jesus' disciples taught there as well.

In addition, we must reclaim important continuity with the covenantal intentionality of *halakah* as it is embodied in these materials by reconnecting with the covenantal history of Israel. Jesus was clearly trying to serve this intentionality, even when he was confronting it. Consequently, we must be alert to ways we cut the Christian witness off from its covenantal context by telling or treating the passion narrative in isolation from that life-orienting context. In other words, we must remain covenantally whole, even when arguing about the shape of covenant life.

Moreover, we should not overlook the conflict generated by Jesus' exercise of authority in relationship to this covenantal history, the shape of the holy as it was manifest in its sacrificial system, and how he understood the boundaries of inclusion and purity in that covenantal way of being and doing. In other words, our post-Shoah perspective does not remove us from recognizing the strong disagreement with regard to authority between Jesus and the religious leaders of his day. But we must identify that conflict accurately, carefully, aware of the ways we can slip into the either-or mentality of us against them, a mentality Jesus opposed on numerous occasions.

In this spirit, then, we are confounded by this figure who takes us back to center, daring us to reconsider how we approach and shape the holy, and whom we include in the boundaries of its domain. We must not be afraid to claim that Jesus is clearly turning the tables on religious authorities in this narrative, but he is not turning the tables on Jews or Judaism per se—and neither may we. Rather, he is turning the tables on anyone (including us) who seeks to fence in the holy and thereby tries to control and regulate it. For Jesus, the holy won't stay inside our fences. It cannot be sealed in our systems or our tombs—more on that later.

Even here, of course, we have to be careful putting the matter this way, since one of the traditional ways of speaking about *halakah* is that it is a fence around the Torah. But the task of that fence is not to keep the holy in; rather, its role is to signal to others, when they are approaching the holy, that the holy is near, and that one should proceed with care and respect. Indeed, pun intended, the role of *halakah* is to alert and proclaim that the holy is served in the ordinary as well as in the extraordinary times and places in which we dwell. That is, there is no place one may not honor the obligation of covenant life. Nonetheless, the point remains. For Jesus, the holy won't stay fenced in, enclosed inside our boundaries.

Being clear about the pastoral task requires that we come to terms with the shape of the conflict disclosed by our approaching the conflict the way we have. Our goal is not to arrive at a final and singular reconstruction of the conflict as it happened between Jesus and the temple authorities or between Jesus and the representatives of Rome. To be sure, the intricacies of reconstruction will be beyond the expertise of most pastors and not a few scholars. But the impact of reconstruction will not be. It discloses the multiple voices that constituted the conflict and the scope of the arena in which their conflict made sense then and makes sense now. Many of those voices were Jewish, and the debate and argument would have occurred among Jews about matters important to their world. Other voices would be distinctly Roman and signal issues regarding power and control more than anything else. Still other voices reflect collusion between representatives of Rome and Jews with invested interests at stake in Jerusalem. But none of the voices justifies indiscriminate caricature of Jesus in conflict with *the* Jews or even all Pharisees. Instead, the work of scholars like Chilton, Borg, and Crossan should lead us to appreciate the complexity of the conflict and the specificity of the voices involved in it, as well as the issues over which they differed. The voice of scholars like Brown will hold us accountable to what the text, as we have it, says in its canonical form. Midrash provides a way of listening and being informed by all of them.

When we enter this orchard, we will recognize ways that we have over-simplified and distorted the scene portrayed in the distinctive Gospel portraits of this last week. What the Gospels presumed as background and texture, we cannot. What the Gospels reshaped, we too easily lose, because the gestalt against which they pushed is too often overlooked or hidden from our view. Our task is to restore as much of that as we can without claiming to know more than we do or can. As we succeed and recognize what we have done in our oversimplifications and distortions, we may discover unintended, or even intended, violence—more often in the form of contempt and disdain, at least in the domain of the biblical text and our interpretations of it. When this happens, we may be moved, adopting the theme that Chilton has tried to restore, to attend to the relational purity of our sacrificial offering.

As we look anew at Jesus in the temple courtyard, particularly as it relates to his actions at table during his last meal with his disciples, we may find that we have distorted the conflict we thought we understood. And if we look closely at the words in Matthew 5:23–24 about putting down one's offering to seek out an estranged neighbor, we will recognize that the interruption Jesus is describing[10] comes as an essential act in fulfilling the relational significance of our sacred obligations. In short, as we limp through Jerusalem, through Holy Week, we will meet such interruptions ourselves—even in presentations like this one. When we do, we may need to attend to the matter at hand before proceeding further. That's the way with life, and with the sacred. We can fence in neither one. In other words, our pastoral tasks may often come as interruptions as well as carefully planned attempts to return with authenticity and compassion to the narrated world of the text.

Our pastoral tasks, however, are almost never encountered without being entangled in specific circumstances. With that in mind, let us ponder a troubling, but easily overlooked, sacramental implication that grows out of examining how we frame the way we gather at the Lord's Table in our own sanctuaries. There is, of course, some risk in this regard. However, there is probably no more appropriate issue to face in the context of these reflections. Before we do, however, let us push away from the table, so to speak, in order to come to terms with another matter that will help us as we move forward.

Pushing Back from the Table—A Hermeneutical Pause

As indicated in an earlier footnote, the German loanword *gestalt* helps us make important hermeneutical distinctions as we move forward through the narrative terrain of Jerusalem. Many readers will recognize the term from either the domain of *gestalt psychology* or exercises on perception conducted a few decades ago, wherein persons would be asked to identity a figure in a simple line drawing. Some would see one character; others would see quite the opposite. The drawings were intentionally constructed to contain both figures, with one or the other coming into focal awareness, depending upon which aspects of the drawing the viewer used as background in establishing a figure-ground relationship. This activity was used to help people recognize the active work of interpretation that accompanies any act of perception. The reality being perceived was described as a gestalt of relationships that took identifiable shape, depending upon how those relationships were constructed. And in these cases, the fundamental relationships being established were those of foreground and background.

At the heart of this activity is the recognition that perception and interpretation are fundamentally related to the reality we experience. Moreover, that relatedness is captured in the wordplay that develops when we consider how we speak about our significant relationships. For example: They configure our lives. They can be disfigured or reconfigured in life-changing ways. Sometimes they undergo transfiguration. In each case, we are speaking of relational gestalts of some kind or other that are both external to us and essentially connected to how we perceive and relate to them. Configure, reconfigure, figure, configuration—which all share the same root, figure—are terms we may use to express the gestalt of covenant life as embodied in and through the ministry and person of Jesus.

Hopefully, using a term like *gestalt* honors the relational view of the world[11] that is at stake in these observations. Perception, interpretation, and the reality in which we live and interact are all fundamentally related. Indeed, Jesus' parables seem to point in this same direction; he employed short narratives to interrupt ways of perceiving situations and interacting with others that froze those circumstances in one-dimensional occasions. With his parables he introduced an alternative way of seeing that offered an abundance of meaning and possibility, breaking open the logic of scarcity operating among those in his presence. Indeed, he told such stories in the presence of gestalts of generosity and hospitality that his stories served to usher into the foreground of shared perception. With his parables, Jesus reconfigured the lifeworlds of those he met and taught.

Peter Hodgson's use of *gestalt* to explain the dynamic character of Jesus' understanding of the kingdom of God has been especially helpful in this regard. Hodgson uses the term to render the Greek word *basileia*, more typically translated as the "kingdom" or "empire" in the phrase "kingdom of God/heaven."[12] In using *gestalt* he captures the relational qualities of God's rule and realm; at the same time he is able to avoid the hierarchical notions of power associated with the monarchic metaphor we more typically employ. The term has been especially instructive in helping me to identify and express the fundamentally relational quality of covenant life as it happens in various ways and circumstances in our own experience and to understand its occurrence as described in the Gospels. For example, hospitality is constituted by a host and a guest or guests linked in a particular kind of relationship; when it occurs, there is a very palpable ethos or spirit that can be felt, even perceived, by others. But it requires the perceiver to put it together in a whole that is larger than its parts. When that happens, the generosity that makes hospitality possible provides possibilities for healing as well. In other words, the rule and realm of God has come near and brought with it a wholeness to reality that blesses those who participate in it. Similarly, I have been helped by Hodgson in his use of *gestalt* to speak of the presence of the risen Christ. He explains that whatever else resurrection might be, the Christ who is experienced on the other side of death is identified with the covenantal gestalt of relationships, teachings, and actions that Jesus embodied with others.[13] I will explore this implication further in chapter 6.

I ask my readers to join me in coming to terms with the words we select to represent important matters like these. While the use of the term *gestalt* may appear jargonistic, I have been unable to find a better way to capture the dynamic, relational nature of reality that we more conventionally refer to in static, substantive ways. For example, the human self is typically identified in substantive terms that treat the self as an autonomous entity solely responsible for the relationships the self inherits and develops over time. However, as Walter Brueggemann has argued so persuasively in *The Covenanted Self*, each human being is an identifiable matrix of relationships embodied and particularized in a single person but never in isolation from others—and always more than the sum of those relationships.[14] Theologians of the early church recognized this too, so they applied Trinitarian thinking not simply to the life of God but also to the life of each human being. That is, each human being is fully encountered in body, mind, and soul, but always more than one or the other of these aspects. However, many of us, as this language suggests, view these triadic dimensions in substantive ways: We have a body; we have a mind; we have a soul. In contrast, the notion of a *gestalt* points us toward relationality itself as a dynamic, yet identifiably embodied expression of individual and corporate existence. Mind, body, soul are dimensions of the relational fabric of human existence, not discrete entities or substances we possess.

Not surprisingly, the theological concept of the Trinity can be rendered with insight and power with the help of the term *gestalt*. For example, when we speak of God as Father, Son, and Holy Spirit, we mean that God is fully encountered in and through each of these moments but also as a Trinity of relationship. The notion of *gestalt* can help us hold this concept together in helpful ways. God as Father means that there is an experience of God in relationship to an Other who can be viewed as children might view their parent. Likewise, in perceiving this relational quality the doctrine of the Trinity claims that there is a Spirit to this interactive reality that can be felt, perceived, and understood, just as wind can be so identified and understood when it is present. That Spirit is likewise an essential dimension of the relational life of Father and Son. If we shift our attention to the reality of hospitality, we can see a similar triadic character at work in this gestalt. Hospitality is the relational reality that binds host and guest together and is known in and through our encounters with the host and the guest; at the same time hospitality can be grasped by attending to the overarching relational configuration that binds host to guest and guest to host.

Indeed, the phrase "turning the tables," which is used in the title of this chapter, is typically used to indicate a gestalt we associate with the waging of conflict toward some specific end. And as this chapter has sought to clarify, how we shape or configure the conflict we see makes an extraordinary difference in the conflict we try to address. Indeed, conflict is a primary example of a gestalt. It is clearly encounterable in its otherness and in its capacity to generate effects of one kind or another. It has agency, even if identifying a specific agent is problematic. It has character and identity as well, though such character and identity are often fully ambiguous and often debatable. Still the encounterable qualities of a gestalt remain. And they remain relational.

Human beings know this reality in another way that is readily familiar. As mentioned before, each human self is more a gestalt of relationships than a substance. We are a mix of complex relationships. Yet we are agents of meaning and action. At the same time, we are fully ambiguous and ambivalent creatures. Still, we have identity, character, and enough consistency to be present to ourselves and to others. And how we present ourselves depends significantly upon figure-ground dynamics.

If we return to the Trinitarian rhetoric of theology, another key term is worth pondering. The Greek word *perichoresis* points to similar dynamics.[15] It refers to the Trinitarian quality of mutual indwelling or interanimation with regard to each of the persons of the Trinity. That is, the fullness of God is present in each of the identities signified by Father, Son, and Holy Spirit; at the same time the identities are upheld in the dynamic relationship that binds them together. And that dynamic sense of relatedness can be experienced as well, much the same way that dancing can be experienced by attending to the dancers and by recognizing the holistic gestalt of the dance. Literally the Greek term *perichoresis* means to dance around while the Latin equivalent (*circumincession*) means to walk around. Yet more is intended than dancing or walking. The term refers to the dynamic, relational character of divinity that can be described as both a singular relationship and a differentiated relating of distinct identities. *Perichoresis* refers to the triadic relational structure of reality that surpasses subject-object and subject-subject dichotomization in favor of a fully relational sense of the whole that also honors the differentiated identities within the relation. That is, the oneness of the whole is a gestalt of pure relationality in which relation is encountered in differentiated subjects that relate, one to the other, and which is not encountered except in the fullness of this dynamic configuration of relating identities. Needless to say, there is no English equivalent to the word *perichoresis*. Likewise, there is no English equivalent to the German term *gestalt*.

Still, the term *gestalt* refers to a phenomenon we can all identify but have difficulty explaining—moments of encountering a reality we can identify by one or more of its components yet always remains more than the sum of its parts. The experience may be difficult to explain; yet, it can be identified by citing examples, or by searching for analogies that capture some aspect of what is being referenced by this German loanword. Enough, however. Let us return to the table, aware that the realities we are trying to understand are fundamentally relational in the ways we encounter them and in the ways that they are constituted in our midst. How we configure them makes all the difference.

Sacramental Implications

The Great Prayer of Thanksgiving of the Eucharist recites in the shaping narrative of its sacramental story what happened and came to focus in the upper room. Far too often that prayer has conveyed what Kendall Soulen has called structural supersessionism, omitting any but the subtlest affirmations of the covenantal story of Israel. Our study calls for a clearer celebration of covenantal solidarity with the people Israel. At the same time, the recital of the so-called "words of institution" at the table is open to alternate readings suggested in the previous analysis. When these are combined, the gestalt that coheres around this table more nearly resembles the shape of the holy manifest in the conflict generated by Jesus in the temple courtyard and extended to the upper room table with his followers.

Consider the conventional wordings of The Great Prayer of Thanksgiving that will be offered by many Christians on Maundy Thursday evening. Roman Catholics, Lutherans, Presbyterians, Anglicans, and other church folk will differ, I suspect, at critical places in the wordings of their prayers, usually to differentiate their understandings of the sacramental character of the meal and to frame their various views of what is happening in the meal with regard to the presence of the risen Christ. However, they will deviate very little with regard to the Trinitarian structure of the prayer, and many will fail to acknowledge the covenantal history of Israel as a key component of this act of thanksgiving, except, perhaps, as a prefiguration of the salvation history that follows and fulfills its promise. They will differ in what they identify as essential sacramental features, but share remarkable consensus in failing to affirm any self-sufficient or noninstrumental significance to the covenantal history of Israel.

To put the matter forcefully, as we limp through Holy Week and its ritual acts, we rarely avoid encountering either a supersessionary or *Judenrein* narrative prayer as the centering act at the Lord's Table.[16] In giving thanks for God's faithfulness, we can no longer skip from creation to Jesus, recalling only a minimalist reference to the Hebrew prophets, or at best, an instrumental acknowledgment of Israel's covenantal walk with God. Surely after Auschwitz we can see the displacement logic in this—to use Soulen's term, its structural supersessionism. Indeed, the historic creeds of the Christian faith embody what he calls the standard canonical narrative at the structural level. They render

> the Hebrew Scriptures largely indecisive for shaping conclusions about how God's purposes engage creation in universal and enduring ways. . . . Israel's history is portrayed as nothing more than *the economy of redemption in prefigurative form.* So construed, Israel's story contributes little or nothing to understanding how God's consummating and redemptive purposes engage human creation in universal and enduring ways. Indeed, the background can be completely omitted from an account of Christian faith without thereby disturbing the overarching logic of salvation history. This omission is reflected in virtually every historic confession of Christian faith from the Creeds of Nicaea and Constantinople to the Augsburg Confession and beyond. [Italics in original text.][17]

Soulen's description requires little imagination for applying his critique to this Trinitarian structure of most eucharistic prayers. Surely it is time to give thanks in this centering and faith-shaping prayer for the covenantal walk of Israel and God's abiding faithfulness to this people. I know I am meddling now. But Jesus' encounter with the heart of Jerusalem and its ritual center can mean nothing less than our willingness to examine the same in our own situations. Can we face the heart of Jerusalem as we know it and examine the integrity of the center of our ritual practice?

The matter does not end, of course, with identifying and questioning the supersessionist logic we find here—though it surely must include that. If it is to be true to the way Jesus turned the tables in Jerusalem, it must also include a confrontation with the sacrificial system we enact in our own sanctuaries as well. After Auschwitz, however, this matter is compounded.

Jesus saw in the gathering of a meal an occasion that could substitute for the sacrificial offerings (*korbanot*) at the temple. The Table became a sanctuary for honoring and sharing the gracious generosity of God's ways with creation. The rule and realm of God was[18] at hand in the gestalt of hospitality encountered in and around a meal. While Jesus had shared this message in parable and enacted it in other settings, on the occasion of this last meal and in the shadow of his encounter in the temple courtyard, he moved to elevate the character of what happened in and through the meal to be equivalent to what was seen as present only at the temple.

Chilton's analysis is instructive. He reminds his reader that Jesus used the social settings of meals as action-parables of his understanding of God's royal rule. Likewise, these meals demonstrated how one might participate in the encounterable gestalt of God's inbreaking domain. With this in mind, Matthew asks his readers to consider that all the meals that Jesus had were conflated into and focused by the story of this last meal with his disciples. They were enacted parables to which Jesus added an intensifying feature after the conflict in the temple courtyard. The prophetic challenge he coordinated at the temple had been ignored. Consequently, according to Chilton, Jesus substituted the bread and its ritual blessings of thanksgiving that were customary offerings before every meal and linked them to the offerings that he viewed to be impure acts at the temple. Likewise, he took the cup of wine in a ritualized gesture of thanksgiving and linked it to the cup in which the blood of the sacrificial animal would have been collected and identified the wine with the offering of blood that would have been poured on the altar at the temple. As Chilton reads the text and this scene, Jesus believes he has made the purer offering even though he has substituted bread and wine for the flesh and blood that were being offered impurely at the temple. The critical issues for Jesus, says Chilton, were the intentionality of the offering and the purity of its expression as an offering. In other words, Jesus challenged the sacrificial gestalt as it was configured at the temple. His actions challenge us to examine ours as well.

Reconfiguring the Sacrificial Gestalt

The emphasis is on the offerer's relationship to the offering. His or her intentionality and the directedness of the offering stand in contrast to the purity of the sacrificial gift or animal, which, as Chilton points out, was presumed in Matthew's story. This contrast invites us to ponder a similar shift in sacrificial emphasis—the substitutionary gift of an innocent lamb of God, versus the full and embodied intentionality of his offering. Such a shift provides help in moving away from views of sacrifice that impute God's need for appeasement on the part of an innocent victim to the sacrificial character of offering one's life in service to others.

When the emphasis remains on a physical, substitutionary, sacrificial gift and its purity, we are left either with a system that finally requires satisfaction of some kind or with replacement occasioned by an act that breaks the cycle of sacrifice. In the former case, classical theologies of atonement, satisfaction, and substitution, are clear examples. In the latter case, René Girard's work provides an example. In neither case is the understanding of divinity operating in the background challenged. Such a God still requires satisfaction. The scales of justice, especially divine justice, must be balanced, and a sacrificial act tipping the scales in the direction of an innocent victim is required.

Theologies of atonement like the Christus Victor model emphasize struggle that overcomes the injustice predominating in life and overwhelming the ways of creation. But the emphasis remains on winning a result—even when love and light are contending with the forces of hatred, evil, and darkness. The outcome is what finally matters. When the emphasis falls on the character of the offering, however, our attention turns to the choices manifest in and through the offering that the offerer is making. This is the breakthrough that Chilton signals with his analysis. When applied to Jesus' sacrificial act, the shift is important. Obviously, this is not a matter of either-or categories, but of emphasis, except that in choosing to risk death either by placing himself in a vulnerable position or by engaging the ways of violence with the ways of peace, the choice is *not for suffering or for death*. The choice is *for relationship, engagement, and life* with the full understanding of the consequences of this choice. Jesus is choosing to give his life to the higher purpose of covenant life in complete dedication to the rule and realm of God. He is not choosing to be a victim but to act on behalf of others in a cause beyond himself. In short, he is not choosing death, even if death results. He is choosing life at the risk of death. More on this as we move into the garden and ponder the testing he undergoes there. But for now, it is important to acknowledge at the Table the shift in emphasis that will enable us to develop a significantly different approach to sacrifice, one rooted in the donation of oneself for the sake of others and committed to life even if death eventually is the consequence of choices made for life.

It is important for us to recognize that the way we shape these actions affects how we understand the shape and substance of the holy. How we configure the conflict reflects what we believe is at stake. In one reading, God requires a particular kind of gift in order to be pleased. In the other reading, the offering signals a kind of life embraced for others and expressive of the kind of life intended by God from the very beginning. The difference is significant and has been all along. However, after Auschwitz, this difference is focused in the extreme.

There is an apparent similarity between the reconfiguration of the sacrificial gestalt that arises from Girardian analysis and critique and the midrashic approach I have been using. However, a midrashic approach avoids two serious flaws present in Girard's project. First, a midrashic approach resists any overarching typology. Girard works from exactly such an abstraction— namely, the scape-goating dynamics of mimetic desire. That typology guides his interpretation across the board. While his insights are often perceptive and helpful, they nonetheless operate as a monolithic prism through which every significant act and text is refracted and understood. In the end, mimetic desire, a hermeneutical construct, replaces the text and its narrated world. Every text yields to this interpretive lens. In other words, the Girardian project is finally a form of interpretive triumphalism within and beyond the boundaries of Christian identity. Or to put the matter in the language of these reflections, the Girardian approach does not limp.

Second, the Girardian reconfiguration turns on the exposure of violence at the heart of the sacrificial system when a purely innocent victim, who fully embodies the divine intentions of creation, is sacrificed as a propitiation for the sins of the world. The system is turned on itself and replaced by a sacrifice that brings an end to all sacrifice. While this observation is instructive, the conventional theistic understandings of divinity woven into the system shatter under the weight of the violence required to break the cycle of violence in it. A midrashic approach, however, allows for contrasting and even contending views of divinity that challenge conventional ones. The book of Job demonstrates precisely this kind of challenge to conventional views of covenantal theism, which Girard's system cannot contain, while addressing the violence Girard has exposed to critique. In the shadows of Auschwitz, we cannot overlook this matter. We will consider these issues more fully in chapter 5.

A Sacramental Orchard

We return to the temple precincts and the upper room table sacramentally, not just homiletically. And there are important implications for the sacramental gestalt that is reconfigured by our confessional return to this scene. As we make our way, we must not forget that we limp. We will stumble. We will make mistakes, but we must also move forward with our walking. Each step is precious as well as perilous. And as we look at the sacramental significance of our post-Shoah return, we proceed with increased awareness of how difficult it is to raise questions about our most sacred acts. After all, what else was Jesus doing if not raising questions about the ritual center of his people's life and how they approached the holy. That is precisely what we do whenever we raise critical questions about our sacramental actions. And now, whatever conflict we may generate remains "in house," among Christians.

In the spirit of midrashic inquiry, I am not arguing for a particular sacramental theology. But I am asking my fellow Christians to enter this gestalt with me by considering what I see as I limp along. I ask only that they venture into this terrain willing to approach it in the same manner we have approached the narrated world of the biblical text. Indeed, this sacramental gestalt is representative of the *PaRDeS* in which we dwell as Christians. And our post-Shoah encounter with Holy Week will be an illusion if we do not risk taking these steps into the heart of Jerusalem as we know it sacramentally.

As we return to the temple and link what happened there with what happened in the upper room, we see a distinctive emphasis on the one who offers, as an essential factor in making a sacrifice that Jesus is willing to identify as pure and appropriate in the eyes of God. That is, the all-important issue of purity shifts, away from the physical offering, to the heart and intentions of the one who makes such an offering. Purity is thereby tied to penitence and forgiveness, because purity rests in the covenantal graces of restored fellowship with the people Israel. In short, purity is viewed as a matter of covenantal relation. When relational wholeness is restored, purity is restored. When covenantal wholeness is absent, when relation is broken, purity is likewise undone.

This shifting, sacrificial gestalt is itself enriched by the parabolic nature of Jesus' teachings and actions with regard to the rule and realm of God, which Jesus had drawn in sharp contrast to the empire of Rome. God's realm operates on the logic of abundance; Rome operates on the logic of scarcity. God's ways are righteous and just; Rome's are not. God's power serves creation and the proliferation of life; Rome's power oppresses and diminishes life. God's ways are hospitable and gracious, making room for the other, making room for life; Rome's are hostile and self-serving, restricting others, restricting life. By confronting the temple policies in parabolic actions as he did, Jesus placed his specific challenges regarding sacrificial offerings and expectations of purity into the larger frame of his concerns for the rule and realm of God, directly challenging the relationship Caiaphas maintained with the representatives of Rome to establish his own sacerdotal authority.

The shape of this gestalt is further enriched as we extend its conflict to include what happened at the table in the upper room. Looking back on this event, the gathering is associated with Passover, and ritualized either as a Seder (as in the Synoptics) or as a *havurah* meal just prior to the Passover (as in John). Either way, the ritualization, if we are not careful, can obscure the more general framework of a meal that underlies the gathering. Jesus saw every meal as a parabolic occasion in which one could embody the dynamics of God's ways with creation. Through the hospitality practiced at table, those who shared meals with others touched the very dynamics of God's ways with creation. God, the host of life, made his children welcome by making room for them as guests in the created domain. Created in God's image, God's children were themselves asked to be hosts to others, welcoming them into God's garden of life. Indeed, the vulnerable character of such hospitality is demonstrated in the footwashing ceremonies that recall the setting in John's Gospel and by Jesus' serving his disciples while telling them they would fail him either by denial or betrayal in the days ahead. The hospitality of the table was being extended and deepened to capture the hospitality behind the very gift of creation and expressive of God's ways with all of creation—a wager Jesus was willing to make in the face of impending disaster.

As Chilton recounts the situation, Jesus took a bold step by using the acts of thanksgiving associated with bread and wine at every meal and identifying them with the sacrificial offerings of the temple. Taking the bread, Jesus used the language typically associated with the sacrifice of meat to be shared as it is offered at the altar. As Matthew reports, Jesus called the bread he took his body, or *soma* in Greek. However, *soma*, as Chilton points out, can be translated either as flesh or body. Before we associate this act with Jesus' death, Chilton explains, we must first see it in the context of a meal following his demonstration in the temple courtyard. This, the bread reserved for a thanksgiving blessing at the meal, would be his sacrificial offering of flesh, using words a temple priest would have used to identify the meat offering that Jesus challenged in the temple courtyard. Jesus did not need to go to the temple to complete the offering he did not make. The social setting of a meal was sufficient, because it is not the place or the object of the offering that matters but the expression of the offering on the part of the offerer. Likewise, Chilton explains that Jesus took a cup and offered it as the cup that would have gathered the blood from the sacrifice at the temple. These actions and the so-called words of institution that accompanied them are typically ignored for their historical significance because of the problematic fit they have between early Christian identification of its significance and their apparent anti-Jewish character. "What Jew would tell another," asks Chilton, "to drink blood, even symbolic blood?"[19] But Chilton, working with the texts of the Mishnah, shows us how the words attributed to Jesus are directly related to the words (in Greek) that would have been spoken by priests over the offerings of flesh and blood in the acts of temple sacrifice. If Chilton is correct, Jesus was substituting bread for the flesh (*soma*) offered at the temple and wine for the blood poured out on its altar.

As I linger with Chilton's comments regarding Jesus' actions at the meal, I am reminded of the many companions who accompany me personally (literally as well as figuratively) in my limping through this orchard. Surely they would tell me that Jesus looks more Jewish to them when viewed this way. But they would remind me as well that this doesn't remove the disagreement that we have as Jews and Christians about the significance of this meal and the person whom I believe to be fully present in it. But it does shift our disagreement to something around which we can have more constructive dialogue and debate.

A Sacramental Offering

The pastoral responsibility for sacramental gatherings during this week will undoubtedly include many of the hermeneutical tasks identified above. How they embody the conflicts of this week will shape Christian identity profoundly. At the risk of introducing further conflict, I wish to offer a eucharistic prayer as a case study to encourage further reflection with regard to how post-Shoah Christians might gather at their sacramental tables. The prayer has grown out of two contexts: university worship in a private, church-related, but diversely constituted campus community and a biennial scholarly gathering meeting under the auspices of the Goldner Holocaust Symposium.

In the university setting, students come from a variety of Protestant backgrounds and occasionally from Catholic and Orthodox ones. The general structure of the Sunday service is eucharistic even on those Sundays the Eucharist is not celebrated. Aspects from a variety of traditions are incorporated in the service, and a worship booklet for Word and Table is provided to explain the significance of the Eucharist and the ways it seeks to represent the variety of Christian identities that gather for it. The Goldner Symposium is an intentionally diverse group of Holocaust scholars—Jews and Christians as well as secular humanists—who meet biennially for four days in the British countryside of northern Oxfordshire to pursue the work of *tikkun olam* as a shared post-Shoah vocation. Meeting over the Shavuot/Pentecost holiday weekend in 2000, the members of the Goldner Symposium chose to celebrate the Jewish Sabbath and the festival of Shavuot in appropriate Jewish ritual on Friday night and Saturday morning and the Christian Eucharist on the following Pentecost Sunday.

As cochair of the symposium, I accepted responsibility for celebrating the Eucharist. The challenge was to celebrate the heart and soul of the Christian faith sacramentally in the full presence and awareness of our Jewish siblings without denigrating their identity as Jews. We sought in our service a way to articulate the boundaries of Christian identity that expressed with confessional clarity what it meant for us to be Christian, while also affirming the larger, covenantal ecology that others might choose to honor and serve differently. The eucharistic prayer and all parts of the service were framed with a sense of open hospitality rooted in our Christian particularity, which was itself grounded in the steadfast generosity of God. An earlier act of corporate confession turned to a simplified version of the ancient liturgical chant of the *Kyrie* (singing "Kyrie eleison" only). During a meditative period following the *Kyrie*, individuals were invited to add their own statements of contrition if they were so moved. Interestingly, our Jewish colleagues joined in this act with their Christian brothers and sisters. Later, when the invitation to the Table was offered, it expressed a profound and shared sense of penitential humility. Furthermore, during the invitation the Table was identified as an open, yet clearly Christian Table where hospitality and presence were articulated as essential features, even for those who did not receive the bread and wine while they stood as welcome guests of their Christian brothers and sisters.

Eventually, the eucharistic lessons learned in that experience were incorporated into the monthly service celebrated in the campus congregation I serve at my university. The text of the prayers, the invitation, and the sensitivities learned in the service and discussion afterwards at the symposium all contributed to the service I now celebrate with my student congregation. The text of its Great Thanksgiving follows as the offering of this chapter, including the statement that regularly accompanies the invitation to come forward and receive the gifts of bread and wine. They are presented for analysis and critique in hopes of stimulating further reflection on how post-Shoah Christians might gather at their sacramental tables and altars.

The Great Thanksgiving

May God be with you.
And also with you.

Lift up your hearts.
We lift them up to God.

Let us give thanks to the Eternal One our God.
It is right to give our thanks and praise.

It is good and right that we give you thanks for all that we have received. Only you are God. You created all things and called them good. You created us in your image. And even though we rebelled against your love, you did not desert us. You walked with our forebears: Abraham and Sarah, Isaac and Rebekkah, Jacob and Leah and Rachel. You spoke through Moses and Aaron and Miriam, and through all the prophets. You called all Israel your people, binding yourself to them in covenant. Even when they stumbled, you kept faith with them, bearing witness to your steadfast love for them and for all your creation. Therefore we join our voices to theirs, and to all your people on earth, as we join the unending chorus of heaven, singing your praise:

Holy, holy, holy, Lord,
God of power and might,
heaven and earth are full of your glory.
Hosanna in the highest.
Blessed is the one who comes in the name of the Lord.
Hosanna in the highest.

In the fullness of time you walked with Jesus, and we beheld him, your beloved son. He healed and taught; ate with sinners; welcomed the outcastes; and saw in every other—even his enemies—the reflection of your image. He brought you near, manifesting the fullness of your presence in our midst.

We beheld your glory.

On the night in which he gave himself wholly to your ways, embracing covenant fidelity even in the face of sure death, he took bread, blessed it giving you thanks, broke the bread and gave it to his disciples and said:

Take, eat; this is my body,
which is given for you.
Do this in remembrance of me.

Likewise, after the (Passover) meal, he took the cup. After giving thanks, he gave it to his disciples, saying:

This is my blood,
poured out for you and for many for the forgiveness of sins.
Do this, as often as you drink it,
in remembrance of me.

And so, in remembrance of these acts and in thanksgiving for the life they embody, we offer these gifts of bread and wine. We give them to you, even as we present ourselves. Infuse them with your Holy Spirit, transforming them as you transform us, that together we might be the body of Christ, given to and for the world, that it too might be transformed in your image.

Thus we pray that our lives may proclaim the mystery of our faith:

Christ has died.
Christ has risen.
Christ will come again.

Bless your church and all who serve you in word and in deed. Confirm and guide us all in our witness and raise us up in the power of Christ's resurrection that we may be faithful disciples of your covenantal way and grateful stewards of all we have received from your loving hand. Bind us together, in Christ, and with all your people, that your will may be done on earth as in heaven.

This we pray in the name of Jesus Christ, your beloved son, in the unity of your Holy Spirit, and in fidelity to your embrace of all creation. For in him, through him, and with him, all glory and honor is yours, now and forever. **Amen.**

Now with the confidence we share as children of God, let us pray as Christ has taught us:

Our Father in heaven,
hallowed be your name,
your kingdom come,
your will be done
on earth as in heaven.
Give us today our daily bread.
Forgive us our sins
as we forgive those who sin against us.
Save us from the time of trial
And deliver us from evil.
For the kingdom, the power, and the glory are yours
now and forever. Amen.

The minister breaks the bread in silence or while saying,

Because there is one loaf, we, many as we are, are one body, for we all partake of the same loaf. The bread which we break, is it not a sharing in the body of Christ?

The minister lifts the cup in silence, or while saying,

The cup over which we give thanks, is it not a means of sharing in the blood of Christ?

The invitation* to the altar/table is given and the minister declares,

Gifts of God for people of God.

The bread and wine are shared with the people; these or similar words are exchanged:

The body of Christ, given for you.
Amen.
The blood of Christ, given for you.
Amen.

When all have received, the altar/table is put in order and a prayer of thanksgiving follows:

Eternal God, we give you thanks for this holy mystery in which you have given yourself to us. May our lives overflow in justice and peace, and so may we go into the world in the strength of your spirit, to give ourselves for others, in the name of Jesus Christ. Amen.

NOTES

1. John Dominic Crossan, *Who Killed Jesus? Exposing the Roots of Anti-Semitism in the Gospel Story of the Death of Jesus* (San Francisco: Harper, 1991), 64f.
2. Marcus Borg, *Jesus in Contemporary Scholarship* (Valley Forge, PA: Trinity Press International, 1994), 116.
3. Crossan, 47.
4. Ibid., 47–48.

* Our table is an open table. All are welcome here. Those of you who come from other covenantal ways, know that your presence with us is precious to us and we are grateful for the ways you enable us to gather in fidelity here. Those of you who would regularly receive communion in your own congregations are welcome to do so here. However, as much as we might wish otherwise, the church is not (yet) one. So if it is more appropriate for you to say, "No, thank you," please know that you will be understood and respected in your decision. It is enough that you stand with us in this act of thanksgiving. If you do wish to receive as a follower of Christ, then come forward with the others, take the bread and dip into the cup, receiving as the body and blood of Christ—gifts of God, for people of God.

5. Ibid., 4–12.

6. Chilton's insights are rendered in three sources, one popular (*Rabbi Jesus*) and the other two more scholarly in nature (*The Temple of Jesus* and *A Feast of Meanings*). See Bruce Chilton, *Rabbi Jesus: An Intimate Portrait—The Jewish Life and Teaching That Inspired Christianity* (New York: Doubleday, 2000), 250–59; *A Feast of Meanings: Eucharistic Theology from Jesus through Johannine Circles* (New York: E. J. Brill, 1994), 24–74, esp. 57–72; and especially *The Temple of Jesus: His Sacrificial Program within a Cultural History of Sacrifice* (University Park, PA: Pennsylvania State University Press, 1992), 110–11, 121–24, 137–54, esp. 150–54.

7. The word *gestalt* will grow in significance as these reflections progress. A loanword from German, it captures the dynamic, relational character of the reality encountered and experienced at the upper room table. The term, poorly rendered in English, is variously translated as figure or form. It refers to phenomena that are encountered as dynamic, relational configurations that are not exhausted by our more typical ways of identifying them. See *Pushing Back from the Table,* 60–64.

8. This distinction is not just a matter of emphasis. It indicates differing ways that the holy may be approached and shaped. The approach typical of Pharisaic reform began with the sense of distance, respect, awe, and even the unapproachable quality of the holy. From this ground, one relates to the everyday and familiar, seeking ways to set the ordinary apart with respect, as one does the sanctuary of the temple. In contrast, Jesus began with the ordinary and familiar in acts like simple meal times, wherein expressions of generosity and hospitality may be seen as reflections of God's ways with creation. In this way, the ordinary is elevated in its ordinariness as an expression of the holy, as God's rule and realm are manifest in the fulfillment of creation coming to full fruition as intended from the beginning. In other words, the kingdom of God comes near, but not in some magical, interventionist way.

9. Most scholars agree that the conflict expressed in the Synoptics between Jesus and the religious leaders includes conflict from a later generation contemporaneous with the communities Matthew and the other writers were addressing when they were compiling their written testimony. Similarly, John scholars view the conflict between Jesus and the religious leaders as reflecting tension between Jesus and contemporary religious leaders as well as later conflict between synagogue leaders and followers of Jesus generated by their inclusion of Gentiles without requiring them to adopt a Jewish identity in responding to their good news about Jesus.

10. See Matthew 5:23–24: "So when you are offering your gift at the altar, if you remember that your brother or sister has something against you, leave your gift there before the altar and go; first be reconciled to your brother or sister, and then come and offer your gift."

11. Here I am referencing what is best termed an interactionist epistemology like that associated with thinkers like Jean Piaget, James W. Fowler, and Robert Kegan. At the heart of each of their projects is a recognition that the ways in which we know the world shape the world we know, while at the same time the world we interact with directly affects how we know it and even calls forth, when sufficiently complex, more sophisticated ways of knowing that world.

12. Peter Hodgson, *Christian Faith: A Brief Introduction* (Louisville, KY: Westminster John Knox Press, 2001), 62, 108–10, and Hodgson, *Winds of the Spirit* (Louisville, KY: Westminster John Knox Press, 1994), 151, 259.

13. Hodgson, *Christian Faith,* 121.

14. Walter Brueggemann, *The Covenanted Self: Explorations in Law and Covenant*, ed. Patrick D. Miller (Minneapolis: Fortress Press, 1999), 18–34.

15. Gregory Scott Gorsuch's discussion of the term is an excellent summary of these issues. See Gregory Scott Gorsuch, "*Perichoresis* as a Hermeneutical Key to Ontology: Social Constructionism, Kierkegaard, and Trinitarian Theology," <http://www.commongroundseattle.org/temp_07.thtml>.

16. There are exceptions to this occurrence, and they are to be commended. But they are generally encountered as options to other prayers provided for presiding clergy that do embody this displacement logic. The essential affirmation of the covenantal history of Israel is thereby still overlooked.

17. R. Kendall Soulen, *The God of Israel and Christian Theology* (Minneapolis: Fortress Press, 1996), 31–32.

18. Rule and realm, while grammatically plural, configure a single reality, a gestalt, rendered in the Greek *basileia*. Consequently, I have used the singular form of the verb to call attention to this singular gestalt.

19. Chilton, *Rabbi Jesus,* 252.

Chapter 4

Confronting the Night

Facing Anguish and Trial in the Darkness

Making Our Way to the Garden

As we leave the upper room and prepare to move forward through the narrated world of Holy Week, our gaze turns toward a garden below the Temple Mount we know as Gethsemane. We move from our table and follow Jesus and his disciples to this next stop, challenged by reconfigured gestalts of conflict and grace, hospitality and power, danger and possibility. Night has fallen in more ways than we may want to admit, and we will face serious choices for how we face the night before us—choices made clearer by our limping along the way and by the changing shape of familiar stories and their conflicts.

Having come to more responsible terms with the multifaceted conflict generated by Jesus in Jerusalem, we leave the protected space of our shared meal and move into the darkness of night beyond the protective walls of that intimate gathering. We make our way, as we have into the city. Liturgically, as well as midrashically, we return to the garden, where once more we will face temptation and anguish. As we make our way to this liturgical space, we also make our way to the narrated orchard of Matthew's story. We walk there awkwardly, for we know the darkness encompasses a night of anguish for Jesus and his followers, a night of testing for those caught up in its drama, and a night of trial for any who would follow Jesus all the way to the consummation of his life. We also know of another night of anguish and trial which challenges this special night that we remember. And so we join Elie Wiesel in asking the ironic question of Passover, with full awareness of the double and triple entendres we have added to it: Why is this night different from every other night?

Of course, the Seder, the ritual meal of Passover, turns on this question and prompts the anamnesis of deliverance. The night Jesus was betrayed, he was delivered to Roman authorities, reversing the logic of Pesach. The vocabulary used by Matthew[1] suggests he knew this association and was making it intentionally. But the irony doesn't end there for us. Many of us have learned of the Shoah reading Elie Wiesel's *Night*, which moves fuguelike in answer to the Seder question. Telling the story of the betrayal and abandonment of his people at the hands of Hitler, Wiesel relates this story as a negative *haggadah*. So, it is not far from the mark for us to understand that when we return to the night of Jesus' deliverance to Roman authorities, we are entering a midrash that turns on a similarly posed question. Matthew intended us to reenter the night of Pesach as well; but now, after Auschwitz, we enter as well that twelve-year night, compounding the darkness and finding ourselves once more at the banks of the Jabbok, wrestling with our shame for the sake of our own integrity and relational wholeness.

In other words, our place in this story is layered with meaning. We have entered the darkness of night, but it is not a simple night. We have entered the domain of an olive grove, but it is not a simple olive grove. It is an ambiguous place, a garden of historic proportion and at the same time a parabolic orchard in which we face ourselves and so much more. We have entered tormented and tormenting territory, but we have also stepped onto holy ground. So we must take off our shoes and walk with great care, especially as we remember that we limp along the way.

Anguish in the Garden

According to Matthew the anguish that Jesus faced in Gethsemane began earlier, in an upper room, in the evening setting of the Seder. The story of deliverance and its celebration in a ritual meal, including a statement indicating his doubt about the constancy of his companions' fidelity, had led to Jesus' dismissing his disciples and moving with them to the Mount of Olives. There, after asking all but three of his disciples to wait for him, Jesus withdrew with Peter, James, and John to pray. He told them that he was troubled and asked them to remain where they were and "watch" with him while he withdrew from them to pray. After a time, Jesus returned to the three disciples whom he asked to watch with him and found them sleeping. This scene, of course, repeats itself three times. During his anguish, Jesus pled in a private and intimate prayer that the cup he was facing pass him by. At the same time he asked for strength to accept and drink from the cup, if it was what God willed.

The action Matthew describes may be straightforward, but the story is far from simple. Like Jacob at the Jabbok, Jesus brought his lifetime to this garden, where he struggled with the consequences of his work and message. Somehow, he knew it was not going to turn out well for him. The story of his last meal recalled his sense of what lay ahead, as Jesus informed his disciples that one of them would betray him. He even identified the blessings of bread and wine with the sacrificial offerings associated with the temple, thereby connecting his own commitments to this covenant fellowship with the sacrificial offering he made in and at the meal. And traditionally we know that the bread and the cup have been interpreted to refer to Jesus' impending crucifixion and death. Now we look back from our critical vantage point and see a compacting of symbolism that signals a night of intensified anguish filled with numerous trials for everyone involved. But what else do we see?

From the traditional site of Gethsemane, one quite literally looks up to Jerusalem. From there, Jesus pondered the consequences of his life and work as he looked out at his cherished city. He was on a collision course with Roman authorities, and he had frightened temple leaders, who relied on the status quo for their sacrificial programs to flourish. In the garden, Jesus dramatically faced the probable outcome of his ministry: rejection and death. He prayed that this not be so, yet always in the context of giving himself to the divine will, which the text implies would require Jesus' death.

Of course, what happened in the garden was also the disciples' story: They were asked to go *with* Jesus to his place of prayer and struggle. There, three of them were singled out to go farther and to *watch with* Jesus as he went still farther into the garden to pray and wrestle with his destiny. The disciples responded by falling asleep, failing Jesus. Jesus had asked only that they stay *with* him or *watch with* him. He asked them to do no more. They failed, falling away, as Jesus, as the story remembers it, expected.[2]

Whatever else it is, the episode in the garden is a boundary story for Jesus—but also for anyone who seeks to follow him. For Jesus, the boundary is often associated with the physical and spiritual sufferings that lay ahead in the trial, rejection, abandonment, and eventual crucifixion awaiting him. However, in the garden (as at the table) the crisis was tied specifically to the relationships Jesus had with his disciples. And because the story is also for disciples of subsequent generations, their crisis becomes ours. What was the limit of the covenantal existence he offered his followers? Would their inability to stay awake and watch, their inability to share his anguish, their inability to face what he must face, destroy what they shared with him and what he had given them? Would Peter's denial break the bond that tied them together? Earlier Jesus had said it would not. Was that not the choice immediately facing Jesus in this episode? How fully would Jesus drink from the cup of covenant life? In a sense, Jesus had promised and advocated a covenantal relationship, a marriage, so to speak, that could not be sundered by the imperfections of those who accepted it. In Gethsemane, that promise was tested with sleep, denial, and even betrayal. Would Jesus choose covenant life in these circumstances, with these people? If so, it would cost his life. And in the larger circle of Jesus' covenantal obligations, the issue remained the same. Jesus had chosen covenant life with all of Israel, and he had chosen to focus his embrace with those usually cut off or living at the margins of covenant community. How deeply would he drink from this cup?

Facing the Cup

For Jacob as well as for us, the central question faced at the banks of the Jabbok was, with whom did Jacob wrestle that night? In Gethsemane, the parallel question is, what was and is the cup that Jesus anticipated with anguish and prayed might pass him by? In the ugly light cast by the Shoah, several traditional answers to this question are now problematic, if not obscene. The cup simply cannot signify a divine expectation that Jesus must suffer and die to restore order and balance to creation. No longer can any human being be used as an instrumental step in some larger scheme of things, even if that grand design is called divine. Nor can suffering per se bear the intrinsic meaning it has carried for Christian belief. It may continue to bear meaning when it is chosen vicariously for others. But in the light of the Shoah, even this assertion requires careful scrutiny, and perhaps qualification. Just as surely, the cup cannot be filled with supersessionist interpretations of God's covenantal embrace of creation or Israel.

What, then, was the cup that Jesus faced in Gethsemane? After a post-Shoah journey to the Jabbok, how can and should the cup that Jesus confronted that night in the garden be identified? With whom and what did Jesus wrestle in the night shadows of that place? And how does our vantage point in the early twenty-first century affect the way we identify that cup? To be sure, the biblical text proclaims that, whatever it was, the cup was a source of anguish. Jesus could feel its presence. In effect, he knew it was coming, but not that it was inevitable; otherwise he would not have prayed as he did. Somehow, somewhere, it involved a choice: his, God's, his disciples', the local authorities, Jewish and Roman—all of them.

Traditionally the church has identified the cup in Gethsemane as an extension of the cup Jesus identified as his sacrifice of blood in the gathering in the upper room. Moreover, the cup of Gethsemane has come to represent Jesus' suffering and crucifixion as a sacrificial death for others in the spirit of the sacrificial system of the temple. But in the light of our reflections on Jesus' conflict with the temple and its sacrificial system, we will want to ponder this identification further.

Of course, Jesus did not introduce, de novo, the imagery of a cup to his disciples. Nor did Matthew. Quite possibly, Matthew may be more responsible for this use of the image than Jesus, since it is referenced in Gethsemane in a moment of private introspection. Regardless, the cup as Matthew renders his account of Jesus' anguish, is layered with significance. In the story he tells, Jesus earlier took a cup in the ritual context of the Seder, a highly stylized meal wherein the cup of thanksgiving is richly bound up with the story and images of Israel—more specifically, Israel's deliverance and identity as a covenant people.[3] The cup was and remains a rich symbol of thanksgiving, recalling a relationship bestowed and yet still promised to God's people. It recalled the Passover gift of freedom and its corresponding relationship of responsible witness. Its meanings were and are cumulative. Every Passover ritual and experience of this wonderful relationship would be poured into this cup, likewise the cup of every Sabbath meal and the cup of blessing with which thanks would be offered at every meal. The point: Israel's entire covenantal legacy is bound up, in thanksgiving, with this ritual act. The cup bears multiple meanings, all of which provide gustatory linkage with the covenantal story of Israel.

In this context, then, we may conclude that just as the cup in the Seder signified divine deliverance and God's gracious choice to be in covenant relationship with the people Israel, so the cup for Jesus would be identified with his appropriation of that covenantal legacy as well as its and his unyielding commitment to liberation and life. Jesus identified his entire life with that cause. His cause was God's cause, and God's cause was Israel and the covenant life that Israel represented for the world. After Auschwitz, Christians must see this cup in all its fullness, not simply as it has been reduced by selective liturgical memory.

From this more inclusive and self-critical perspective, the cup would still include the suffering Jesus was anticipating and the cost of his life; but those components would be derivative, no matter how important they were and remain. They would be consequences of covenant life fully chosen and abundantly lived. The cup represented the gift and calling of covenant life, embodied in his own life and that of his people. The question confronting Jesus then would be, Would Jesus drink from the cup of covenant life so completely that it would bind him irrevocably to those who followed him and to those he sought to reach with his message? Like Jacob, Jesus faced a lifetime in one night, symbolized in the cup. What would it mean for Jesus to drink deeply from this overflowing symbol of his life and everything to which he was committed?

If God intends life—since God intends life—God would not intend that which diminishes it. Since the cup was given by God—and that is surely the implication of this imagery—the cup would not represent crucifixion per se, but all that Jesus chose and embraced in his life and the consequences of those choices, consequences that also signify and include crucifixion along with the fullness of life he served as he made this choice. After Auschwitz, this qualification, though subtle, is critical.

Another caution should be noted as well. As we read this story in the context of Christian liturgy, we must be careful not to bring Jesus' anguish in the night to premature closure by identifying it too simply with the eucharistic cup that we use to recall this night. Jesus' cup is distinct from ours, even though ours brings his near by participating symbolically in its overflow of meaning. For example, if we see Jesus' cup through the lens of a medieval eucharistic cup, a chalice, we may skew our perception of the choices Jesus faces in the garden and alter them to fit a predetermining view of atonement that undergirds the sacramental action framing our understanding of the chalice. Our sacramental theology should be accountable to Jesus and his actions, not the other way round.

Trials in the Night

Jesus has faced a trial not unlike the one at the beginning of his ministry in the high desert overlooking the Jordan River valley. Indeed, as Matthew tells the story, we should be struck by the midrashic way these two trials frame his Gospel. The story of Jesus' ministry moves from the baptism of John to the baptism of crucifixion. Jesus' ministry is bounded at one end by the temptation in the wilderness and the other by his trial in the garden. In the first case, Jesus was tempted to distort his ministry in three ways. In that setting, he wrestled with progressively complicated issues of power, all related to ethically important matters symbolized by bread, temple, and palace. That is, the temptations Jesus faced in the wilderness were manifestations of the seductiveness of power in noble disguise. In the garden, Jesus once again was confronted with three moments of crisis. In this case, they were relationally focused. Three times he asked his disciples to watch with him. Three times they failed, falling asleep. Jesus was struggling with a lifetime of choices, all linked to a life lived for others. Yet as he faced the probable consequences of his choices and commitments, he found himself alone, isolated from the very ones on whose behalf he had risked so much.

In each case, Matthew describes intimate moments no one could possibly have witnessed. Scholars like Crossan view such scenes as evidence that Matthew has once again historicized prophecy. On the other hand, scholars like Raymond Brown emphasize the possibility of what he calls "ear witnesses"[4] repeating and stylizing what Jesus has related to them. Once again, a midrashic approach recognizes in the stylization a conscious use of Moses' story to tell Jesus' story, remembering Moses' time and the people's time in the wilderness. Matthew has shown us how Jesus stood at the threshold of what he had promised and looked into the promised land of God's domain. There he chose life, covenant life, in and with all its implications.

But Jesus was not the only one undergoing a trial. Peter and all the disciples were as well. First, they were asked to wait and watch through the night. They slept, instead. When Jesus was arrested, they fell away. Peter followed, but at a safe distance. He was identified by some bystanders in the crowd, who confronted him. But Peter, out of fear, denied the relationship with Jesus. His story is stylized too, framed in prediction and punctuated by a rooster's announcement of the approaching dawn. Peter's *ish*—himself, his fear, his impetuousness—wrestled him to the ground. And Peter did not prevail—at least not yet. Peter's trial exposed Peter and every other disciple to what we have seen unfolding throughout Matthew's story.

Of course, Matthew reports two more trials. The first unfolds at the house of Caiaphas as Peter hides in the shadows, watching from a distance. The action unfolds inside the house as Matthew describes the presence of some who served in the Sanhedrin, the council of scribes and elders entrusted with ruling on matters of *halakah*. Many scholars question the probability that the Sanhedrin was formally called to meet and hear the case against Jesus. Such a gathering would have contradicted the legal code setting up the guidelines for their meeting, not to mention the same code of expectations that Jesus was being accused of violating. More likely, the high priest, in collusion with some council members, confronted Jesus with his actions at the temple as well as those at the table, and then turned Jesus over to the Roman authorities, who eventually sentenced him to crucifixion. Bruce Chilton suggests that Judas may very well have been especially motivated by Jesus' bold move at the table and reported this to Caiaphas, believing that Jesus had gone too far. Regardless, the action that Matthew describes unfolds at a distance and inside a location whose access is denied the followers of Jesus. Yet Matthew describes the little detail he reports as if he were there. Furthermore, when compared to the accounts from the other Gospels, the testimony is inconsistent and reminds us that the historical information about this night is sketchy at best. Consequently, as we limp through the text and its testimony, we are wise to remember the stylized way in which this testimony is framed.

Matthew next reports Jesus being brought before Pilate, the Roman prefect whom other records describe as ruthless in his dealings with the Jews of Second Temple Israel. According to Matthew, Pilate confronted Jesus with the accusation, "Are you the King of the Jews?" (Matt. 27:11). Jesus responded with his only answer in this setting, "You have said so." Pilate then confronted Jesus with the accusations of Caiaphas and his cohorts, but Jesus did not respond. While many have interpreted Jesus' silence to be composure, that Jesus was at peace with the events that were unfolding around him, we may also view Matthew trying to point us to other dynamics present in this scene—perhaps preparing us for the multiple ironies that we find in the text.

For example, before Pilate washed his hands of responsibility for the decision that only he could render, he toyed with the crowd, offering to release one of the prisoners he presented to them. He cited a figure called Barabbas and asked the crowd to choose between the one called Barabbas, Aramaic for son of the father, and Jesus, who was called the Messiah. Embedded in the names is a choice between two figures, each of whom claim to be "son of the father." Which one will they choose? As Michael Goldberg has observed,[5] the crowd is placed on trial by such a query, but, ironically, so is Pilate, who does not understand what he has done. His act of washing his hands, which immediately followed, could not wash away his responsibility for the death sentence that he imposed, or what he had failed to grasp.

Finally, we must face the language of self-incrimination voiced by the crowd, "His blood be on us and on our children" (Matt. 27:25), and their preceding plea to Pilate that Jesus be crucified. The text attributes both statements to all who were assembled in the crowd. Even if everyone in the crowd spoke these words, which in itself is doubtful, we cannot equate that crowd with an entire population or with a category of people, whatever label we give them. Scholars help us, in this regard, reminding us of the conflict that existed at the end of the first century between the leaders of the synagogue and those who believed Jesus had fulfilled the messianic expectations of their people. That conflict, they contend, spilled over into the story of this conflict as Matthew used the language of 2 Samuel 1:16 to identify Jesus' opponents in the crowd with Amalek. We must be more careful. In other words, the crowd, even if they recognized their own complicity, probably never uttered the words that Matthew used from 2 Samuel. More likely, Matthew was using them midrashically, and in debate with a later generation as he did so, arguing that like the Amalekite who stood before David in an earlier time, they had participated in taking the life of God's anointed one.

Differentiating the Crises

In the darkness of this night, it appears that Jesus faced two major crises: one covenantal the other political. At the closest, most intimate level, Jesus had asked Peter, James, and John (his closest companions) to go a step further into the night and to watch and pray with him. To be sure, what he faced, he faced alone, as the story relates. Nonetheless, he asked his three intimate friends to go the extra distance and to stay awake and watch with him—nothing more. They were not asked to change things or to do anything other than to be present, to stay awake and to watch. Yet they slept. And the others, whom he asked to go only partway into his night of anguish, fell asleep as well, failing to give even a more limited presence. In contrast, Jesus was fully present—to himself, to his cause, to God, and even to his sleeping companions.

The covenantal crisis extended to the people and to the city that Gethsemane quite literally faced. What was Jesus' commitment to that place and to those people? Would it be as complete and unreserved as his commitment to his disciples? The answer was yes. There was no turning back on his commitment. There was no holding back on embracing covenant life as fully and intensely as he had chosen. He had filled the cup full, to overflowing, and he would drink it.

The other crisis, distinct from the covenantal one, was political. Jerusalem was not simply occupied; it was also not infrequently compromised. Whom did Jerusalem honor and serve? God or Caesar? All of her children or only an elite few? Still, the city remained holy and the center of his people's life. This crisis swallowed up the others and then receded into the background in the later stories of Jewish complicity and responsibility for Jesus' death—responsibility that recent scholarship points out has been misapplied to the Jews as a people, and in later generations has supported an operative myth of deicide.[6]

In other words, Jesus faced a multifaceted crisis. On the one hand, the crisis was covenantal. It involved those people to whom he was covenantally bound, from the most intimate members of his disciples to the most marginal members of Israel's second commonwealth. On the other hand, his crisis was political. His beloved city and land were occupied by Rome. The leadership of the temple had collaborated with Roman authorities to stay in power and to secure what they thought was needed for their people. Collaboration and oppression were palpable. How committed was he to the message of God's inbreaking reign and to those to whom he was covenantally committed, especially those in Jerusalem, the heart of his world? He was absolutely committed—even if it cost his life!

Yet the story of crisis has been distorted, confusing some subtle but important distinctions. The covenantal crisis that Jesus resolved in favor of those who fell away, denied, rejected, and abandoned him, has been confused with the political one, especially as it was focused in the breach between Jesus and Judas. The blame for Jesus' death has been too easily shifted from the executioners, that is, the Romans, to an intimate collaborator. Similarly, blame has also been shifted from Caiaphas to the Jerusalem crowds and all the religious leaders who may have collaborated with Pilate. Therefore the political crisis with Rome has been all but removed from the story, certainly placed in the background, while parts of the covenantal crisis have been brought to the fore.

Given what can be critically discerned about Jesus' situation then, as well as what must be faced about the distortion and hatred carried by Christianity's legacy of anti-Judaism and its myth of deicide, how should the crisis and its conflict now be understood? To be sure, the issue is covenantal, but on a much larger scale. Now it includes not simply individuals and/or parts of the covenantal story of Christianity, but the overarching covenantal framework of life to which Christians bear witness. The covenantal crisis that confronts critical and thoughtful believers—Jews as well as Christians—is whether or not the world can be embraced covenantally at all. Indeed, this is the heart of Irving Greenberg's point that the Shoah is a reorienting event moving Israel [and Christianity] into an age of voluntary covenant.[7] According to Greenberg, covenant life must hereafter be voluntary, recognizing fully that in "covenant life" God has completely embraced human agency. Divine partnership and presence are to be found in the covenantal experience and process, but no longer can the divine partner be expected to act, except through the "*called* human response"[8] of faithful people. Moreover, covenantal wholeness must hereafter include the full people of Israel—even those Jews who reject the claims of the included ones in Israel's story that the one who included them did so as their messiah!

Another Night

As our encounter with Jacob at the Jabbok has made clear, another more recent historical night casts its shadows on our interaction and interpretation of the texts of faith. Jesus' followers must face the unsettling recognition that to follow Jesus after the *Shoah* is to follow Jesus into the camps and its kingdom of night. With this in mind, the story takes on a frightening dimension. If the night and its garden now include the world of the whirlwind (or its reverse, the whirlwind now includes this story), then the trials and its accusations now include the torment of Nazi prosecution and persecution. Each stage along the path is a stage in the immersion of this world. To be asked to enter the night in Gethsemane with Jesus is frightening enough. To be asked to stay awake and watch, more so. To be asked to go a little farther, and then to watch and pray, increases the challenge even more. To face the betrayal and arrest cruelly extends the matter even further. But to draw the night in Gethsemane together with the night of Shoah and then ponder their relationship is something else altogether.

After Auschwitz, following Jesus means following Jesus into a Gethsemane renamed Majdanek or Sobibor or some other frightening appellation. It means discovering that one can just as easily be standing by as authorities come for any Jews, not simply Jesus, and arresting them in spite of their innocence before God and creation. Similarly, the trials rehearsed in these episodes call to mind the humiliating trials endured by Jews during the long night of Nazi persecution. What else was going on when Jews reported to public assembly areas to have their papers stamped for work or deportation? Was not Josef Mengele conducting a trial, playing judge and jury, as he sentenced men, women, and children to death and others to the harshest conditions of life, when they lined up before him upon arriving at Auschwitz?

Historically, we know that only a few Christians followed Jesus into the night of the Shoah and most of them did so problematically. Members of the Confessing Church, for example, attempted to follow Jesus in confronting Hitler's claims for power, but many of them failed in recognizing the pervasive poison of antisemitism in their land and culture. The issue for them was idolatry and church autonomy.[9] Jesus, the Jew, would have been rounded up with others, sentenced to work or deported, and targeted for eventual annihilation. Even the Confessing Church, like Peter, could not escape denying Jesus—that is, the *Jew* from Nazareth, whom they called Christ.

Bonhoeffer, however, provides us with yet another way of reading the story of sleeping disciples. The historic night of the Shoah was longer than one evening, lasting twelve dark years. Although Bonhoeffer may have dozed early in its shadows, he awoke enough to join his companion and teacher in solidarity with his people, eventually giving his life as a consequence. Because of his witness, we know that others who fell asleep could have awakened. Though difficult, it was possible to break the hold of sleep, even deep within that long night. Still, most of Jesus' followers in that time and place simply fell asleep, even those who tried to stay awake. Some participated in the betrayal more actively than we or they realized.

A Post-Shoah Cup

Let us return to the matter of the cup over which Jesus anguished the night his trials were so intensely focused. As I suggested earlier, our Christian notion that suffering might contain inherent meaning is transfigured by Jesus' choices and concerns that night as we view them in a more self-consciously Jewish framework—perhaps one even more Jewish than that of Matthew. The goal is to clarify that Jesus' choices and anguish were life-directed, both individually and on behalf of his people, even if they were made in the face of death. That is, they were not acts of resignation and giving up, but moments of resistance to death and its power as it was experienced in denial, rejection, abandonment, and betrayal. Jesus was choosing life, covenant-oriented life, even if his fidelity to covenantal existence risked probable death.

The options facing Jesus all emphasized that the covenantal framework of his life was now completely in his hands. Divine intervention did not come from someplace else, heaven or otherwise, to confirm or deliver Jesus from his night of anguish. The cup from which he chose to drink did not contain a magic potion capable of removing Jesus from his circumstances. Instead, what lay within his power was whether he would choose the covenantal quality of life that characterized life with God and neighbor in an ecology of faith, even if it was confirmed by no one else. This cup, like the sacrifice that Jesus approached relationally, had a covenantal shape. Moreover, it had a voluntary shape that embraced the crisis at hand in spite of what was happening. In a sense, this is Irving Greenberg's point about entering an age of voluntary covenants after Auschwitz. And it was embodied in Jesus' choices in Gethsemane. Intervention did not come; nonetheless, Jesus chose and extended covenant life at its point of crisis. This is the cup we see Jesus choosing to accept as we wrestle with these questions after the Shoah.

Instead of seeing Jesus in anguish over whether or not God wanted him to be a sacrifice for others, this reading sees the crisis confronting Jesus to be one of risking probable and imminent death as a consequence of fidelity to a covenantal relationship with God, Jesus' own followers, the people Israel, and even those most marginal in Israel's covenantal community. Just as his conflict with the temple authorities centered in a relational understanding of sacrifice as offering, so too did his understanding of the shape of the holy, which he sought to honor in covenantal loyalty and integrity. This is the cup we are called to see Jesus choosing and accepting as we return to this night.

Jesus was facing the incredible cost of grounding his own life in a radically hospitable and inclusive commitment to covenant life at the point of extreme crisis. That crisis included impending death. Perhaps more significantly, that crisis included the betrayal of one intimate companion, denial and falling away of eleven others, and rejection by the larger numbers of people whom Jesus sought to embrace. And as the crucifixion scene eventually portrays, the crisis included in the end even the feeling of absolute abandonment. Moreover, a covenantal reading of this story distinguishes this aspect of the crisis from the political crisis, the more direct reason for Jesus' crucifixion. Jesus faced the choice of affirming his covenantal commitments at their point of violation and in the face of a distinct, even if related, political cost. His passion was a radical and intense commitment to covenant life and its way of hospitality. Consequently, this interpretation sees Jesus' prayers in Gethsemane not as moments of resignation and submission to God's will but as moments of wrestling with the implications of embracing covenant life so fully that he embraced its multiple violations—in denial, betrayal, and even abandonment. Essentially, the underlying question confronting Jesus in Gethsemane was, how committed was he to this inclusive and unyielding way of embodying his Father's will? The answer, the story reports, is completely.

The Midrashic Task

So far we have seen that the pastoral task in this approach is thoroughly midrashic. That is, we are called to enter the orchard of Gethsemane and the night of trials as a participant in its gestalt of images and flow of questions. Furthermore, we make our way to this orchard with the pastoral task of guiding others into its domain, that they too may stand in this place. Our task is to help others recognize and differentiate the related crises that arise there and to find ways to pose the challenge of watching through the night with our companions in this garden.

Just as there was a more complicated conflict to portray surrounding Jesus and the various groups with whom he interacted in Jerusalem, there was more involved in the trials that he and we must face as we enter and reenter this night of anguish. If we are successful in this regard, we will face our own trials, just as the first disciples did. While we may look over their shoulders and learn from their mistakes, we will make our own. Our trials, like theirs, will extend from relational matters to religious and secular domains of authority and power. We will do well to keep before us the complexity of this mixed arena and its ecology of issues, as we are called to stand before the representatives of religion and culture. Here we will confront the relational character of the covenantal and the power dynamics of the political as we limp into its difficult territory, wounded by our knowledge of what has happened here before in the recent past. The midrashic task is to face the multiple trials of this night and early morning, but to move beyond the accusational mentality in which we have read them before.

Throughout, the overarching concern will be to hold ourselves and these images in dialogical tension with each other. Critical faith calls for hermeneutical self-consciousness that can situate its interpretive dynamics faithfully within the tradition and at the same time avoid making the mistakes of the past, even if such mistakes were once faithfully motivated. What is required is a double-edged hermeneutic, with distinct but related moments of critique and correction. That is the critical spirit incorporated from midrash.

Indeed, the critical leverage of midrash resides in the biblical text itself, freed from ideological readings of it. Careful attention to the shape of the text and its telling gaps helps us differentiate the crises, clarifying the covenantal and political dimensions buried within. The political conflict with Rome has been driven to the background, fronted by the covenantal challenges faced by Jesus and his followers. Still, the conflict with Rome resurfaces in the narration of the crucifixion, even if its political character is downplayed. Of course, even a midrashic strategy like this one limps. But it is strong enough to clarify that Jesus' choices were life-directed in the midst of a complex mix of interpersonal and political turmoil. They were not acts of resignation but resistance to death and its power.

Entering this combination of nights we are asked, as in the story, to go a little farther—deeper into the garden, deeper into its anguish and trial to watch with Jesus of Nazareth. That task was daunting for the first disciples. It is intensified for us. For example, after the Shoah, the cup with which Jesus' followers have to contend overflows with increased anguish. Gethsemane's locations shift to places with names like Majdanek, Belzec, Sobibor, Ravensbrück, and questions of staying awake and staying with Jesus during the night take on new, unsettling meaning. Stylized trials in the domains of religious and secular authority remind us of testing in places named Nuremberg, Berlin, not to mention Munich, as well as Oberammergau, and even Barmen. Of course, including Barmen in this regard opens another midrashic door, leading us to ask what it means to remember that a smaller number of disciples walked farther into the night with Jesus than the others did. While the three who accompanied Jesus deeper into the garden eventually fell asleep as well, Barmen reminds us that we can fall asleep even as we are expending energy trying to stay awake![10] Even with this caveat, however, the choices in the garden and in the centers of religious and secular power take on increased significance as places where the covenantal shape of our world was tested in crucibles of power and corporate identity.

Practical Matters

As we attend to the great issues that confront us in this multishadowed night, we must also be alert to the more mundane as well. The familiar, if we are paying attention to the one we have followed to this place, carries significance far beyond our expectations. In the case of Holy Week's practices and liturgies, we are challenged to apply our big perceptions to the simpler tasks of selecting hymns, crafting prayers, planning movement, and developing publicity. How will these necessary and mundane concerns unfold as we take them into the domain of this complex night of anguish?

Mary Boys, in a masterful book titled *Has God Only One Blessing?* has devoted several chapters to linking the larger issues we have been pondering to the actual work of pastors and priests in education and liturgy. She suggests several liturgical forms that require critical evaluation:

- the typological pairing of lectionary texts
- gestures of respect that build on a logic of comparison and contrast
- creeds and other formative and authoritative statements of Christian identity that deny the covenantal story of Israel its rightful place in Christianity's master narratives
- hymn lyrics and other forms of liturgical music that convey problematic relationships with Jews and Judaism

In short, she is asking pastors to give close scrutiny to the unintended consequences of our liturgical choices and actions. Where possible we should consider how the texts we read will speak to each other on their own accord and with regard to the external logic that will be imposed by the setting and the themes we celebrate in our liturgies. As we seek to lift up certain aspects of our tradition, we should think about how we do that. For example, when we emphasize our own culpability in the denial and betrayal of Jesus, do we point fingers of accusations at others who do not bear such responsibility? In the case of Christianity's historic relationship to Jews, our conventional confessions have told a shadow story that we can no longer let go unchallenged. Consequently, when we tell or sing the story of complicity and betrayal on this night, we must be especially alert (awake) to implications we do not intend.

Kendall Soulen has raised similar concerns with his critique of the structural supersessionism present in our liturgies and creeds.[11] Citing the historic creeds of the church as examples, he points out that supersessionism is present in structural ways that are often more difficult to recognize, but nonetheless problematic. Following a historic Trinitarian pattern, they begin with an affirmation of God as creator, then move to the life and ministry of Jesus, and culminate in an affirmation of the gift of the Holy Spirit. Father, Son, and Holy Spirit provide the background for reciting the master story of Christian identity. But the covenantal relationship of God with Israel is overlooked. By omission, the covenantal history of Israel and its God is left behind or taken for granted, as if it were not an essential component of the life of Jesus and those whom he served and who first followed him. In the same spirit, we might consider the liturgical practice of standing for the Gospel lesson while sitting for the Old Testament and Epistle lessons that precede it in high church settings. Even when each reading is followed by "the Word of God" or "the Word of the LORD," the act of standing for one reading but not for others privileges the one for which we stand. If Soulen is correct, supersessionary attitudes can be fostered and supported by a practice meant to convey respect for the Gospels as primary witnesses to the life of Jesus, by inadvertently privileging one lesson over another.

Whereas Soulen refers to this as structural supersessionism, Boys identifies the problem with conventional salvation history, contending that it is in need of reform and revision. While they have diagnosed the problem differently, they have put their finger on the subtle ways the issue is embedded in our practical expressions of Christian identity. Indeed, they force thoughtful Christians to examine taken-for-granted assumptions about core matters and to ask if they must necessarily be expressed as they are. For example, Boys' critique of the christocentric structure of the *Lectionary for the Mass* is telling as she exposes the structural supersessionism that Soulen has sought to disarm. She writes, "A key way in which christocentrism operates in the *Lectionary for the Mass* lies in the pairing of the Gospel and Old Testament lections governed by the concepts of salvation history (*Heilsgeschichte*)."[12]

She explains, "*This means . . . that the history of Israel is proclaimed principally as anticipation of the Christ event. The history of the Jewish people appears to have meaning only insofar as it points to Christ."* [italics in original text][13]

In other words, the typological pairing of lectionary texts according to the christological lens of salvation history often sets up the Hebrew lections for supersessionary interpretations of the Hebrew Bible. For example, the four Servant Songs of Second Isaiah are typically paired during Holy Week with Gospel lessons according to a christological identification of Jesus with Isaiah's Suffering Servant. To show that this association is one interpretation among others, instead of it being the foreshadowing of a prediction that comes true in Jesus, requires careful exegesis and focused work on the part of the preacher in his or her sermon. When this pairing is simply taken for granted, the interpretational moves required for the association are lost and supersessionism is unwittingly supported.

Boys's critique is incisive. While she writes as a Roman Catholic, Soulen's perspective as a Protestant underscores the pervasiveness of the problem. Their point: supersessionism permeates the liturgical life of the church.[14] Boys offers three rather bold proposals that are worth pondering as we consider how we might be more watchful in our liturgical passage through Holy Week.

1. Ordinarily, select passages from the First Testament for proclamation on Sundays that do not relate typologically to the Gospels.
2. Eliminate a second, intermediate reading and lengthen the first reading from the First Testament (or occasionally from non-Gospel books of the Second Testament).
3. Approach our sacred texts with greater sensitivity to their poetic quality.[15] [I would add, as a friendly amendment, their midrashic dimensions.]

Similar issues can be identified when, as we examine the lyrics of cherished hymns and other forms of liturgical music, we recognize the formative role they play in shaping Christian spirituality and identity. Whether one looks at the language of sovereignty accompanying entrance rites and palm processions that begin the week, or the language of sacrifice punctuating classic hymns associated with the latter part of the week (Maundy Thursday and Good Friday), staying awake and alert in the garden of worship takes on new dimensions as we limp through the tasks of planning and preparing for worship. Sometimes the task may be to rework lyrics. Sometimes the task may be to find other hymns. Sometimes the task may be to try other ways of entering the narrated world of this week. But the practical challenge will remain the same: to dwell in this liturgical garden alert and awake. Sadly, we know too well how we have fallen asleep on this job in the past.

A Liturgical Offering

Our journey through Holy Week has taken us deep into a richly textured night. Layered with multiple meanings, the experience of this night begins in the early evening with the events of the meal at sundown and extends into the late night anguish of the garden and beyond. As, led by Matthew, we made our way to Gethsemane and then to the domains of the religious and political leaders of Jerusalem, we encountered a number of stylized trials, each with its own subtle dynamics drawing us into its dilemmas and testimony. It became more and more apparent that we were participants in the story with choices to make in how we enter and what we see when we do.

Entering the garden liturgically most surely means responding to the call to watch with Jesus through the night. Following the meal as it does, the biblical journey to Gethsemane suggests a liturgical model linked with the Eucharist. For many congregations, the Last Supper is commemorated on Maundy Thursday/Holy Thursday evening in a special sacramental service. With little difficulty, the sacrament of Holy Communion could also include some form of "Watch Night" liturgy, either to conclude the service or to follow the sacramental meal. For congregations that celebrate a ritual footwashing, there would be some need to differentiate and link that commemoration with the night in the garden as it is described by Matthew—unless the scene in the garden turns to the text of John for the remainder of the gathering. Still, a clear articulation of the shift in witnesses would be important for the integrity of the narrative being developed in the liturgical journey through the week. Nevertheless, the opportunity to provide a time of introspection focused on the significance of "watching through the night" can follow.

As in previous chapters, the liturgical option with which we conclude this reflection is offered to encourage thoughtful consideration of how the hermeneutical concerns of this chapter might be implemented in the worship life of a local congregation. Moreover, the following suggestion should be read as building on the work of the previous chapter, incorporating the reflections on the sacramental action at the Table articulated there. The liturgy described below is therefore presented as an extension of those earlier reflections and presumes the text of the Great Thanksgiving considered in the last chapter.

To be sure, such a period of introspection is open to a variety of forms. It could be circumscribed by the sacramental liturgy, as presented in the following option. Or the period could be open-ended, with participants leaving the experience when they decide. Just as easily, the invitation "to watch through the night" can lead to a more focused experience of reflecting on the biblical lessons read earlier and their application in the present. Or a more intensive experience of meditational prayer, even journal writing, could be introduced for the introspective work of an overnight retreat.

The option provided here follows the Matthean witness and links Jesus' struggle in the garden with Jacob's wrestling at the Jabbok. It provides a way of moving from a service commemorating the Last Supper to confessional activity that enables the participants to examine their lives vis-à-vis a number of possible dilemmas: staying awake to the dangers of the night, facing the night at its shadowy threats, wrestling with the cup, and coming to terms with one's own betrayal and complicity. In each case the issues would be encountered by entering into the garden of the text, not by imposing them on the participants in thematic fashion. The goal is to open the text to those who have gathered for the evening and to enter its narrated world of significance and challenge.

Note the use of silence in this liturgy. Silent prayer is designated as an appropriate form of preparing for hearing the Scriptures and for the time of confession that follows. Likewise, the time typically designated for a sermon or homily is offered as commentary in the expectation of dialogue, which could very constructively be punctuated with more silence. The worship leader should be comfortable with this format and able to provide minimal instruction and enough silence for the open space in the service to provide room for the spirit to have its say in the time together.

Maundy Thursday

Holy Eucharist with Watch-Night Liturgy

GREETING

> **Leader:** Bless the Eternal One, whose hospitality welcomes us all;
> **People: and whose mercy endures for ever.**
> **Leader:** May God be with you.
> **People: And also with you.**

OPENING PRAYER

HYMN/SONG

TIME OF SILENT PRAYER AND CENTERING

WITNESS OF SCRIPTURE   Genesis 32:22–33   Matthew 26:17–35

COMMENTARY

RESPONSE

PRAYERS OF CONFESSION

Brothers and sisters, we all have sinned and fallen short of the glory of God. Let us be still and confess our sin, remembering that God is gracious and loving, and always reaching out to us. Embodying God's love, Jesus has invited us to his table knowing full well our weakness and fallibility. In silence, therefore, let us pray.

Concluded by announcement of Good News.

PRAYERS FOR OTHERS[16]

Merciful God, on this, the night Jesus was betrayed, your Son welcomed to his table those who would deny him, and even the one who betrayed him. As we commit ourselves to following his example of love and service, teach us to embody his courage and hospitality.
>   God of grace,
>   **hear our prayer.**

On this night, Jesus prayed for his disciples to be one.
As we grieve for the divisions in the church, unite us.
>   God of grace,
>   **hear our prayer.**

On this night, Jesus prayed for those who would come to follow him.
As we take up the mission of your church, temper our zeal with humility and deepen our commitment to you.
>   God of grace,
>   **hear our prayer.**

On this night, Jesus commanded his friends to love, but he suffered rejection himself.
As we open our hearts to the rejected and the unloved, fill us with your compassion and understanding.
>   God of grace,
>   **hear our prayer.**

On this night, Jesus reminded his people that, if the world hated them, it had hated him first.
As we face our own fears, we pray for those who are persecuted for their faith; so we pray, give us strength and your abiding peace.

God of grace,
hear our prayer.

On this night, Jesus loved his friends to the very end.
As we open our hearts to all who face darkness tonight, we pray for the sick, those who mourn, those trapped by violence, addiction, or pain: give healing and hope.

God of grace,
hear our prayer.

Faithful God, receive our prayers.
We offer them trusting and hoping in you.
Hear and help us, challenge and change us,
through Jesus Christ our Lord. Amen.

PEACE

OFFERING

Bread and Wine
Other Offerings

THE GREAT THANKSGIVING   (full text pp. 73–75)

Let us welcome one another as Christ has welcomed us.

Leader: May God be with you.
People: And also with you.
Leader: Lift up your hearts.
People: We lift them up to God.
Leader: Let us give thanks to the Eternal One, our God.
People: It is right to give our thanks and praise . . .

LORD'S PRAYER

TAKING THE BREAD

TAKING THE CUP

COMMUNION

HYMN

THANKSGIVING AFTER THE MEAL

INVITATION TO WATCH THROUGH THE NIGHT

Leader: Then Jesus went with them to a place called Gethsemane.

PROCESSION TO WATCH-NIGHT LOCATION

WATCH-NIGHT LITANY

Leader: And he said to his disciples, "Sit here while I go over there and pray."

The community gathers in silence. After an appropriate interval the silence is broken.

Leader: Then he said to them, "I am deeply grieved, even to death; remain here, and stay awake with me." And going a little farther, he threw himself on the ground and prayed, "My Father, if it is possible, let this cup pass from me; yet not what I want but what you want."

A period of silence follows.

Leader: Then he came to the disciples and found them sleeping; and he said to Peter, "So could you not stay awake with me one hour? Stay awake and pray that you may not come into the time of trial; the spirit indeed is willing, but the flesh is weak." Again he went away for the second time and prayed, "My Father, if this cannot pass unless I drink it, your will be done."

A period of silence follows.

Leader: Again he came and found them sleeping, for their eyes were heavy. So leaving them again, he went away and prayed for the third time, saying the same words. Then he came to the disciples and said to them, "Are you still sleeping and taking your rest? See, the hour is at hand, and the Son of Man is betrayed into the hands of sinners. Get up, let us be going. See my betrayer is at hand."

SENDING FORTH INTO THE NIGHT

NOTES

1. The Greek word translated as "betrayed" also means "delivered" and "handed down."

2. It is interesting to note that in this episode the characters are all male. Later, as the crucifixion draws nearer, the women of Jesus' circle will emerge from the background of the narrative as those few, in contrast to this scene, who did not fall away or fail to watch with their leader and their friend.

3. Christians are challenged by Jewish friends to recognize that the Seder is more than

an historical *Sitz im Leben* for this story. As my colleague Zev Garber has explained, the Seder has an abiding significance for any who would participate in it. That is, the Seder should have an active, living presence in readings which are faithful to the context that Matthew provides. Garber calls it "an unending Seder." See Zev Garber, "Night Encounters: Theologizing Dialogue," *Shofar* 15, no. 1 (Fall 1996): 46ff.

4. Raymond E. Brown, *The Death of the Messiah: From Gethsemane to the Grave* (New York: Doubleday, 1994), 1:13–17.

5. Michael Goldberg, *Jews and Christians: Getting Our Stories Straight* (Nashville: Abingdon Press, 1985), 179–83.

6. William Nicholls, *Christian Antisemitism: A History of Hate* (Northvale, NJ: Jason Aronson, 1993), xix.

7. See Irving Greenberg, "Religious Values after the Holocaust: A Jewish View," in *Jews and Christians after the Holocaust*, ed. Abraham J. Peck (Philadelphia: Fortress Press, 1982), 63–86, esp. 82ff., and "History, Holocaust, and Covenant," in *Remembering for the Future: The Impact of the Holocaust and Genocide on Jews and Christians*, Proceedings of an International Conference, Oxford and London, July 10–17, 1988 (Oxford: Pergamon Press, 1989), 2920–26.

8. Greenberg, "Religious Values after the Holocaust," 83.

9. See Franklin Littell, *The Crucifixion of the Jews: The Failure of Christians to Understand the Jewish Experience* (New York: Harper & Row, 1975), 44–60, for a classic analysis of this chapter in the history of the Christian church.

10. My friend Martin Rumscheidt reminds me that even with Barmen's primary concern regarding idolatry, they were not ignoring the Jewish question as a component of Nazi idolatry. Rather, for strategic reasons they focused their concerns on idolatry and confused allegiances between church and state. Still, as Barth has remarked in retrospect, Barmen failed to confront the oppression and suffering of the Jewish people in any direct manner. And in this regard, even those who courageously crafted the Barmen Confession slept.

11. R. Kendall Soulen, *The God of Israel and Christian Theology* (Minneapolis: Fortress Press, 1996), 31–32.

12. Mary C. Boys, *Has God Only One Blessing? Judaism as a Source of Christian Self-Understanding* (New York: Paulist Press, 2000), 208.

13. Ibid.

14. Ibid., 200.

15. Ibid., 217.

16. Adapted from "Prayers of Intercession for Maundy Thursday" from *Lent, Holy Week and Easter* (London: Church House Publishing, 1984), 188–89. Also available online at http://www.oremus.org/liturgy/lhwe/mt.html.

Chapter 5

Coming to Terms with a Good Friday World

Facing the Cross and Its Aftermath

On the Way to the Cross

As we limp into the final days of Holy Week and take our place in its story, we pause outside the palace of Pilate, the Fortress Antonia, to await the outcome of the rapidly unfolding events of the night before and the early morning that followed. Once more, we limp as we take our place following Jesus on his path toward crucifixion, accompanied by ever-present Jewish companions, past and present, who remind us that they too have experienced the taunting we see aimed at the one we follow on this wretched path.

The trials of the night and early morning continue for Jesus as well as for his followers. Pilate's sentence of crucifixion has been rendered. In its wake, Jesus faces ridicule and humiliation. Roman guards, enamored with their power, lampoon the accused "King of the Jews." Their abuse is physical but also verbal. How will Jesus respond to their hostility—he who has challenged others to turn their cheeks in the face of violence done to them? How will those standing by respond? Will anyone interrupt or challenge the abuse? One tried earlier in the garden, but his recourse was to violence in return. And Jesus interrupted that action even though he had been placed under arrest. Will anyone dare follow (except at a distance) under these circumstances?

Of course, we cannot review this scene and its interrogations without extending the trials to our own time. Just sixty years ago, Jews were rounded up, arrested, detained, and often ridiculed by uniformed soldiers of the Third Reich. From Kristallnacht on, the scourge was carried out in public view, even though much more occurred behind barbed-wire fences and brick walls. Every Jew was a target, if not an actual victim, of this abuse.

The walk to Golgotha loops through every street in the Third Reich and every *schtetl* of eastern Europe. When we return to Holy Week and the final leg of our walk through Jerusalem, we limp with the knowledge of this modern path of shame and destruction—a path Jesus would have walked if he had been born two millennia later. The taunting of bystanders and the shouts of ridicule that rain down with wrath from angry spectators only add to the unsettling comparison. The outskirts of Jerusalem look more and more like the outskirts of Warsaw, Lublin, Ościwęcim, Kraków, Berlin, Oranienburg. The hillside of Golgotha looks more and more like the camp sites of Majdanek, Birkenau, Bergen-Belsen, Sachsenhausen.

As we gaze at those lining the way, we stare at bystanders in disbelief, but we cannot escape recognizing that the face of the bystander looks more and more like our own reflection the deeper we venture into Jerusalem. As we return to the story and to our place in its domain, we simply cannot dismiss our place in it. The story is familiar—too familiar.

Approaching the scene we continue to limp, wounded by an increased sense of complicity and collusion punctuating the text and its narrated world. We stumble into the picture behind vocal and silent bystanders who line the way. Others peek out from the safety of their homes. Shrill voices shout epithets and fill the air with adrenalin and fear. As we take our place, we can just make out a beaten and bruised figure stumbling from the gates of the Fortress Antonia. He is carrying the crossbar of his cross, made to bear the weapon that will take his life, forced to cooperate in his own execution. But he is too weak to make it on his own. He stumbles and slips down. The guards turn to another and force him to take the crossbar from Jesus. As the guards push both men toward the execution site, Jesus says nothing, though occasionally his eyes fall on curious bystanders along the way.

Standing among the bystanders, we cannot point an accusing finger at others. The complicity of everyone present is too strong. There is enough blame to go around. Still, it would be wrong to blame anyone not present for what is happening here.[1] That language must be resisted. Yet it is in the text, having crept in from Matthew's time as he responded to the contentious give-and-take between synagogue leaders and followers of Jesus by incorporating their polemics into his descriptions of what happened.

As we ponder the characters attending this odious procession, we take our place in the background as Jesus approaches and then arrives at Golgotha. However, we cannot help but notice the absence of Jesus' closest companions. Judas, of course, has fallen away. According to the text, he has taken his own life out of grief and guilt. But the others have also fallen away, even Peter, James, and John. Peter, especially, wrestled with his denial. It was personal and poignant, even anticipated by Jesus. Matthew's text is clear in this regard. At this portion of the story, these close friends and followers are simply not present. They are missing.

As we continue to look around, we should not overlook Pilate, though Matthew appears to shield him from our view. Nonetheless, he would have been looking down on the scene from his vantage point in the Antonia. His wife, some say, warned him to beware of getting too involved. So he made a show of washing his hands of the affair. But the sentence was still his. The cross Jesus approaches was Pilate's decision—no one else's—no matter how much collusion there may have been.

Beholding Crucifixion

The transition to the execution site is abrupt. Matthew's description of the crucifixion is stark. It is simply presumed that the reader or hearer understands what is involved in a crucifixion. The detail to which Matthew gives his attention has to do with other matters, such as the guards offering Jesus a palliative of sour wine to help him confront the agony that lies ahead. Jesus refused, Matthew tells us. Likewise other details speak to how Matthew views the crucifixion in its theological context. Still, we should not avoid the stark reality of the execution and its brutality—facts that confronted the earliest followers of Jesus. They were features of the cultural and political landscape that Matthew could presume.

From a number of extrabiblical sources we know how cruel and brutal crucifixion was. The suffering was intense—physically and mentally—as the victim hung with little or no clothing, exposed to the elements and to animals that might be attracted to the scene. If the victim hung unsupported from the cross bar, the shoulders would dislocate and pain would be intense. Death would come slowly by asphyxiation, as the weight of the body bore down on the lung's capacity to take in fresh oxygen. Little by little, the body would be starved of oxygen. If the body's weight was supported, then death would take longer, and exposure would be a greater factor. Either way, death by crucifixion was torture.

The irony in Matthew's description of the crucifixion is not lost on the attentive reader or listener. Those whom he sought to serve, misfits and sinners, were on his right and left hand—not his disciples. Roman guards watched over him without falling asleep, though gambling for his clothes and continuing their sarcastic ridicule. And when the soldiers gambled for his clothes, the two others with whom he was crucified even participated in the humiliation—both according to Matthew, one according to Luke. Even some religious authorities were present, taunting him with words that recalled his challenge to the temple and its sacrificial system. Only the two Marys,

Magdalene and the mother of James and Joseph,[2] along with the other women in the group remained close. The disciples were missing in action. Jesus' abandonment was nearly complete.

While the crucifixion itself was sparsely described, the elements accompanying the scene are highly stylized, as in previous moments of the passion. As Matthew relates the events, the sky darkened from noon to three in the afternoon. Then, at three, Jesus cried out "Eli, Eli, lema sabachthani," speaking the opening words of Psalm 22. And he died. The death scene is framed in the language of Amos 8:4–6 and Psalm 22, while the approach to Golgotha has been clothed in the language of Second Isaiah. In fact, the description of the events accompanying his death—the tearing of the temple curtain and the opening of the graves—is the strongest indicator of the midrashic character of this stylization. That is, the events that Matthew relates are cosmic and cataclysmic. Yet no one except a Roman centurion takes any notice of them. These cosmic events appear inserted into the story without any narrative impact on the flow of what happened. Instead, they seem to set up the ironic commentary of the Roman centurion ("Truly this man was God's Son!"), in contrast to the crowd and the grieving Marys and the other women (including a possible veiled reference to his mother). In other words, the narrative resumes as if none of these earthshaking events happened. Crossan concludes that this is evidence of "prophecy historicized." He writes:

> By 'prophecy historicized' I mean that no such *historical* three-hour-long midnight at noon accompanied the death of Jesus, but that learned Christians searching their Scriptures framed this ancient description of future divine punishment . . . and so created that *fictional* story about darkness at noon to assert that Jesus died in fulfillment of prophecy.[3]

Crossan argues that this kind of material, with its heavy reliance on the language of Second Isaiah, Amos, and Zechariah is strong evidence that we are not reading history remembered as it happened. For example, Matthew, or his source, has used the words of Second Isaiah to tell the story of what happened as Jesus approached Golgotha, adopting the poetic language of Isaiah's prophetic vision as if it were history. Then subsequent readers or listeners encounter the material and read or hear it as history. In that way, the poetic discourse of prophecy is transmuted into the seemingly factual record of history.

I find it more helpful, however, to conclude that Matthew is telling this story midrashically. That is, Matthew is self-consciously using the language of Isaiah to tell the story of what happened to Jesus in order to help his listeners/readers recognize what was hidden in the plain sight of the events that are not yet understood. In other words, the language of Scripture was used to cast light on an otherwise inexplicable event, revealing a way of seeing what happened "according to the Scriptures." But the key is not that Matthew or his precursor knew the significance of what happened first, then sought out the prediction in Isaiah, and consequently told the story to show what was predicted from before. Rather the anchor of understanding resides in the prophetic discourse that was used to make sense out of the terrifying vision of what happened to Jesus. The directionality of the knowing is critical. The prophetic knowing provided leverage for understanding the meaningless suffering undergone by the innocent victim who died such an ignominious death.

If Matthew is telling his story midrashically, as I believe he is, then he is telling the story of what happened to Jesus using the larger story of prophetic discourse. He is using what he knows to make sense out of what he wants to understand. Standing within the prophetic perspectives of Amos, Isaiah, and Zechariah, he shines the light of their discourse on the problematic events of this week, especially its tragic outcome. He reads the events "according to the Scriptures." But we must be clear that what he knows first are his Scriptures. What he seeks to understand is what happened to Jesus. By reading the *as yet not understood* events in the light of previously understood Scripture, he uncovers what he is now able to see in the experiences he could not previously understand. That in turn leads him to return to the Scripture he knew before, but now recognizing new dimensions in it he had not seen earlier.

Perhaps a more contemporary example would help interpret this dynamic. Elie Wiesel's *Night* features a scene in which he describes the hanging of three camp inmates who are being punished for their attempts to blow up and destroy facilities at Auschwitz III, Monowitz, where rubber was being manufactured for the Nazi war effort. As a lesson, all the inmates were made to stand and watch the hanging. Then they were ordered to pass by the victims left hanging before them all. As Wiesel describes the scene, he tells of a young teenager, a *pilpul*, whose body weight was so slight his death was prolonged in tortuous agony. As Wiesel stood among other inmates watching this gruesome sight, he tells of hearing someone behind him ask, "Where is God now?" to which Wiesel said he recited to himself, "Where is He? Here He is—He is hanging here on this gallows."[4]

A few years ago, Alfred Kazin criticized Wiesel for taking liberty with his narration in *Night*, eventually accusing him of inventing this scene. Wiesel responded to this criticism with anger and passion, explaining he could identify the people by name.[5] Kazin's critique, to my mind, had failed to understand what Wiesel was doing in *Night* and led Kazin to place the stylized nature of the narrative over against a historical recounting of what happened in the camp. Wiesel, however, was writing midrashically, telling not just his own story but also the story of an entire people caught up in the twelve-year-long night we now identify as the Shoah. He had woven the text of his story and that of six million others into the haggadic character of the exodus story, in effect portraying an anti-exodus haggadah. He was answering the question, "Why is this night different from any other night?" using his people's paradigmatic story of liberation to tell the story of their nearly total destruction. Wiesel had layered his narrative in order to tell a gestalt of stories in a single narration. His critic, by failing to understand what Wiesel was doing, placed history as testimony over against fiction, thereby missing the point and setting up a conflict between history and a very sophisticated interpretation of history. A dichotomy such as the one set up in Kazin's reading of Wiesel can obscure other ways of entering and viewing history. I fear that Crossan sets up a similar possibility.

Using this example points up another important issue. In being instructed by Wiesel's midrashic approach, we cannot then turn to a scene like the one cited in *Night* and usurp it for our own purposes, turning it into something it isn't. Moltmann, in his book *The Crucified God*, takes this very scene and uses it in just this way, as God choosing to enter into human suffering in a potentially transformative way.[6] But Wiesel is telling his story to describe the very loss that Moltmann wants to resist. For Wiesel, the scene does not disclose divine solidarity with his or his people's agony, thereby breaking the suffering open with meaning it otherwise would not have. Instead, the scene is a description of the "useless suffering" that destroys meaning, even divine purpose. Indeed, Wiesel ends the chapter that frames this scene with the statement, "That night the soup tasted like corpses."[7] If we are going to behold the cross and Jesus' crucifixion after Auschwitz, we must be willing to confront the meaninglessness that it embodied for those who returned to it midrashically for help afterwards.

This caution illustrates another feature of midrash. Even though midrash promotes multiple interpretations, not all interpretations are equally valid. Indeed, some should be resisted. For example, Moltmann has overlooked the limits the text of *Night* places (its *peshat*) on its interpretive possibilities and has read the passage in a way that opposes the plain meaning of the text. Kazin's interpretation, that the scene in question is fiction, likewise overlooks another critical feature provided by the text. Though stylized, *Night* is identified by Wiesel as testimony (*temoinage* in the original French version).[8] That is, *Night* is not a novel but the testimony of a witness. Consequently, Kazin's comment that the scene could be made up challenges the factuality of the event Wiesel has described as well as the integrity of his witness. In his published reply to Kazin's allegation Wiesel, therefore, adds additional information, the names of the people depicted in the scene Kazin has questioned. In doing so, Wiesel supports the plain meaning of his text with specific information to underscore further the nature of the text as testimony and to refute the allegation that the testimony could be false. In other words, even if a text can be interpreted in more than one way, some ways can be identified as unfaithful renderings of it. Just as there are limits that we must learn to face in the raw experience of human suffering, there are limits proffered by the text to which we must attend as well—even with midrash.[9]

Meaningless Suffering

Any honest attempt to face the crucifixion must come to terms with the utter destruction of meaning and hope that crucifixion represents. Or to put the matter another way, we must recognize that what happened on that occasion was utterly destructive to the hopes and dreams that had been focused on Jesus by his followers. Furthermore, the abandonment and forsakenness that Jesus experienced were complete. After Auschwitz, we who follow a crucified Messiah must be willing to face the collapse of meaning and hope that confronts us at the cross. Likewise, we must be willing to face the full crisis of meaning that is occasioned by the Shoah. To put it bluntly, there is no way to find meaning in the burning children of Auschwitz.

This mandate challenges us to recognize that Matthew's descriptions of the crucifixion are acts of return, not original, unmediated encounters with raw suffering. Indeed, his midrashic rendering of what happened is already a narrative way of returning to a setting of meaninglessness that provides a frame for confronting the event itself and the problems it poses. Whether one withdraws and returns in a very short span of time or returns sometime later, the hermeneutical reality remains the same. The encounter, the approach, will always be a return, even when we make it for the first time, because others have shaped even our first approach by their return. That is, the midrashic response is exactly that—a response, a return, mediated by Scripture, seeing what happened not in its raw form but "according to the Scriptures." In other words, when one beholds the crucifixion reading or hearing the story of Matthew, our beholding is always a returning to the scene according to a scriptural frame that holds what we see. Still, we must come to terms with the first encounter that we can access only by way of the mediated narrative. And that first encounter is one that evokes midrash, precisely because it is bereft of meaning otherwise. Embedded in the midrashic return, the meaninglessness of suffering is present as that which calls forth the midrash itself.

After Auschwitz, this hermeneutical caveat is not just a clever act of theological posturing. Rather, it is a compassionate willingness and moral mandate to face the reality that some suffering is not meaningful, but useless. It is a recognition that suffering can be utterly destructive; that suffering can be the exact opposite of God's intentions for creation—indeed, the undoing of creation.

If we insist on viewing Jesus' suffering as intrinsically meaningful, then we place the suffering of Auschwitz and that of all other victims caught in the grips of meaningless suffering beyond the reach of what has happened in his crucifixion. However, our distinction between the raw experience of what happened and the midrashic return that Scripture uses to narrate that suffering provides us with the leverage for recovering the crisis of meaning that is embedded, though hidden, in the text that describes Jesus' crucifixion.

Emmanuel Levinas has identified this crisis as occasioned by "useless suffering," meaning "pain in its undiluted malignity, suffering for nothing." He explains,

> It [useless suffering] renders impossible and odious every proposal and every thought that would explain it by the sins of those who have suffered or are dead. But does not this end of theodicy, which imposes itself in the face of this century's inordinate trial, at the same time and in a more general way reveal the unjustifiable character of suffering in the other, the outrage it would be for me to justify my neighbor's suffering?[10]

Just as disturbing are intended "uses" one makes of suffering to destroy life. Jean Amery has described his encounters with torture as crushing blows to the victim, stripping him or her of any fundamental sense of "trust in the world."[11] In torture the victim is reduced to the physical phenomenon of pain. "Only in torture," he writes, "does the transformation of the person into flesh become complete."[12] Terrence Des Pres captures the humiliating character of raw victimization in his description of the torturous actions of death camp personnel as "excremental assault." He explains,

> The exercise of totalitarian power, in any case, does not stop with the demand for outward compliance. It seeks, further, to crush the spirit, to obliterate that active inward principle whose strength depends on its freedom from entire determination by external forces.[13]

He continues,

The death of the soul was aimed at. It was to be accomplished by terror and privation, but first of all by a relentless assault on the survivor's sense of purity and worth. Excremental attack, the physical inducement of disgust and self-loathing, was a principal weapon.[14]

Any return we make to Jesus' crucifixion will be mediated by our encounters with the suffering represented by texts like these and their witness to human cruelty. Through their lenses, we must now look at Jesus on the cross and hear his midrashic cry, "My God, my God, why have you forsaken me?" challenged by knowledge of utter, meaningless suffering propagated on others simply because they were defined as not being worthy of life. Any attempt to cloak the most extreme forms of human suffering with a view that sees in it intrinsic meaning fails to address the suffering we meet at the heart of the Shoah. Indeed, after Auschwitz we may say that it is a moral and spiritual outrage to justify anyone's suffering, whether the most despicable human being or the Messiah himself, for some transcendent reason. More on this in a moment. For now, it is sufficient that we face the utter meaninglessness of suffering that our post-Shoah perspective forces us to examine when we approach the crucifixion from the shadows of Auschwitz. The meaninglessness of suffering is there, hidden in the text, in the midrashic response to an experience so empty of meaning that it could not be faced any other way but midrashically.

The Aftermath of Crucifixion, Burial and Despair

We must be careful as we recognize the depth of what is at stake at this point. Too easily we as Christians move from the tomb in which we place Jesus, our accompanying hopes and dreams, and our accompanying images and understandings of God, to return to the tomb to proclaim that the tomb is empty, that God has raised Jesus from the dead, that death could not hold Jesus who was placed there, or the hopes and dreams that we buried with him, or our understandings of God. Easter comes too quickly, as we omit the aftermath of this cruel experience and its tormenting images. In fact, the biblical story does very little to discourage this, by moving quickly past the interim period of the Sabbath that precedes Easter morning. We cannot.

As we limp from the scene of crucifixion to the grave site and prepare to return two days later, we stumble over the awareness that the aftermath of crucifixion could not have been seen as an interim period by those who tried to rest on that bitter Sabbath immediately following the death and burial of their friend and teacher. Their hopes and their dreams were destroyed along with their beloved rabbi.

Our limping return to the crucifixion prepares us to see the despair and grief that were undoubtedly being experienced by Jesus' close companions—the two Marys (Magdalene and possibly his mother)[15] and the other women. Like Jesus, they had been left alone by his so-called disciples. For whatever reason, the disciples were not present to remove Jesus from the cross, to take care of his body, to carry him to a tomb, or to prepare him for burial. Another figure is introduced, Joseph of Arimathea, who offers his tomb for Jesus' use. As a result, a new irony appears. Jesus is dependent, even in the end, upon the hospitality of another, perhaps a stranger,[16] to provide him a final dwelling place.

However, we cannot linger with this irony, except to contemplate its bitterness on that original occasion. The text tells us very little about what happened except to say that Jesus was buried in a borrowed tomb, that a stone was rolled into place to seal it, and that guards were secured to stand watch. And almost as an aside, we are told that Jesus' followers went home, or wherever they were staying, to rest, since it was the Sabbath. We are left with a gap in the story that we must fill when we ponder the aftermath of what happened and how deeply the despair of that day penetrated the stillness of the Sabbath that followed the crucifixion. It would not have been a day of delight. It would not have been a day to ponder the abundance of creation. It would have been a bitterly ironic day, a Sabbath of stillness, but very little, genuine rest.[17]

When we pause for this Sabbath and sit Shivah with those experiencing utter despair because of what happened, we risk being still long enough to confront the full aftermath of what happened at Golgotha. When we experience not an empty tomb but a full tomb, holding not just Jesus' body but everything else that was lost that day as well, and then move to sit with a grieving mother, then we limp into unexpected shadows. More than Jesus was buried in his tomb. That rather simple statement points to the theological crisis facing those who have dared to venture into the shadows of the crucifixion and its aftermath. To be sure, his dreams and hopes were placed in the tomb with him, but for those of us attentive to the covenantal dimensions of his ministry and the questions raised by his suffering, as well as the suffering of so many other innocent victims throughout history, the very presence of God comes under question. Wiesel's question before the hanging *pilpul* in Auschwitz returns to haunt not simply our first encounter with the crucifixion but any return to a scene of meaningless suffering. Where is God now? More pointedly, where is the covenantal God of creation now? To put the matter starkly, the God of covenantal theism is buried in Jesus' tomb along with Jesus.

The absence of rescue in Jesus' situation accentuates the absence of rescue in other situations when innocent victims suffer. When that is linked with the injustice of 1.5 million children who perished in the Shoah, then we must ask about the absence of divine intervention in all these cases. Likewise, we must ask about the understanding that God's action may be a relinquishment of judgment because of the satisfaction of God's passion for balancing the scales of justice with the life of an innocent victim. That understanding is challenged by Jesus' own message that God's love and mercy are abundant fountains of grace. But when Jesus' crucifixion is viewed in the company of the burning children of Auschwitz (Greenberg's criterion), such a view of God's action is morally and spiritually untenable. And when we approach this recognition limping with our knowledge of how we have held so many persons hostage to our theologies over the centuries, then we find ourselves challenged even further. If we are honest with ourselves, we find that the challenge extends to our understanding of God and the model of covenantal theism by and through which many of us have learned to view the events of this week and the theology that has grown out of them.

Theological Implications

The dilemma is not unlike that faced by Job in earlier centuries, except that for Christians Jesus bears the face of God in such a way that in the aftermath of crucifixion we must ask, what happens when his face is distorted not just with pain but also with the sense of being forsaken and utterly alone? When he cries out, "Why have you forsaken me?" do we not hear God cry out the same lonely lament to us? To borrow a phrase from J. B. Metz, we must ask, "With such a catastrophe at one's back, is there a God to whom [we] can pray?"[18] In other words, when this Jesus is buried, then the God of covenantal theism is buried with him, yet crying out to us about being forsaken too!

The Job story is most instructive for us in this regard. Job buried his ten children and knew they were unjustly taken from him. By insisting on the wrongness of their suffering he brought forth logical protest from representatives of the conventional piety of his day. They intervened where God did not, seeking to help Job examine his life to see how he was responsible for what happened to his family. But he knew otherwise; he was not the cause of what happened. What happened could not be justified by his or even his children's behavior. What happened did not fit the conventional logic of God in covenant with the world, rewarding them for good and punishing them for bad. When Job sought to challenge God that the suffering his family had experienced was unjust, Job was challenged again by conventionally religious friends. They declared that his protest was unacceptable. But Job wanted a chance to plead his case with God, to set things right, to correct what had to be a mistake. At this point, Job too was operating within the same model of covenantal theism. As the story unfolds, God entered into intense encounter with Job, putting Job under interrogation. "Where were you when . . . ?" (Job 38:4). In the process, Job's conventional framework for understanding God collapses, yet the collapse of belief allows room for the relationship to seek another form. That is, Job's way of understanding God shattered even when he did not give up on the one whom his belief could no longer hold. The God of conventional covenantal theism had to make room for a God who would join Job in protest and lament.

One of the theological strategies Christians use to avoid this crisis of belief has involved our view of Jesus as a sacrificial offering who sets things right with the God of covenantal theism. Typically, Christians focus on the suffering Jesus underwent, concentrating on the sacrificial character of his life and death. In doing so, we assign meaning to his death as an act of expiation or propitiation, to use terms we Christians often hear in our liturgies; or as an act of satisfaction or substitution, to use terms from the traditional models of atonement. The emphasis, of course, is on the meaningfulness of Jesus' death as a substitute payment to God or a representative offering to balance one sinless life against all others who otherwise deserve punishment. In either case, the meaning is in Jesus' sacrificial death, with Christians referring to this act as Christ dying for our sins. Moreover, this is good news that many of us in the church proclaim in Jesus' name.

In the face of what we know about suffering in our age, viewing Jesus' suffering, much less anyone else's, as having intrinsic meaning is problematic and serves the glorification of victimization. Our earlier encounters at the temple, in the upper room, and in Gethsemane help us see another way, viewing Jesus' passion as a radical commitment to covenant life that retains the power to heal and transform even in the face of rejection and death. Liberated from the lens of viewing Jesus' death as a sacrificial requirement of God, we are free to see Jesus' choices for life, particularly covenant life, as an offering he makes so that his followers may share in the abundance of life he knows in his relationships with others. The extent of that commitment is manifest in his decision to take his message to the city that he deeply loves but that is filled with danger to him. Likewise, it is embodied in his commitment to disciples whom he expects to deny, fall away, and even betray him. In this way, the meaning of sacrifice shifts from the death of an unblemished victim to the pure offering of oneself a person can make for the sake of others.

In other words, Jesus' passion does not need to glorify suffering and vic-timization. Instead, without changing any of what happened, our midrashic return helps us recognize in Jesus' earlier actions in the temple courtyard and at the upper room table a radical passion for covenant life *in the face of death* and abandonment, even in the face of covenant life's greatest threat, betrayal. Moreover, that choice was confirmed yet again in Gethsemane and immedi-ately thereafter, as Jesus faced the trials that grew out of his choices for covenant life. To choose covenant relationship in such circumstances, there-fore, breaks the cycle of rejection and betrayal (i.e., the power of death) at its point of violation. But the cost is much higher than we may have thought.

Pastoral Tasks and Implications

As Christians, we live not only in a Good Friday world, but also in a Holy Sat-urday world, between the first encounter with the tragic tale of violence and the post-Easter encounter with a resurrected Christ. As Alan E. Lewis has put it:

> This is a story which must be told and heard, believed and interpreted, *two different ways at once*—as a story whose ending is *known*, and as one whose ending is discovered only *as it happens.* The truth is victimized when either reading is allowed to drown out the other.[19]

While Lewis is undoubtedly correct in this assertion, we have to be careful after Auschwitz, knowing how easy it will be to hear only the Easter side of the dialectic. We want urgently to remove the pain of an empty Sabbath. Yet not to attend to it would be to deny the very faith that drives me to insist that we must hear the haunting cries of crucifixion day and its aftermath. How then do we attend to both without undoing the tension Lewis says we must maintain?

Perhaps the word *promise* is helpful here. We know the promise of Easter through what has been shown to us in an empty tomb and a continuing story. But we know its victory of life over death as promise, not as a final, completed act. It has begun, yet it remains tenuous. Having happened, it is real and not a pipe dream. Not having happened for all, it remains as yet a promise of what might be for all. During the interim Sabbath we dwell in that promise with thanksgiving and in intercession for a tormented world. Even so, it may be too soon to linger here. We must beware of premature closure.

What then is our pastoral task? How are we to proclaim Christ crucified? We need to honor the vantage point by which we view his death as the consequence—but not the gift—of his sacrificial offering of and for life for the sake of a world in need of just what he has to offer. At the same time, we need to confront the starkness of the first encounters with this *world-and sanctuary-rending* event that stalked his followers and friends immediately following his death. We know we cannot slip into easy formulations, particularly the easy confessions of faith, what Douglas John Hall calls cheap hope.[20] We know also that we must beware the language of blame and any rhetoric of caricature when we talk about what happened during Jesus' last week, whatever we say. For example, the midrashic use of 2 Samuel 1:16 extending David's condemnation of the Amalekite for taking the life of Saul, God's anointed, must not only be understood as midrash, but must also be resisted otherwise.[21] We know with discomforting clarity that we must repudiate any language that blames Jews for what happened. Similar care must be taken when we apply the language of sacrifice to what happened. What do we say about the sacrificial offering of his life?

One of the most important pastoral responsibilities that comes from our limping through Jerusalem must be learning to resist locating the meaning of Jesus' passion in his death. Instead, we must direct our attention and that of our parishioners to the choices Jesus made and the actions he took in the face of death. The reconfigurations of Easter will likewise include these moments as they transform what happened and declare that death did not have the final victory—even in a theology of sacrifice. The meaning resides in the moments before and after crucifixion. The suffering of the cross is meaningful—if that is the best term for what is otherwise meaningless, useless suffering—only in the light of meaning brought to it in choices for life, not death. And in Jesus' case, those choices were for the sake of covenant life, his life in devotion to others and to God, tested in the most extreme moments of covenantal crisis.

Perhaps I can illustrate this with a story from years ago. I had been meeting with a woman who was experiencing intense depression over the breakup of her marriage. At one very significant point she quoted Paul's words about suffering, but not in hope; instead, with the deepest frustration, she said something like this: "I just don't have enough faith. All things are supposed to work for good for those that love the Lord. All I can think is how wrong this is. I guess I just don't have enough faith." I remember saying something like, "Paul said those words after, not before. Those are words of confession, description. They are not a prescription. When it's Good Friday, you don't see Easter morning."

That moment, giving her room to suffer on her own terms, without her pain having to be part of some intended expression of God's will, allowed her to be whole. To be sure, the wholeness was a wounded wholeness, but the wholeness of that covenantal wounding had to be risked and claimed if she was ever to know the healing that came afterwards. The good news of that healing did come later, in its own time. Neither she nor I had to force the meaning. Instead, we had to face the suffering without it having to have meaning, trusting only the moments of meaning that frame the emptiness of despair to be sufficient.

In other words, we had to trust the power of covenant relation to be strong enough to face its own crisis in her failing marriage. We had to trust the unfolding gestalt of hospitality and grace in which we participate when one makes room for another to be fully who he or she is. If Jesus was right before, that in our gestalts of generosity the rule and realm of heaven is[22] in our midst—or alternatively, we are in its midst—then that gestalt will sustain us in the present.

Our pastoral task will include portraying the complex frame of the cross and its aftermath well enough so that those with whom we work can recognize its multilayered significance while discovering in the shattering of life and their loss of trust in the world, that life may yet be embraced in spite of the rejection and abandonment they have experienced in their Sabbath of despair. While our pastoral task is more than hermeneutical or midrashic, it will never be less than that. Still, it will require courage to accompany others into this terrain and to refrain from shielding them from the pain of crucifixion's aftermath. Pastoral action will join, without cheap hope or predetermined answers, in covenantal solidarity with others in their suffering, risking the despair that one must face in such an act.

Healing, like salvation, flows from an embrace of covenant life that includes us in its fundamental and relational promise of life—forgiving, fulfilling, empowering, restoring, and challenging us to participate in the ongoing work of creation. As a Christian, I view this as good news. It is an embrace that Jesus embodied and extended to those who followed him—and that, in his name, has been extended to us. The good news of post-Shoah faith remains the good news of inclusion in God's covenantal embrace of life in and through God's representative one, Jesus. Yet it cannot be an embrace that tries to undo the pain of radical destruction and humiliation. Instead, it must confront that pain again and again in profound sadness and grief, needing the response of partners in hospitality to make it real.

Facing the Cross—An Unfinished Story

We live in a Good Friday/Holy Saturday world. We dwell there on the other side of the first Easter, yet facing an as yet unredeemed future. Its time of fulfillment is present only as promise. Peter Hodgson has captured this quality succinctly:

> Jesus' project of announcing the inbreaking kingdom of God failed; the transfigured world of the parables was interrupted and displaced by scenes of betrayal, false charges, political dealings, weakness and vacillation, an angry mob, and an ugly finale on Golgotha. . . .
>
> The shape of the cross is a question mark or a cancellation sign, a large X, which must be written across the shape of the basileia, reminding us that its vision of inclusive wholeness, of a liberated communion of free persons, forever remains marginal in this world, unable to dislodge the economy of domination and violence but only to disturb it, to disclose it for what it is, to reduce its scope and hegemony, perhaps to modify it somewhat, and above all to empower people to maintain a compassionate solidarity for and with one another in their struggle to make things better—as Jesus himself did, who died for the sake of all those who had joined or would join his cause, and indeed for those who would not. . . . The shape of the cross *crosses*, is superimposed on, that of the basileia vision, lending it the realism, clarity, and toughness necessary for its endurance in history as a transformative factor.[23]

In other words, we may return to the cross theologically and liturgically, but it returns to disturb our lives as well. When we return to the cross, it is an act we have chosen to undertake. We are returning to a time and place circumscribed by narrative, by interpretation. Consequently, we are not facing what others faced, or face still, when devastation and suffering have been thrust upon them. For us, choosing a cruciform life can mean at most that we accept the vulnerability we share with others and choose to risk it in relation with them, even if and when it means rejection, betrayal, or death. What we cannot do is choose that kind of victimization that came without choice. That requires a larger, farther-reaching framework.

Emil Fackenheim has captured the tragic dimensions of this by describing the victimization of the children during the Shoah as resulting not from their actions or choices but from the decisions made two generations before them on the part of their grandparents. According to Nazi definitions of Jewish identity, anyone with a Jewish grandparent was a Jew by blood; that person, regardless of circumstances or claims, was sentenced to suffer the fate of every Jew coming under Nazi jurisdiction. That is, the youngest generation of victims suffered because of choices made two generations before them. Therefore, they had no role in choosing to risk their lives by being Jews. That decision was made by others before they were even born. As a result, Fackenheim concluded that there was a moral imperative for surviving Jews to choose to remain Jews, lest the immeasurable price paid by the children be dishonored by subsequent generations, thereby granting Hitler a final victory in destroying Jewish life. Fackenheim called this the 614th commandment.[24]

For Christians seeking to honor the same children and the essential wrongness of their suffering, a similar demand is posed. We must find a way to acknowledge the jagged nature of innocent suffering at the same time we proclaim the power of a cruciform life. We begin by rethinking any form of return to Good Friday and its aftermath that finds or seeks intrinsic meaning in the suffering of innocent life. We look for ways to affirm the cruciform shape of Jesus' life that can likewise shape our protest against such suffering. Job's story may once again be instructive here.

As Job faced the aftermath of tragedy in his family, he was approached by well-meaning representatives of conventional covenantal piety. They offered frameworks of meaning in their interpretations that required Job to see meaning where meaning was absent. They offered interpretations of God's ways with creation that required Job to withdraw his protest against evil and abandon his sense of justice and the moral wholeness of life. More directly, they demanded that he betray his children by seeing them as deserving the tragedies that they suffered. And yet his views of divine providence and God's ways with the world were not unlike those of his erstwhile counselors.

Scripture preserves Job's story in a sometimes puzzling framework. The story is introduced by a scene in the council of heaven. God is visiting with one of the members of the divine court, one the text simply calls "the Adversary" (*haSatan* in Hebrew). God asks the Adversary where he has been. The answer: roaming the earth. Then he is asked if he has seen God's righteous and faithful servant Job. An argument, of sorts, evolves with the Adversary contending that Job is good only because his life has been blessed. Job and his family have known only good times. They have thrived. The Adversary therefore asks God if he may challenge Job to see if he will remain faithful. God declares that Satan may do so, imploring him not to harm his servant personally. And the story begins.

Typically, this scene is interpreted as God and the Adversary entering into a wager, with Job a pawn in this divine demonstration of wisdom. The Adversary asks for and receives permission to test Job. However, this view participates in exactly the same logic that is being challenged by the story. Not until that logic is shattered does another option break through. Perhaps the so-called wager was much earlier—at creation. From this perspective, Job's anguish would be an anguish that God knows and has known from the beginning and more deeply than Job could ever know. God, in making room for creation, has been making room for that which is other than God. Creation, as a radical act of hospitality, makes room for a plenum of otherness that stretches from the smallest to the largest expressions of creation—even those creatures that oppose the very spirit of hospitality that makes for their contention with others. In this reading the heavenly figure of the Adversary is a figurative expression of this radical wager for life. That is, the risk that willingly embraces not just death but the power of death waged against life, is made at creation. For Job, his recognition of this theological fact came as a radical shift in perspective in the face of a whirlwind of suffering. For those who live self-consciously in the face of a cross, our neatly framed theological worlds are shattered by the presence of burning children. But like Job, we may find that the choice that redefines our perspective may drive us back to the divine wager for life we call creation. To be sure, such choices may be cruciform for us, but they need not reduce the suffering around us to fit in our theological systems. To the contrary, they may lead us to open our systems to the wager for life that frames creation itself.

In other words, for many in our world, the cross and other meaningless forms of suffering continue to return in our world, even as we talk about returning to its domain with meaning and hope. We are not finished with the cross, nor the shadow it casts across our theological landscape and everyday world. Whether one is hoist on its crossbar or dwells in its aftermath, the specter of despair continues to haunt unsuspecting victims, taking too many hostages too many times. As Christians sensitized to the Good Friday/Holy Saturday world of our post-Shoah time, we must be prepared to embrace more than the theological crosses that mark our confessional horizons. We must also acknowledge and accept a cross that takes new victims, more victims, holding them for ransom to every manner of human evil.

Liturgical Offerings

The symbolic landscape of Good Friday is rich; but making our way liturgically and homiletically through the last hours of Jesus' life can be treacherous. A number of traditions—from the Stations of the Cross to meditations on the Seven Last Words—are associated with the day and provide uneven terrain that must be negotiated with care, sometimes extreme caution. At stake is the core witness of the Christian gospel; but misdirected passion toward innocent others, particularly Jewish others, can have violent and far-reaching consequences.

In the case of the historic liturgy referred to as *The Reproaches*, for example, the theme of human complicity on the part of God's people is recited by way of selected references from the Hebrew Scriptures. The gathered faithful are thereby encouraged to acknowledge, according to the Scriptures, how they have opposed God's will as they stand at the foot of the cross of Jesus. However, the cumulative impact of the rite builds a strong and negative witness against the Jewish people. All too clearly they are depicted as a people opposing God, instead of the more authentic portrait developed in their Scriptures as a limping people with whom God remains faithful in spite of their stumbling. The Roman Catholic Church has recognized this danger and cautioned against the continued use of this rite. The Inter-Lutheran Commission on Worship has recommended reform,[25] adding biblical expressions of Christian failure and opposition to God's will. However, even this revision remains problematic. On the one hand, it will too easily fail to counteract the cumulative impact of negative stereotypes, especially when they are expressed in the symbolic garb of liturgical acts. On the other hand, even when the liturgy adds biblically based reproaches against the Christian church, the unintended consequences of retaining biblical accusations against the Jewish people will continue to foster the attitudes the liturgy seeks to avoid.[26] For this reason, *The Reproaches* and other traditional liturgies that portray the passion by way of using Jews as negatively significant others should be avoided. The danger of using them, even when amended, is too great. Indeed, there are other traditions available to us that can be used in authentic and healthy ways.

Some congregations will gather for a service in which the passion account from John is read in its entirety. As on Palm/Passion Sunday, the focus is on the immediacy of the narrative, not the interpretive power of the sermon, though a brief homily may be given. If this option is developed, a midrashic reading of the John account could be developed by the local priest or pastor in charge, using the model offered earlier with regard to Matthew's text. Some of the commentary could be replicated, but clearly there would be a need to help the congregation recognize the distinctive voice and emphases of John's account and the issues that lie embedded in the text.

Some congregations may turn to the tradition of Tenebrae, providing a service of readings linked with the progressive diminishment of light in the sanctuary as the death of Jesus approaches in the readings. Obviously, an evening setting is anticipated in a service like Tennebrae, with its use of candlelight and music to punctuate the story of the passion. When such a ritual is planned, it can be developed using guidelines that guard against the incorporation of structural supersessionism and unchallenged stereotypes of key figures in the story. Midrashic readings can be developed and used as well, adding the drama of extinguishing candles as the story is told in progressive stages of diminishing light. Likewise music can be sung that expresses the challenges and sacrifices of the day without taking unintended hostages with careless expressions about others.

A few congregations might even dare to face the issues posed by the Shoah itself in a service of penitential accountability for Christian sin vis-à-vis our Jewish siblings, linking the suffering of Good Friday with the suffering of other generations. But care must be given to guard against imposing Christian meaning where it is not present. One commendable example that local congregations can ponder is offered on the World Wide Web by the Evangelical Sisterhood of Mary[27] at http://www.kanaan.org/israel5.htm. An explicitly post-Holocaust Christian sisterhood, the group has published a penitential rite of confession for 2000 years of Christian complicity in anti-Jewish and antisemitic attitudes and behaviors. It may be downloaded from their Web site. The service rehearses the shameful legacy of Christian complicity and provides liturgical expression for the kinds of issues being discussed in this book.

Some may find themselves committed to understated and somber settings for the day. Altars may be stripped, even shrouded in traditional ways as congregations gather to hear special music and ponder brief devotional meditations. As we conclude our reflections, but certainly not our encounter with the cross and its aftermath, we present a Good Friday option for reflection and critique. As in previous offerings, the so-called Seven Last Words of Jesus are presented as opportunities for midrashic devotional encounter. Their testimony is differentiated and shared as distinct perspectives on the event of the crucifixion. They are not meant to build a single, coherent image. Critical interaction is likewise encouraged, but the aim is for the worshipper to enter into the multifaceted biblical story and via its richly textured witnesses to open his or her world to include the dramatic events of this difficult day.

As in previous chapters, the offering presented here is meant to evoke further reflection on how we commemorate the story of Jesus' death. Hence, the meditations are open-ended and unfinished, awaiting responses by those who read or hear them being read. They could be dramatically presented by readers in a service. In fact, that would probably be the most effective way to render them. The service could be brief, focusing on just these readings. Or it could be longer, utilizing appropriate music and penitential readings like Psalm 51. Just as easily these meditations can be used for silent encounter, as written guides for worshippers in the pew. In my own congregation, they have been used during a midday organ recital that we hosted for Good Friday. Printed programs containing the readings were made available for silent reflection and prayer. Musical selections appropriate for the day were played while members of the congregation came and went during an open time for silent prayer and contemplation.

Good Friday

Midrashic Meditations on the Seven Last Words[*]

Taking our place in the drama of Good Friday, we look over the shoulders of the biblical witnesses. Indeed, most of us enter the events of this day by way of more than one witness. In the meditations that follow, we stand in the cumulative presence of the canonical witnesses, aware that they offer distinct perspectives; like most witnesses, their testimonies vary as they report different experiences that grow out of their specific vantage points. And as we enter into their narrated experience, we must eventually come to terms with their distance from the events they describe, since their testimony includes their report of Jesus being abandoned by those who followed him. At best, the Gospel witnesses are themselves looking in on these events by way of others who were there. While their place in the story they relate may give us some interpretive difficulty, their willingness to locate themselves as they do invites us to do the same.

In this spirit let us take our place in the events of the day, according to the Scriptures; but also let us do so aware of our role in choosing to enter these events as we take responsibility for our place in this difficult drama and its place in our lives.

Mark and Matthew, relating their story "according to the Scriptures," use the language of Amos 8 and Psalm 22 to tell this story. They report, one in Aramaic and one in Hebrew, Jesus crying out, "My God, my God, why have you forsaken me?" They may be framing a pleading cry to God in the language of the psalm, stylizing the cry to underscore its agony. Or they may be reporting Jesus' utterance as they heard it reported to them. Either way, the irony of identifying the opening words of this psalm with this figure who was steadfast to the end, is intensified by their witness.

---

[*] Three voices are used: the voice of the text in regular type, a voice of commentary in bold, a midrashic voice of meditation in italics.

When it was noon, darkness came over the whole land until three in the afternoon. At three o'clock Jesus cried out with a loud voice, "Eloi, Eloi, lema sabachthani?" which means, "My God, my God, why have you forsaken me?" (Mark 15:33–34)

From noon on, darkness came over the whole land until three in the afternoon. And about three o'clock Jesus cried with a loud voice, "Eli, Eli, lama sabachthani?" that is, "My God, my God, why have you forsaken me?" (Matt. 27:45–46)

If we listen to the white fire between their words, perhaps we might hear these words*:*

> *When we looked deeply at him, we saw the very face of God. What more can we say? So when he cried out, "My God, my God, . . ."we can only wonder if was he reciting Psalm 22. We were struck dumb by those words. Actually, we must confess, we weren't even there; some of the bystanders heard it and talked about it. The women told us about it too. That made it worse. So much worse. We had forsaken him. Then when we heard that he cried out that God had forsaken him, all we could think about was that we had forsaken God too. If he brought God near to us, and he did, then we had forsaken God as well as Jesus, and because we had forsaken Jesus, he felt abandoned by God. All along, he pointed us to relationships. Relationships. He was steadfast in that regard; we were not. My God, my God. . . . How have we forsaken you?*

❧❧❧❧❧❧❧

Luke, writing about one who included the outcasts and the unclean, shows us a figure who even in the most extreme conditions remained faithful to the end, practicing hospitality even to a criminal hanging beside him. Crucified and hanging in disgrace, they were all unclean in the eyes of *halakah*, yet looking beyond to the rule and reign of God, in which Jesus dwelled and which he brought near, we glimpse something else. Jesus had reminded us again and again that those who showed generosity to others recast the notions of clean and unclean, holy and profane. And now, in reply to the wounded generosity of a thief—a fellow victim—Jesus showed that even in the disgrace and humiliation of capital punishment, the orchard of God could be promised and brought near. And so he gave himself, completely, into the hands of God even as he gave himself into the hands of others . . .

When they came to the place that is called The Skull, they crucified Jesus there with the criminals, one on his right and one on his left. Then Jesus said, "Father, forgive them; for they do not know what they are doing." (Luke 23:33–34a)

Again, listening to the white fire between Luke's words, we might discern these:

Early on, we, his disciples, fought with each other over who would sit at his right and at his left. He wasn't happy with this. Indeed, he chastised us about our pettiness and our inability to see beyond ourselves, even when we were pondering the coming rule and reign of God in our lives and in the lives of our people. He would have none of that. Now we have acted in such fashion that when he needed us, we were neither on his right nor on his left. We were absent. Look who is on his right and left now. Look. Dare I say, behold? We should be with him. But we are not. And look again; look at him hanging there. He is flanked by criminals, outcasts; and even there he accepts his place among them. We just never understood. Perhaps we still don't.

Luke continues:

One of the criminals who were hanged there kept deriding him and said, "Are you not the Messiah? Save yourself and us! But the other rebuked him, saying, "Do you not fear God, since you are under the same sentence of condemnation? And we indeed have been condemned justly, for we are getting what we deserve for our deeds, but this man has done nothing wrong." Then he said, "Jesus, remember me when you come into your kingdom." He replied, "Truly, I tell you, today you will be with me in Paradise." (Luke 23:39–43)

Once more the white fire invites us to listen:

Listen to them. Even on a cross, the self-serving preoccupations continue. That could be us. Perhaps it should be us. But wait. What's the other one saying to him? Even in the midst of such pain, how can a thief like him see beyond himself? Yet he has—even there. Once again I have judged too quickly. Wait again. What did Jesus say to him? Paradise? How can he speak of paradise from a cross? How?

Luke is not yet finished:

Then Jesus, crying with a loud voice, said, "Father, into your hands I commend my spirit." (Luke 23:46a)

And the white fire glows:

There is no triumph here; but neither is this resignation. Still, he summoned all the strength he had left and cried out, calling God the way he taught us: Abba. Then he gave his life up to God. He let go. He let go. But God wasn't there. God wasn't doing anything. We weren't doing anything. In fact, we were as far away as we could be; the women told us what he did, what he said. How could he surrender to God when God did nothing to stop what happened? Worse still, how could we even ask such a question when we did nothing? How? I am lost.

John, writing about the word made flesh, presents us with images of relationships and of a thirst for their transformation. He describes a final gesture that presents us with the ironic portrait in its fullness. Behold the one in whom God was pleased to dwell. When we behold him, we behold the One whom he represents.

When Jesus saw his mother and the disciple whom he loved standing beside her, he said to his mother, "Woman, (behold) here is your son." Then he said to the disciple, "(Behold) Here is your mother." And from that hour the disciple took her into his own home. (John 19:26–27)

There is white fire here, too. Listen:

As we behold him, he beholds us and challenges us to turn to his mother and see her as our own and ourselves as her children. Perhaps he is telling us to reconfigure our relationships with each other, accepting each other as members of one household. One last gesture to make sure she is not abandoned, but cared for by those whom he saw as his extended family. Surely she will be the object of the same or similar derision and ridicule that was focused on him. He, a victim of crucifixion, the oppressor's form of political execution, has suffered because he is a Jew committed to God's rule and realm happening among us. So we must be prepared to take on the risk of reaching out to her as he asks.

John continues:

After this, when Jesus knew that all was now finished, he said (in order to fulfill the scripture), "I am thirsty." A jar full of sour wine was standing there. So they put a sponge full of the wine on a branch of hyssop and held it to his mouth. (John 19:28–29)

The white fire in John is palpable. We can almost feel it on our lips.

He says he is thirsty, he who came to quench our thirst. How is that so? The guards offer a panacea; but he doesn't take it. They don't understand his thirst. Perhaps we haven't either. He thirsts now as he did throughout his ministry. He thirsts for different kinds of relations. He thirsts for righteousness. He thirsts for justice. He thirsts for liberation, for change, for life. And instead, we responded—we—the authorities and followers alike, the Romans, the leaders of the temple, the pilgrims around us, those who loved him—we (How can I be more blunt?), we did not quench his thirst. He is thirsty for the very same thing he offered us, water from the fountain of the water of life. We did not return what he offered us. He is thirsty for what we did not give him. And now, it is too late. He thirsts. Perhaps I'm beginning to understand. I am thirsty now. I thirst.

Once more John speaks to us:

When Jesus had received the wine, he said, "It is finished." Then he bowed his head and gave up his spirit. (John 19:30)

And the white fire glows stronger, fanned by an unexpected rush of air. If we listen closely we can hear it simmer:

"It's finished?" It's over. He said, "It's finished." That's what they said he said. All I know is that it's over. The dream, the hopes, the promise . . . it's all finished. Everything. We weren't strong enough to hang in there with him. It's all over. He's finished. We're finished; what will we do now? What? Heaven help us. Heaven help us.

NOTES:

1. Of course, one not originally present can choose to take his or her place in the story along this path, as I am doing.

2. Interestingly, Matthew names one of the Marys as the mother of James and Joseph. But earlier, Matthew cites the people in Jesus' hometown asking about the figure speaking to them, pointing out that he is the son of Mary and the brother of James and Joseph as well as Simon and Judas. John, in his Gospel, identifies Jesus' mother as present in this scene. Is this a coded or veiled way of Matthew referring to Jesus' mother being present but identifying her by two of Jesus' brothers? One would have to know the story or the family to catch the connection. Is this a way of veiling the story in the face of Roman oppression? By itself this is an invitation for further midrashic thinking. See Matt. 13:54–56.

3. John Dominic Crossan, *Who Killed Jesus? Exposing the Roots of Anti-Semitism in the Gospel Story of the Death of Jesus* (San Francisco: Harper, 1991), 4.

4. Elie Wiesel, *Night*, trans. Stella Rodway (New York: Avon Books, 1960), 76.

5. Wiesel's text is powerful. He writes:

> In a text in which [Kazin] recalled "what he owed" to Primo Levi and me, he wrote that he would not be surprised to find that the episode in *Night* describing three inmates who were hanged together had been invented. How dare he? There were thousands of witnesses, some of them still alive, among them Yaakov Hendeli, who now lives in Jerusalem, and Freddy Diamond of Los Angeles, whose brother Leo Yehuda was the youngest of the three victims. (The two others were Nathan Weisman and Yanek Grossfeld.) Of all the vile things this bitter man who has aged so badly has written in his life, this is the most intolerable.

See Elie Wiesel, *All Rivers Run to the Sea* (New York: Alfred A. Knopf, 1994), 336.

6. Jürgen Moltmann, *The Crucified God: The Cross of Christ as the Foundation and Criticism of Christian Theology* (New York: Harper & Row, 1974), 273–74.

7. *Night*, 62.

8. Elie Wiesel, *The Night Trilogy* (New York: Hill and Wang, 1972, 1985), 3.

9. Midrash clearly includes the interpretive strategy of resisting a text, reading against its grain. However, when this strategy is used, the reader typically holds himself or herself accountable to the plain meaning of the text being resisted and utilizes some gap or anomaly in it, or its context, to express that resistance. Furthermore, in generating alternative interpretations, other readers and their views are acknowledged in the process. The current reader is, therefore, invited into the interpretive dilemma and encouraged to engage the friction between the *peshat* and the alternative way the text is being read. When resisted in this manner, the text is not violated, even though it may be turned against itself in creative ways.

10. Emmanuel Levinas, *Entre Nous: On Thinking of the Other*, trans. Michael B. Smith and Barbara Harshav (New York: Columbia University Press, 1998), 98.

11. Jean Amery, *At the Mind's Limits: Contemplations by a Survivor on Auschwitz and Its Realities*, trans. Sidney Rosenfeld and Stella P. Rosenfeld (Bloomington and Indianapolis: Indiana University Press, 1980), 28, 40.

12. Amery, 33.

13. Terrence Des Pres, *The Survivor: An Anatomy of Life in the Death Camps* (Oxford: Oxford University Press, 1976), 60.

14. Ibid.

15. Matthew identifies the two Marys, Magdalene and Mary the mother of James and Joseph, but does not identify the second Mary as Jesus' mother.

16. Even though Matthew identifies Joseph of Arimathea as a disciple, we cannot conclude that he was not a stranger to Jesus. Indeed, it is entirely possible that Joseph's act of hospitality in this final moment is what drew Joseph into the circle of those who followed Jesus. Matthew, identifying Joseph as a disciple, may be pointing to a disciple known by those he was addressing, but at the time of Jesus he may not yet have made himself known as a follower of Jesus. The point: Joseph of Arimathea is an unknown figure, introduced in the story in its final chapter, embodying the kind of hospitality for which Jesus lived and gave his life.

17. See Alan E. Lewis, *Between Cross and Resurrection: A Theology of Holy Saturday* (Grand Rapids: Wm. B. Eerdmans, 2001) for a thoughtful discussion of the significance of this interim Sabbath.

18. Johann Baptist Metz, "Between Remembering and Forgetting: The Shoah in the Era of Cultural Amnesia," in *Good and Evil after Auschwitz: Ethical Implications for Today*, ed. Jack Bemporad, John T. Pawlikowski, and Joseph Sievers (Hoboken, NJ: KTAV Publishing House, 2000), 21.

19. Lewis, 33.

20. Douglas John Hall, *Confessing the Faith: Christian Theology in a North American Context* (Minneapolis: Fortress Press, 1996), 466.

21. "Your blood be on your head; your own mouth has testified against you, saying, 'I have killed the LORD's anointed' " (2 Sam. 1:16). It appears that Matthew, with his midrashic use of this passage, has accused the Jews of Judea of being Amalek, setting up the demonizing logic that follows from this passage in subsequent generations.

22. See chap. 2, n. 7. The use of the singular verb form is intentional.

23. Peter C. Hodgson, *Christian Faith: A Brief Introduction* (Louisville, KY: Westminster John Knox Press, 2001), 118.

24. See Emil L. Fackenheim, *God's Presence in History: Jewish Affirmations and Philo-sophical Reflections* (New York: Harper Torchbooks, 1970), 83–98, esp. 84–89.

25. Hoyt L. Hickman, Don E. Saliers, Laurence Hull Stookey, James F. White, *The New Handbook of the Christian Year* (Nashville: Abingdon Press, 1986, 1992), 190.

26. The following text (originally published in *From Ashes to Fire Supplemental Worship Resources 8*) from the *The New Handbook of the Christian Year* illustrates both the attempt to correct for an antisemitic reading and the difficulty of overcoming it in the context of this liturgy. We must ask, Can the cumulative impact of the imagery be undone even by the explicit acknowledgment of anti-Jewish attitudes and behavior in *Reproaches* number 9?

1. Is it nothing to you, all you who pass by?
    Look and see if there is any sorrow like my sorrow
    which was brought upon me,
    which the Lord inflicted on the day of his fierce anger.
    Holy God,
    Holy and Mighty.
    Holy and Immortal One,
    Have mercy upon us.

2. O my people, O my church,
    what have I done to you,
    or in what have I offended you?
    Testify against me.
    I led you forth from the land of Egypt
    and delivered you by the waters of baptism,
    but you have prepared a cross for your Savior.
    Holy God,
    Holy and Mighty.
    Holy and Immortal One,
    Have mercy upon us.

3. I led you through the desert forty years,
    and fed you with manna:
    I brought you through tribulation and penitence,
    and gave you my body, the bread of heaven,
    but you have prepared a cross for your Savior.
    Holy God,
    Holy and Mighty.
    Holy and Immortal One,
    Have mercy upon us.

4. What more could I have done for you
    that I have not done?
    I planted you, my chosen and fairest vineyard,
    I made you the branches of my vine;
    but when I was thirsty, you gave me vinegar to drink
    and pierced with a spear the side of your Savior.
    Holy God,
    Holy and Mighty.

Holy and Immortal One,
Have mercy upon us.

5. I went before you in a pillar of cloud,
and you have led me to the judgment hall of Pilate
I scourged your enemies and brought you to a land of freedom,
but you have scourged, mocked, and beaten me.
I gave you the water of salvation from the rock,
but you have given me gall and left me to thirst.
Holy God,
Holy and Mighty.
Holy and Immortal One,
Have mercy upon us.

6. I gave you a royal scepter,
and bestowed the keys to the kingdom,
but you have given me a crown of thorns.
I raised you on high with great power,
but you have hanged me on the cross.
Holy God,
Holy and Mighty.
Holy and Immortal One,
Have mercy upon us.

7. My peace I gave, which the world cannot give,
and washed your feet as a sign of my love,
but you draw the sword to strike in my name,
and seek high places in my kingdom.
I offered you my body and blood,
but you scatter and deny and abandon me.
Holy God,
Holy and Mighty.
Holy and Immortal One,
Have mercy upon us.

8. I sent the Spirit of truth to guide you,
and you close your hearts to the Counselor.
I prayed that all may be one in the Father and me,
but you continue to quarrel and divide.
I called you to go and bring forth fruit,
but you cast lots for my clothing.
Holy God,
Holy and Mighty.
Holy and Immortal One,
Have mercy upon us.

9. I grafted you into the tree of my chosen Israel,
and you turned on them with persecution and mass murder.
I made you joint heirs with them of my covenants,
but you made them scapegoats for your own guilt.

Holy God,
Holy and Mighty.
Holy and Immortal One,
Have mercy upon us.

10. I came to you as the least of your brothers and sisters;
    I was hungry and you gave me no drink,
    I was a stranger and you did not welcome me,
    naked and you did not clothe me,
    sick and in prison and you did not visit me.
    Holy God,
    Holy and Mighty.
    Holy and Immortal One,
    Have mercy upon us.

The New Handbook of the Christian Year, 187–89.

27. The Evangelical Sisterhood of Mary is an international, interdenominational Protestant organization founded in 1947 within the framework of the German Evangelical Church. For more information on the organization, see http://www.kanaan.org/main_frames.htm.

Chapter 6

Returning to an Empty Tomb

The Holy Ground of Easter in the Valley of Dark Shadows

Back to the Garden

Back to the garden. As before, our way and destination merge as we enter the pluriform landscape of the biblical world. The tomb, borrowed and hewn from rock, was near the site of execution (not to mention its proximity to the storied location of the near-sacrifice of Isaac[1]). Its textual domain resides for us in the narrated world of Matthew, awaiting our liturgical, methodological, and confessional return to its witness. But this time our return is complicated by the post-Shoah legacy we bring with us. In the past, we have walked with expectant joy, assured that we approach an empty tomb—emptied of death's devastation and power. This time we return aware of ways that the empty tomb's triumphant spirit has been used in the denial of life and in the service of death. We face the irony that we have served the diminishment of life even when proclaiming the triumph of life over death. Therefore we limp.

We return emboldened by the promise of past Easters, to be sure. But this time we return in the shadows of a catastrophic event that, as Franklin Littell reminds us, shatters our practiced confidence and occasions a crisis of credibility and hope.[2] Can the story of Easter, and its witness to life in the face of death, rise to the challenge put to it by our post-Shoah times? Like Ezekiel's dream, we hover over the scarred landscape of our post-Shoah world and find ourselves being asked, perhaps in our own voices, certainly in the voices of those who have perished at the hands of religious violence, can this story, this orchard of meaning and hope (read, "these bones") live? Let us take our place in the story, then, to see how this question might be posed to us and how we might be bold to respond.

In the receding shadows of the coming dawn, Mary Magdalene and the other Mary (the mother of James and Joseph, and by inference the mother of

Jesus) return to the garden where they, along with their friends and perhaps other disciples, have left the body of Jesus sealed in a tomb. Their return has to have been undertaken with the heaviest of hearts. As we look over their shoulders, we are struck that, even with the knowledge we have of previous returns to this scene, their journey from a Sabbath of loss and despair is undertaken with shattered hearts and broken spirits. As we accompany them along this path, they limp, as it were, burdened by the weight of all they carry with them in their long journey to this garden tomb. They limp because of what they have experienced. We limp because of what we have seen, by way of Matthew, through their eyes and what we have learned about ourselves by facing our own history. That confessional knowledge, of course, comes from taking our place in the story and discovering how we deny, betray, abandon, and fail the one we follow. That knowledge is compounded, however, when we make our return by way of the River Jabbok.

We limp because we also know how we have used our knowledge of this story. We know that the journey of these women leads to an empty tomb and an eventual affirmation that death has been vanquished. In that knowledge, we too easily dismiss their anguish to move to the triumph we see on the other side of this grave. When that happens, we have raced before them, eager to get to the empty tomb and then to run ahead announcing the good news of God's triumph, in spite of what happened that fateful day. Limping, we find we can follow them to the tomb or accompany them only when we recognize that they are limping too.

As we noted early on, how we approach something has everything to do with what we see and hear as we make our way. Our approach sets the tone and orients our senses. When we approach limping, we are reminded in the most tangible ways of our limitations and imperfections. When our limping combines with the narrativized limping of others (i.e., returning disciples), then our understandings and sensitivities are compounded all the more.

Approaching the Tomb

As we make our way to the empty tomb, we join the two Marys as they make their way in the early morning shadows that follow their long Sabbath of grief and loss. As we join them, we must remember that on their return they are not headed to an empty tomb symbolic of a resurrected Jesus but to a sealed tomb in which they have left the body of Jesus. Matthew's report takes us quickly through the events of that morning. However, our limping slows us down. Indeed, our limping provides us an opportunity to ponder the two Marys returning to the tomb that morning in such a way that we might recover a more insightful view of what happened that day.

As we take our place beside them in the dawning light of that day, we begin by pondering their reasons for returning to a tomb the two women expect to contain their beloved Jesus. While Matthew's focus remains elsewhere, theirs would be on a life they are grieving and, most probably, their final obligations to this one whom they loved. Indeed, if the other Mary was Jesus' mother, it is her final act of taking care of her son, whom she has been asked to surrender to his prophetic/messianic cause and now death. Though Matthew does not develop it, Mark's description, which Matthew appears to know, indicates that the women have secured ointments and perfumes to complete the religious burial functions, cleaning and anointing the body according to *halakah*.

As we join them in this regard, we join two Jewish women approaching a Jewish grave site. While this may seem like an exaggerated concentration on the obvious, it helps us see what might otherwise remain hidden in plain sight. What the two women find is not what they expect. Matthew reports an earthquake caused by an angel who rolls away the stone that has sealed the tomb. The angel then sits on the stone, presumably to wait for the women and then to interpret what has happened to them. The imagery is rich and stylized in the same fashion as Matthew's report of the crucifixion, and we might wish to ask if this is the same kind of earthshaking event that Matthew recounts happening then. After all, the guards, paralyzed with fear, appear to hear nothing. Later they will report to their superiors what happened, but not in a way that indicates that they have witnessed what the women experience. In comparison, Mark's description helps us reconstruct a situation in which they find a tomb already opened yet still in need of interpretation. In other words, the evidence of an empty tomb in itself is insufficient, even when stylized in a supernatural framework. In Mark a robed figure inside the tomb interprets the significance of an absent Jesus. In Matthew a dazzling figure in white, sitting on the stone, provides the needed interpretation.

However, behind both stories is a disturbed tomb. The stone has been rolled away and the body is not present. When we approach this scene from our post-Shoah vantage point in the company of two Jewish women, we cannot see just a single, empty tomb. Thousands of graveyards were plundered and desecrated by the Nazis during their assault on Jewish memory during the Shoah. Any return to a disturbed Jewish tomb calls to mind other desecration and causes us to ask of the two Marys if they encountered a sense of defilement in their return, a defilement like that experienced by thousands of Jews in later times. In other words, before the empty tomb would ever be holy ground, it would be seen as desecrated ground.

To understand their dislocation before such a scene, we may recall what the two women bring with them as they approach the grave site. To be sure, they bring their tears, their grief to the tomb. They also bring their despair. And the other Mary, if she is indeed Jesus' mother, also brings her hopes for Jesus as her son, not just as the Messiah of Israel. We may presume that they bring their hopes for what Jesus represented for Israel. But the other Mary, if she is who Matthew implies she is, also brings deeply personal dreams for her son, dreams from the very first moment she felt him move in her womb.

The women also bring their fears. Guards have been placed at the door of the tomb, ostensibly to prevent Jesus' followers (or opponents) from taking his body. But surely their presence also suggests the political tensions that have been generated by Jesus' teaching, his arrest, and now his crucifixion—all in the face of Passover and what it represents. What more might the Roman authorities do to Jesus' closest companions, his mother, his friends, his followers? The two women simply cannot know.[3]

They also bring their anger; we can be relatively sure of that. And it would be directed in more than one way: toward those religious authorities who colluded with Pilate; toward Pilate; toward the disciples who disappeared; toward the false witnesses; toward Judas; toward Peter, if his denial has become known; even toward Jesus, for not defending himself, for placing himself in a predicament he could have avoided. And we cannot overlook the possibility of anger directed toward God for abandoning one whose passion and devotion for God were so absolute, so extensive, so unrestricted and transparent. And of course, there is anger toward death itself. The point: the anger is intense as is their grief and their despair.

The two Marys and their companions bring more than we can possibly imagine to that tomb, expecting it to be sealed, worrying about how they will gain entrance to do the only thing left for them to do for their beloved Jesus. As we join them in facing a disturbed tomb, we must acknowledge the full measure of what would be disturbed, and deeply disturbing, about what they encounter in that place on that morning. When we allow them to approach a disturbed tomb, not yet aware of what it might mean, we are forced to recall other disturbed tombs with a fuller awareness of the despair such a scene can evoke. Perhaps it signals one more travesty. Accompanied by contemporary Jews from a post-Auschwitz generation, we are alerted that the image of an unsealed, opened tomb is also a disturbed tomb—a sign of one more degradation. From the shadows of Auschwitz, a disturbed tomb can mean nothing less than this, for we know that even the dead can be attacked and defiled.

Approaching a disturbed tomb now includes the memory of Nazi attempts to disfigure cemeteries and to remove even the trace of Jewish life. The sense of victimization is compounded—for the two Marys as well as for us.

Facing An Empty Tomb

Only as they draw closer do they discover that the disturbed tomb is empty. The body is absent. The burial cloths remain, neatly set aside. Unlike Mark, who describes the women discovering the disturbed tomb, Matthew reports that the women approach the tomb just as the disturbance, an earthquake, is taking place. It is accompanied by a descending figure, a messenger of God, arrayed like lightning. Not surprisingly, the language Matthew uses to describe this scene echoes the language he uses to describe the crucifixion. It is highly stylized and apocalyptic. Imbedded in it is the implication that what is happening requires interpretation. The women are told that Jesus is no longer present in the tomb. They are directed elsewhere, to Galilee, where they will meet him, for the messenger explains further that Jesus has been raised from the dead. They are invited to see the place where he was placed, then they are sent away to tell his disciples.

In the biblical account the women run to find the disciples. However, we are still limping as we follow them. As a result we have longer to take in the landscape—narrative and cultural—of the story. Matthew's version, like Mark's, depends upon the interpretive work of a messenger, which he identifies in the vivid imagery of a dazzling presence—"like lightning"—and whose clothing was "white as snow" (Matt. 28:3). Mark, in comparison, is less exuberant with his account, describing a man dressed in a white robe caring for the place in the tomb where Jesus had been placed in repose. His description resembles that of a liturgically garbed figure whose role is to announce and interpret the significance of the emptied tomb. In either witness, the meaning of the empty tomb is not self-evident. It must be interpreted.

The textual material is rich with midrashic possibilities. The attending figure is an apocalyptic figure in Matthew, a robed figure in Mark, two figures in Luke, and two robed figures in white in John. And of course, in John, the risen Jesus is mistaken for a gardener by Mary Magdalene. But in each episode one or two attending figures interpret the significance of the now-empty tomb. They assure the returning women—as well as the listeners and readers of this story—that the body was not stolen, that Jesus was indeed crucified, that what happened was more than a vision. Indeed, they testify that some kind of embodied event occurred—an encounterable gestalt of some kind that involved more than one person and in some sort of shared experience. But we are getting ahead of the story.

If we make our return biblically, that is, "according to the Scriptures," our approach will always be in the company of the two Marys and the other women. This means that we will always be joining those who loved Jesus and lost everything they associated with him. It should also mean that every approach is rightly made in the company of faithful Jews, returning to anoint Jesus' body and fulfill the sacred obligations of *halakah*—even in the most bereft of circumstances—daring to walk faithfully even then, even there. They approach with Jewish eyes as well as with broken Jewish hearts. In other words, even this most Christian of places, the so-called empty tomb, is a thoroughly Jewish place first. How can we approach it otherwise?

To say the tomb is empty is not to say that as a tomb it is a place devoid of meaning. That would be a caricature at best, a lie at worst, and a theological oversight either way. The tomb was and remains a Jewish tomb, made by a Jew, made for a Jew, and approached by Jews, even when it is later found to be empty with regard to the body of Jesus. The tomb was made available by Joseph of Arimathea, who constructed it out of rock for himself. He made it available for Jesus in an act of hospitality to Jesus and his family in their need. As such, it was a mitzvah; it was an act of charity (*tzedaqah*). Even this gesture was thoroughly Jewish. The tomb was a Jewish tomb. The two Marys return to that tomb after their agonizing Sabbath in an act that is at once an act of personal devotion and fidelity to *halakah*. And they find *that* tomb empty. Their beloved Jesus is not where they left him, but the significance of his absence is framed by that particular, emptied place.

Unexpected Encounters

Matthew's report is brief, but intensely stylized, and begins with the intention of the women to "see the tomb" (Matt. 28:1). His preoccupation appears to be with the miraculous action at the tomb—an earthquake accompanying the opening of the tomb by an angel of God who then sits on the stone that has been rolled away, causing the guards to freeze in fear as if they were the ones who belonged in a tomb. Matthew then recounts the messenger of God telling the two Marys that the one they seek, Jesus, who was indeed crucified, "is not here; for he has been raised" (Matt. 28:6). The women are then shown the place where he has lain and then are sent away with a message to give to his disciples: Jesus has been raised and "he is going ahead of you to Galilee; there you will see him" (Matt. 28:7). So the women leave quickly, hurrying away from the tomb in fear and excitement to find and tell Jesus' disciples their news. However, as they run from the tomb, Jesus meets them, calling out to them. Matthew reports that they "took hold of his feet, and worshiped him" (Matt. 28:9). Then Jesus sends them on, assuring them not to be afraid, reiterating the message they are to tell the disciples: to return to Galilee, where they will see Jesus.

Limping behind the hurrying women, we have time to ponder the significance of several unexpected actions: first, the directive to return to Galilee; second, their encounter with the Risen One on the way; next, their taking hold of the Risen One as they make their way; and then, their final meeting, which like the first is a sending forth. As if to underscore the importance of these moments in the story, Matthew tells of the two Marys meeting the risen Jesus immediately after leaving the tomb as they were instructed. This encounter confirms the first instructions given by the attending messenger outside the tomb. Once more they are told to go with the disciples to Galilee, to the place where Jesus has directed them.

Just as the tomb is a thoroughly Jewish place, so too is this movement. It recalls the dynamics of Abram's call recounted in Genesis 12. The first moment of whatever it is that happens at the tomb is for the two Marys a summons to go forth to a promised reality that they will later be shown. Then in a brief encounter with the one they originally were seeking to serve, they are sent forth once more to a designated mountain in Galilee, deepening the textual reverberations with Abram's call.

Similarly, we cannot read or hear the description of the two Marys' taking hold of the Risen Jesus without pondering the potential significance of this act. While we may understand the affection and intense grief caught up in this gesture, we should not overlook the resistance in it as well. They are holding on to the one they are called upon to release—in love, in mission, in service, in life, and then in death. But they must surely be holding on to one they thought they had lost, utterly, as well. And we who come to this material by way of the Jabbok cannot help seeing another act of resistance expressed in taking hold and holding on. Jacob held on to the *ish* with whom he wrestled and insisted that this contending other bless him. We, reading midrashically and post-Shoah, hold tightly to this text at the same time we hold on to the Shoah-scarred world we have come to know. We hold on and wrestle with our texts and with contending others whom we insist bless us. Are the two Marys showing us a way of holding on to the risen Jesus, whatever that gestalt of meaning might appear to be for us, insisting that it bless us by our learning to let go precisely as we take hold and grapple with it?

This last moment paradoxically links us to where we began and to where we are called to venture. Indeed, we are summoned to go forth to Galilee, where we are promised we shall meet the one who goes before us. We return to this summons to go forth like Abram and his descendants. Yet we do so by way of a fleeting encounter with one whom we hold only briefly as we are sent forward on our way. Seemingly the only added feature in the structure of these two stories appears to be Jesus attending to the fear with which the women approach and leave the tomb. Assured of the identity of the one they meet on the way, the women are told not to fear but to continue on with the others. Our midrashic aside, however, suggests otherwise. There is more here than meets the eye.

Before we rejoin the two Marys and the disciples in Galilee, however, let us return to the images of desecrated graves and defiled tombs. A single announcement of a reconfigured life, even on the other side of such degrada-tion, does not undo that wounding. We cannot appropriate the experiences of past Shoah victims and incorporate it so crassly into the story of an empty tomb. Instead, that memory must become a reminder of the pain and its sense of deep defilement that must be allowed to question and challenge any hur-ried or easy approach to any empty tomb, especially if it is a Jewish one. We must allow its disturbed and emptied quality to wound us deeply if we are ever going to understand its other dimensions. This feature, quite simply, must remain jagged and wounding.

As we return to Matthew's story, we join the remaining eleven disciples as they and the women together make their way to Galilee to a certain mountain to which they have been sent (Matt. 28:16). As in previous revelatory moments, Jesus meets his disciples on a mountain. There he confirms his pres-ence and sends them out, extending his ministry to all the other nations (*panta ethne*). That is, what Jesus proclaims and embodies for them, with them, they are to proclaim and embody for those beyond their borders, beyond their boundaries. And that final sending forth happens atop one final vantage point: a mountain in Galilee.

Coming to Terms with a Risen Christ

As we come to terms with what happened at the empty tomb and with the women afterwards, we are faced with an event that pushes us to the boundaries of our language—indeed to the limits of our knowing. Expecting to find the corpse of their beloved Jesus, the women encountered something, someone, that challenged them to rethink, to remember, who and what they had left at the tomb, as well as who and what they met there and immediately following. The presence of the interpreting figure at the tomb (the angel, or messenger of

God) tells us that what they experienced was not self-evident. The several stories reported in the Gospel narratives differ with regard to who this figure was and the number present. They concur, however, at the need for its presence. The recounting of interactions with an unrecognized, risen Jesus tells us that the identification of a risen Jesus was also not self-evident. Together, these observations lead us to recognize an embedded ambiguity in the story that preserves a sense of its original mystery. This ambiguity can also be upsetting, since the ambiguity is foundational. But it is nonetheless an opening preserved in the text and its testimony by which we may reenter the experience to wrestle with its meaning for ourselves. Indeed, this ambiguity allows us to join the two women in taking hold of the one they meet there and, like Jacob at the Jabbok, insist that this strange figure bless us in our wrestling with him. Our *ish*, the risen Jesus, is eventually named, but not in a way that removes the mystery of what it means to talk about a resurrected life. For the language of resurrection works figuratively to identify and point to something that is real and encounterable, yet somehow beyond the capacity of language to capture fully.

According to the text, the two women are immediately confronted by an unsettling fact. The one they seek is not in the tomb. He is not where they left him and expect to find him when they return. But the bare fact that Jesus is not in the tomb is interpreted immediately by an extraordinary figure who introduces an unexpected dimension. The apparent desecration of the tomb has given way to something else: an announcement that death has not consumed the one who has been crucified. Matthew—like Mark, whose language Matthew often adopts—is keen to point out that Jesus *was* crucified. The statement "He has been raised," uttered by the angel in Matthew and the robed figure in Mark, follows the equally important assertion "who was crucified." Whatever reality Matthew is describing occurs in the face of that fact. *Jesus was crucified.* He died a horrendous death. And yet he is acting in a new way, even though he was crucified. The language is the figurative language of resurrection, which points to a reality and presence beyond death. But it does so from the human side of dying. Consequently, it is necessarily figurative, but about something that is itself more than figurative. Still, it can be addressed and communicated only metaphorically. That is, while the testimony is figurative, the experience is more than that; it overflows the cup of language and with it, the cup of our ordinary ways of knowing.

The language of resurrection bears witness to the power of God that works even beyond and with the reality of death, testifying that it was at work in the life, now the death, of the one whom Matthew and Jesus' disciples regard as God's Son. As we grapple with its meaning for us, we are led to ask, toward what does this language point? An important clue resides in what the two

Marys expected to find and then anoint as they approach the tomb that morning. To be sure, they expect a corpse. But they are returning to tend to much more than a corpse. They seek to remember and honor one whose life and presence are much more than that. As the interpreting figure at the tomb reminds the two women, they seek "Jesus who was crucified." The one they left in the tomb and returned to anoint is more than his body. The one who was crucified is more than his crucifixion. The two women come to tend the one whom they loved and who loved them. To be sure, they come to tend the corpse, but not simply so. Thorwald Lorenzen has put it well. The body present in that tomb "was [Jesus] himself, his identity, his mission, his effect on the world. It included all of his life; a life shaped in relationship to God, to human beings, to nature, to history."[4] In other words, the full, covenantal gestalt of Jesus' life was buried in the tomb with him, and that full and embodied covenantal gestalt is what they sought to anoint—not just his body.

To say that Jesus goes before the women and then meets them on the way and afterwards meets the disciples on that designated mountain in Galilee is to say that they meet the covenantal gestalt that Jesus fully embodied on the way and on that mountain in Galilee. In the shadows of devastation and death, the two women expect to find a corpse, but they find themselves facing an embodied gestalt of generosity and grace, of hospitality and healing that they had known and shared with Jesus—the covenantal reality Jesus identified as the rule and realm of God.

Still limping, we may approach this scene via another path. Like the path followed by the two Marys, it too is thoroughly Jewish; but it involves an additional detour. From the Jabbok it turns to the base of Sinai to stand before a burning bush. In fact, we might even argue that approaching the empty tomb by way of Moses' encounter at the burning bush is an appropriate hermeneutical strategy, given Matthew's use of the Moses/exodus traditions for telling his story of Jesus.

When we return to the tomb by way of the burning bush, we are invited to view the empty tomb and its transformative announcement through the images of that story. Moses was confronted by an event that summoned him to return to Egypt in order to lead his people into freedom in partnership with the God of Abraham, the God of Isaac, and the God of Jacob. He was summoned into action by a burning bush that, while engulfed in flame, was not consumed by the fire that threatened it. In earlier work, I have suggested that Israel be identified with that bush, as a living entity engulfed in historic flames of hatred and oppression. Israel was utterly threatened in Moses' time and once again in the fires of Nazi policies and actions. Yet Israel was not consumed; Israel survived.[5]

In the case of the empty tomb story and its attendant announcement that Jesus has been raised, we may read that even though Jesus was crucified, dead, and buried, death and the powers aligned against him did not consume him. Jesus, in the full gestalt of his identity and covenantal project, was still present, acting and relating in the lives of his followers, even though he died. He was tortured, abandoned, humiliated, forsaken. What the powers aligned against him opposed was not, in the end, defeated. He prevailed. Indeed, we may borrow a concept from Peter Hodgson to declare that the full gestalt of his life, teachings, and actions with others has not been consumed.[6] In adopting this language we are identifying Jesus as our burning bush, the one through whom the God of Israel speaks and calls. The full gestalt of Jesus, buried with him in the tomb, is neither consumed in his death nor confined by his tomb. Instead, it continues as we identify it with Jesus, to lead and guide us in a reconfigured encounter with the domain of God that he brought near and embodied in our midst.

Death has taken Jesus, but it has not consumed him. The covenant fidelity in which and with which he embraced his followers was not undone by death nor by their falling away—even in that extreme trial. Covenant life as Jesus embraced it prevailed. The community, the *chavurah*, that he forged among them, though shattered by the events of the last three days, returned on the other side of its loss—no longer whole and yet whole in a new way as those who remained began to grasp the gift Jesus had been giving them in this fellowship from the beginning. Though the heart of this gestalt was torn from it and its physical makeup decimated by death, they discovered the heart and soul remained, but transformed by what happened. They had been born anew; their physical makeup, their body, was similarly transfigured. Only now, they were able to receive with more complete understanding the embodied life that Jesus had been giving them all along.

Jesus was their burning bush. He had not been consumed, though he had been taken from them. But he also returned in the covenantal gestalt in which and with which he embraced them before. He was in many ways like Moses to them, and yet now they knew he was more than that. He was their burning bush, and he was calling out to them. All they could say at first—all we can say at first—is, "Hineni." Here I am.

Facing the Risen Christ

The risen Christ, whatever else we may claim for him, is an encounterable gestalt that spoke and called forth the first Easter witnesses and then went before them as they returned to the disciples and then to Galilee. That gestalt was covenantal—thoroughly relational. It embodied the critical and identifiable facets that distinguished the pre-Easter gestalt that Jesus brought into existence and relationship. It was rooted in generosity, operated with a liberating logic of abundance, and expressed a strong sense of radical hospitality to others. What the two women encountered, and then the disciples, was a gestalt, not a resuscitated body. This gestalt, embodied in Jesus, was attacked, denied, rejected, and even abandoned in Jesus' crucifixion. Yet that Easter gestalt met and embraced the two women, and later the other disciples, as they left a disturbed and empty tomb.

We learn from other testimony that this gestalt was constituted in a number of ways. Central among them was and remained the gestalt of their table fellowship, as Luke is bold to portray in his Gospel. It is the same gestalt to which Matthew refers as he describes Jesus' teachings in the temple precincts and then in his report of Jesus' consecrating its presence with his words of offering at the table in the upper room. At the table, the disciples gathered and participated in a gestalt that become for them the resurrected body of Christ.

As our previous analysis has demonstrated, the shape of that gestalt is inclusively covenantal and life-oriented. Rooted in a spirit of generosity and hospitality and operating with a logic of abundance, not scarcity, that gestalt leads the reconstituted disciples back to Galilee and overflows its boundaries. Moreover, as a covenantal gestalt it would have been thoroughly relational.

In effect, the return of this gestalt, in spite of the attempt to deny its power, was a confirmation of the relational shape of the holy and the power of hospitality to hold and shape life, even when that hospitality was betrayed, denied, or opposed. Indeed, the staying power of that hospitality provided and still provides a way of imaging God's way with the world and our participation in it that does not require an excluding and finally violent attitude toward others who dwell differently in the same world. Furthermore, it was this gestalt of hospitality that the disciples were sent forth to share with the nations (*pante ethne*, that is, all the Gentiles) in their final summons.

Furthermore, this gestalt was and remained a compelling and a summoning presence, calling others to join in its unfinished covenantal project that still includes the Jewish people. The sending forth of Matthew 28:19 was oriented toward other peoples, Gentiles, those who were other. In other words, the summons to Jews was not to convert them to Christianity. Rather it was to bear witness to the rule and realm of Heaven that included Gentiles in the household of God. In this way, the work of resurrection is unfinished and covenantal, unfolding in discrete but interconnecting moments.

The power of this gestalt to transform everyone and everything in its midst confronted them on the other side of crucifixion. While it did not undo the cru-cifixion, it did transcend it and its negative gestalt of terror and death. It would also be unfinished, albeit filled fully with the relational promise of creation. As we meet this gestalt, we find it addressing us. It is other and in its other-ness reaches out to us for relation. That is, while the gestalt is intensely exis-tential, it is also more than that. It meets us as we meet it. And as we recognize it, it calls out to us for recognition. But we must be careful, especially here.

After Auschwitz, the danger of triumphalism stalks the path that leads from the empty tomb. So we limp here too, alert to the ways we have abused the good news of this walk. But our limping also provides us an opportunity to recognize that the story itself challenges any overzealous confidence regard-ing what one finds at this place/in this story. Jesus is not there. He goes ahead. Our going forth still limps, however. As we proceed from Jerusalem and return to Galilee (read "home base"), we do so with the knowledge that this path has been traveled many times before and its pilgrims have taken hostages or prisoners along the way. Indeed, the liturgical path provided many con-temporary Christians sets up this continuing possibility, albeit inadvertently. As we go forth on our way, we limp with this awareness charged with the responsibility of sharing what we have learned and how we have been changed. The risen Christ is a still encounterable gestalt of life being affirmed in the face of and in the aftermath of death. As such, it meets us; embraces us; and calls or sends us forth in a continuing venture of life lived for others.

The Pastoral Task

What then is our pastoral task? The most direct way to express it may be to say we are to announce the good news of Easter: Christ has been raised from the dead. But in our post-Shoah context, limping not just to but from an empty tomb, how do we do that and remain faithful to the first Easter witness and firmly committed to the victims of triumphalistic distortions of that same good news? That is the dilemma we face as post-Shoah Easter witnesses.

The risen Christ is a covenantal gestalt with Jesus at its heart, but his pres-ence is a presence linked essentially in relationship with others. To announce that this Christ is risen is to affirm the full covenantal gestalt that he embod-ied as a Jew. To be sure, he challenged the shape of the holy and the configu-rations of purity that distinguished his time. He challenged contemporaneous renewal movements with his own interpretation of what was needed. But we cannot forget that he did so as a Jew and focused, however inclusively, on the people of Israel. The inclusive generosity that now includes us starts from that particularity. Covenantal wholeness, after Auschwitz, as it should have been from the beginning, includes the entire people Israel, even when Jews and Christians challenge and disagree with each other about our most fundamental understandings of the sacred. Whatever else we may add, the pastoral task is rooted in a sense of covenantal wholeness that always includes and extends from Israel. Of course, that may make matters awkward and sometimes difficult with our Jewish siblings. It will certainly not remove the conflict. But it does categorically forbid us from viewing them as standing outside the domain of God's covenantal embrace of creation.

Second, our recognition that the risen Christ is a covenantal gestalt invites our participation in his partnership for life. Likewise, that recognition points us toward another dimension of this partnership that we must be sure we understand. The transformation that we experience is an essential and constitutive aspect of this covenantal gestalt. The transfiguration of life beyond death and its power in our lives is happening not simply to the crucified Jesus and his disciples but also to us. We participate in its power too. Our pastoral tasks grow out of this recognition, to be sure, but they do not lead us to try to force the healing and new life to happen before their time. Rather, our tasks are rooted in nurturing the covenantal gestalt that Jesus embodied and gave his life to serve, trusting that the risk we take in this regard is warranted by what we have seen as its fruit in our lives and the lives of others.

However, when we trust and proclaim the significance of this covenantal gestalt, we must remember what the attending figures at the empty tomb declared to the very first witnesses and what Thomas demanded in John's Gospel: the risen Christ is the one who *was crucified* (my emphasis). Any good news that avoids a full confrontation with the atrocity of crucifixion and all that accompanied it is false news. The announcement of Easter faith is accountable to the tragedy that preceded it. Likewise, after Auschwitz, the good news of Easter is accountable to the burning children remembered by Irving Greenberg. His post-Shoah call for theological circumspection is not unlike that which distinguished the first witness to Easter. However, to be faithful after Auschwitz to that circumspection is to remind ourselves how often we have failed to remember that suffering accurately and honestly. Consequently, in addition to holding Easter accountable to the face of a crucified Jesus, Easter must also be credible in the face of the 1.5 million children who perished without choice because they were Jewish.

As we recognize the essentially Jewish character of this sacred ground, we will find the story of Moses and the burning bush to be more and more instructive. Jesus is our burning bush, and the gestalt of generosity and hospitality that he embodied is our holy ground. As we look at the covenantal gestalt that

Jesus embodied, the Easter message declares that even though he died, the gestalt that was particularly constituted in and by his life was not consumed by his death. But what was raised was not a corpse. The resurrection was not a resuscitation of a dead body. It was something new; something more. Peter Hodgson describes it this way:

> On the one hand, the Resurrection of Jesus is something more than mere historical influence [that continues after his death] or memory or a mere psychological event in the mind of believers. . . . On the other hand, [the resurrection of Jesus] is something other than a miracle of bodily resuscitation and quasi-physical immediacy. . . . What is risen is not the corpse of a dead man but a gestalt, a socio-historical dynamic that coalesced in, around, [and through] Jesus of Nazareth and those whom he touched.[7]

Our pastoral task will be to mediate experiences whereby that gestalt can be reconstituted in our midst—at the table, in the market place, on the margins of society. It will require our participation, so we must be prepared and willing to risk our actions in those places. But it will not be simply our doing. And often it will require the same willingness to risk the powers of denial and death that Jesus faced. But the choices for life must be risked precisely there, if the one who was not consumed by death is to go before us.

Typically we conceive of the pastoral task associated with Easter as one of announcing the good news that death has been vanquished and that Jesus is risen from the dead. We may even be precise enough to insist on claiming that even though Jesus was crucified, he was raised by God, as Christ, from the dead. Still, the pastoral task focuses on the act of announcing the good news of Easter. However, as we return midrashically to the empty tomb and move from it limping, we are obliged to recognize and incorporate its dynamic, covenantal character in our witness and to distinguish unfolding moments in our pastoral task, not unlike the covenantal moments that characterize our coming to terms with the risen Christ. Adapting the work of Kendall Soulen, who differentiates several key moments in the unfolding reality of resurrection, we may distinguish five such moments (openness, recognition, articulation, participation, and going forth) to guide our thinking about the covenantal nature and dynamic character of what we mean by resurrection.[8]

Openness

Even in their grief, the two Marys were open to something more and practiced a hospitality of spirit that allowed them to move beyond the image of a disturbed tomb to an empty one. While this may seem like a minor point, it is not. Even in a moment of compounded grief—one more act of degradation—the two women were able to respond to the surprise of possible defilement in this moment without lashing out and thereby cutting themselves off from the triumph of life that was being offered them even at the grave. Even there, they were open to life.

The text does not tell us about their grieving—whether they had experienced intense grieving or even anger. But Matthew does report that they were able to attend to the figure at the tomb's threshold and possibilities at the tomb other than the obvious, including the interpretation of the absence of Jesus' body by the figure at the threshold as a sign of blessing not curse, life not death. They remained open to the gestalt of God's generosity they had known in Jesus' presence and now encountered in confusing and frightening circumstances at the tomb.

For those of us who follow them to this place, our task is to remain open to new possibilities, even when everything around us proclaims they are exhausted. We may identify this as an openness of spirit that Paul described as "hope against hope" (Rom. 4:18). Similar to what Douglas John Hall develops as "costly hope," openness is neither overly pious nor naively optimistic. Rather, openness expresses an insistent realism on the other side of tragedy that, while not hardened, yields a wounded spirit still able and open to welcome and walk with others.

Of course, the two Marys could, and quite possibly did, experience intensified anger when they approached the tomb. The grave had been disturbed. After Auschwitz, we must ponder this possibility seriously—as we did earlier. But we must also be able to distinguish the difference between rage and outrage in such circumstances. In the former, the one who is enraged is trapped, at least for a time, in the reactive emotions of rage. In outrage, one is drawn out in anger on behalf of others. Its "other-orientation" leads to concern for more than satisfying one's own emotional needs at such a time.[9]

In other words, before we can recognize the significance of a disturbed and emptied tomb, we must first be open to the unexpected, capable of being surprised. That is, we must be fundamentally hospitable to the other/Other/life, whether or not the other is a person or an event or an experience—a gestalt of relationships. Kendall Soulen explains that whatever resurrection is, in itself,[10] it begins for us in a moment of recognition. However, any recognition of resurrection requires a prior openness to the other/Other that is an essential feature of this covenantal event.

Recognition

Recognition happens when and where death is confronted in its covenantal starkness—as a covenantal or relational crisis of ultimate proportion. But it cannot be forced; it must be allowed to grow out of the honest and painful approach we make in the aftermath of crucifixion to the place where we have laid our shattered dreams and broken hearts. That approach can be made vicariously as we attend to the story or stories of those who have faced this crisis before. Their story becomes our approach. In this case our task is to enter this story in order to walk with them and to listen to what they experienced and saw in their walking.

We join them limping, already wounded. Hence we are alert to their wounds, their limping. If we are attentive, we recognize that their good news begins in our coming to terms with their anguish as fully as we can. When we do, we reshape our lives in a new way. We may even discover that our good news is rooted as well in our facing our own woundedness and pain, likewise reshaping our own lives. A pastoral task that fully honors this moment, therefore, begins in attentive hospitality to the other, able to recognize the other before us as well as the other within.

As we follow this story, we will come to a disturbed tomb. Things are not as they were left. Death is not in its place. It may even be one more experience of degradation. But there is more. A relational gestalt confronts us even here—especially here. Indeed, like the first time, we encounter this gestalt before we understand it. So our first task is to recognize that it is present and to acknowledge its relational character. That comes first. We encounter this gestalt before we understand it. That is, we recognize the gestalt and that this gestalt is relational. We encounter it as a gestalt, and our first act is to encounter it in relation, open to how it may address us before we understand the significance of what is happening to us. As we meet this gestalt, we find it addressing us. It is other and reaches out to us in its otherness for relation. Although the gestalt is intensely existential, it is also more than that. It meets us as we meet it. And as we recognize it, it calls out to us for recognition.

Articulation

At the heart of the biblical story is an interpreting figure at once heavenly (read "mysterious") and liturgical who announces that the one we seek is not where we left him. Indeed, he has been raised from the dead and has gone on before us—to Galilee, in Matthew's story. We may interpret that to mean that he will meet the disciples where they began their journey with Jesus, where they lived and worked—at home. We may similarly read this as return to the promised land after exile, only *from Jerusalem* instead of *toward Jerusalem,* reversing the typical direction of that movement. Either way, as we confront this interpretive act, we should notice that just as the two Marys are called upon to tell the disciples what has happened—as interpreted by these other figures—so too are we. Likewise, we are summoned to our Galilee, our home, our familiar territory—the place where we were called into our ministries with others. We are summoned to our promised land, and it is embodied in an act of return to the familiar to be known again in a new way.

Having recognized this presence, we, like the two Marys, are called to pass on what we discover to other disciples. We are to give expression to what has happened to us and to articulate its significance vis-à-vis what has happened to Jesus: he was crucified; he has been raised; he is going on before us. We join the story by adding our voices and our presence to it. Then, as we risk articulating our good news, it is confirmed more directly by the one whom we now behold anew in the gestalt that goes before us and guides us in our going forth. That confirmation comes as we venture to make connection ourselves. We take hold, we dare to make connection, but we do so in a paradoxical way that lets go in recognition of a mystery we cannot manipulate or control. Jesus did not remain in the tomb, nor did the risen Christ remain within the grasp of his earliest witnesses. And we are to give voice to that discovery, interpreting its paradoxical power for the sake of others.

Participation

As we move forward, first, recognizing the gestalt as something new at the place where we left all that Jesus had been and meant to us and, second, coming to terms with its significance for us and for others who loved and followed him, we find ourselves drawn into the gestalt itself. We step, as it were, into the gestalt, participating in its relational wholeness and its healing power. Where we bring remorse and guilt, we find a generosity of relationship that embraces us in spite of ourselves. We give expression to that generosity by declaring our sense of being forgiven and being restored to relationships we had broken. We give expression to its healing power for life by referring to the healing of wounded relationships and broken hearts. The participation is restorative and our task is to participate in that restored wholeness, recognizing the gestalt, naming it in its promise for new life, and then stepping into it, daring to participate in its power. Our pastoral task, even and especially at the threshold of this gestalt, is to attend its threshold, announcing its promise and welcoming those we serve in its domain. In other words, even here, especially here, we are called to participate in its hospitality as welcoming hosts who bear witness to the promise of creation that even death cannot destroy.

In quite specific ways, we will participate in that gestalt as we invite others to share food at the sacramental table, to undergo baptism, to enter into the sacramental domain of the body of Christ. In more general ways, we will offer that invitation wherever we have the opportunity to serve others hospitably and to embody generosity and grace to those who are other and excluded from life's wholeness. And as we do, we will participate in the other moments as well, for they are not sequential steps in an organic process as much as they are aspects or dimensions of an embodied and dynamic experience we may approach from numerous vantage points.

Going Forth—Limping toward Galilee and Beyond

However, resurrection remains an unfinished act, and therefore we are called to more than participation. As the story recounts, we are called to go forth, not unlike Abram in Genesis 12, seeking to extend the reach of the life-giving gestalt we have come to know as the rule and realm of God and now identify with Jesus as the risen Christ. Our going forth is in stages: first, seeking other disciples with whom to share the story and, then, joining them in going forth to share with all other peoples [*pante en ethne*] the full implication of this restorative gestalt we know as the fully embodied will and way of God that we have met in Jesus and in which the very promise of creation dwelled in its fullness.

Our speaking and our acting are to embody the same reality. Yet, even here, going forth as healed and restored children of God, we continue to limp. We know even this wonderful story can be turned from a testimony of healing to a weapon of spiritual conquest. So we limp, still. But our limping, if we will allow it, can be part of our healing, our wholeness.

As Mary Boys so clearly identifies in *Has God Only One Blessing?* those who follow the Roman Catholic and Protestant lectionaries in their worship settings will encounter two structural forms of supersessionism as they make their way through the Sunday readings of Easter. She writes:

> In many respects, the lections of the Easter cycle present even more diffi-
> culties than do those of Holy Week. During the Sundays after Easter, the
> lectionary replaces its customary first reading from the 'Old' Testament
> with selections from the Acts of the Apostles (emphasizing the early part of
> Acts rather than the latter half). Not only does this replacement implicitly
> suggest that the First Testament has nothing to say about God's redemptive
> action in raising Jesus from the dead, it means that the congregants again
> hear the accusation that the Jews killed Jesus.[11]

In other words, the Hebrew lection is replaced with a reading from the book of Acts that is, itself, troublingly polemical, especially if it stands alone while another text is interpreted in sermon or homily. As Boys explains, "even if congregants had heard an adequate explanation of the passion accounts during Holy Week," they will now hear texts that declare statements like "this man, handed over to you according to the definite plan and foreknowledge of God, you crucified and killed by the hands of those outside the law."[12] However, more often than not, preachers and homilists will interpret the Gospel lection for the day, leaving the polemical statement of Acts unaddressed and heard with little attempt to put it in context. In addition, Boys notes an additional problem in the selection of these texts. They are chosen "with christocentric eyes" as ways of portraying the promise-fulfillment motif of salvation history.[13] Typology replaces the richer texture of a multi-voiced narrative. And once more supersessionism does violence to our Jewish other as well as to the text from which the selection is taken. In short, even in the light of Easter, there is still work to be done as we limp forward into a new day.

As we venture into the future trusting and serving the resurrection gestalt, we participate in its healing and life-giving power. Nonetheless, we still risk what Jesus risked in his life and ministry, and a measure of what God risked in the wager of creation.[14] We discover a new understanding of divine providence, and divinity as well, that leads us into different ways of conceptualizing our faith and how we view the covenantal project of creation. The commanding monarch who stands above the give and take of his or her domain, and who deigns to enter into a special relationship with a segment of that domain is replaced by a radically hospitable host of life who acts in and through the embodiment of the hospitality of others. When that hospitality and generosity are fully embodied in human life, the fundamental wager of creation is represented anew and calls forth further participation in its gift. Going forth in the spirit of an empty tomb, empowered by a gestalt that reorients our lives, we should not forget that this gestalt could not be buried. The holy could not be fenced in. It does not remain where we place it. As we go forth, so too does the one we follow. So too does the hospitality that makes room for life to grow and flourish.

Limping into the Promised Land

What then may we conclude about our post-Shoah journey to and from the empty tomb? Several points stand out.

Just as we are to announce the empty tomb and its significance, we are to identify and announce the open places in the biblical story, offering them for interpretation to those who venture their respect for that open space. Recognizing the importance of leaving the tomb empty, we must learn to know what to name and what to leave unnamed in our trips to this biblical garden. In the case of an empty tomb, we are called not to fill it with explanations, but to leave it open as the place that could not contain what had been sealed within it.

Just as we are called upon to take off our shoes before the burning bush, we are called to tread in this domain carefully and with respect, even as we limp. We are called upon to remember that this ground, like the dimension of the holy that Jesus has helped us acknowledge, is thoroughly relational. Our respect will manifest itself in how we approach others.

Throughout, we are called to value our limping. It slows us down, allowing us to see what in our excitement we tend to race through or grasp far too quickly. We still limp, even in the light of Easter morning. Our limping reminds us of the way Israel has told its story of not being consumed by a hostile world, while avoiding a triumphalistic way of claiming its unique story on behalf of a wider world. They remembered their limping at the heart of their storied walk with God. What does God require of us but to "do justice, love steadfastly, and to walk humbly with our God"? We are to remind our parishioners again and again that we approach this sacred ground limping and we leave it limping, always oriented outward, toward others in generosity and hospitality to an ever larger world. We are called to continue an unfinished journey, limping toward the promised land at the same time we dwell in its promise.

Eventually, the pastoral responsibilities of a limping, Easter faith will lead to the celebrative worship of Easter morning. What follows, therefore, is another offering along the path that began with our detour to the Jabbok. In this case, the offering is a sunrise service used at the campus community where I serve as chaplain. The service honors the essential power of the biblical story but acknowledges the need to engage that story and its power as responsibly as we can when we articulate the good news of resurrection. In our case, the service is a shared experience with several congregations who are neighbors of our university. We begin in the plaza between the university chapel and the university library, where we gather before a descending stairwell to a basement entrance. The area is shaded by large trees and nicely landscaped, evoking the feeling of a formal garden. The service begins with a choral call to worship and then the reading of Matthew's account of the empty tomb. Then a brief meditation or midrash follows. Its intent is not to explain away the events of Easter morning but to open the Scripture so that we may enter its narrated world. The service then moves with a processional hymn across the plaza into the chapel sanctuary, where the Eucharist is celebrated as a resurrection meal. Again, the Matthean narrative is read and followed by a brief meditation or midrash. Then the Eucharist is celebrated, the story resumed, and once more a congregational procession moves to another location. In our case, we move a few hundred feet to an outdoor plaza that literally overlooks our city. There prayers for the world are offered, the Great Commission is read, and once more a brief meditation or midrash interprets the passage and its implications for our lives.

In each section of the liturgy, a brief meditation is offered to help worshippers enter the Easter narrative, ever alert to the ways the story remains unfinished and to the ways we limp in our encounters with it. In reproducing the service I have included sample meditations that reflect the midrashic spirit of this chapter. As in previous offerings, these examples are not intended as prescriptions that should be followed but as options for analysis and critique. I hope they will evoke other options and suggest even more ways of moving forward in the wounded walk of Easter faith.

Easter Sunrise Service

GATHERING

CHORAL INTROIT   Appropriate Hymn

Encountering the Empty Tomb

Leader: After the sabbath, as the first day of the week was dawning, Mary Magdalene and the other Mary went to see the tomb. And suddenly there was a great earthquake; for an angel of the Lord, descending from heaven, came and rolled back the stone and sat on it. His appearance was like lightning, and his clothing white as snow. For fear of him the guards shook and became like dead men. But the angel said to the women, "Do not be afraid; I know that you are looking for Jesus who was crucified. He is not here; for he has been raised." (Matthew 28:1–6)

"EMPTY TOMB"   Meditation or Midrash on the Empty Tomb

Sample Meditation: As we make our way to the tomb of Jesus, we are guided in our journey by the selective hand of Matthew. He recounts the scene for us in stylized fashion, helping us see the important details. Our approach is made as dawn is breaking. And our approach is made with the two Marys. He does not tell us what they expected to find but we can guess: unfinished grief, anger, confusion, and a jumble of other emotions. The other disciples remain missing. Our approach is interrupted by an earthquake. Is this world-shaking experience, like the one on crucifixion day, more like a brushstroke in a Van Gogh portrait than an observable phenomenon for all to experience? We are left to work this out for ourselves, but it appears that the only ones recoiling from its occurrence are those at the scene. Regardless, Matthew tells us that the event is not self-interpreting or self-evident. Whatever it is, it requires another figure, one clothed in white, radiant like the fire of the sky, and speaking on behalf of God—and the one who is no longer discoverable in the grave. Jesus is not where he was left. Funny thing, if we ponder it a bit. Jesus seems to have made this a habit—never staying put, where others, where we, have left him. Such is the case here. He is not present in the grave. Likewise his grave clothes no longer bind him. Nothing binds him now. Not the grave. Not the guards. Not the grief that consumes the two Marys, one of whom may very well have been his mother. And not any other expectations or fears. And so the attendant announces to his returning companions: He is not here. But he is not simply missing. No. This is not the case of a disturbed tomb and desecrated tomb. This is the story of an abundance that overflows even this cup too. He has been raised. To what, for what, for whom, with whom? That is for us to find out. Let us return to the story and see where it leads us.

> **Leader**: He is not here; for he has been raised, as he said. Come, see the place where he lay. Then go quickly and tell his disciples, 'He has been raised from the dead, and indeed he is going ahead of you to Galilee; there you will see him.' This is my message for you." So they left the tomb quickly with fear and great joy, and ran to tell his disciples. (Matthew 28:6–8)

PROCESSION INTO THE SANCTUARY   Appropriate Hymn

Celebrating the Resurrection

> **Leader**: Suddenly Jesus met them and said, "Greetings!" And they came to him, took hold of his feet, and worshiped him. (Matthew 28:9)

ACT OF PRAISE   CHOIR

"THE RESURRECTION MEAL"   Meditation or Midrash on the Upper Room

Sample Meditation: There is more to the story than Jesus being free from the grave. To be sure, he is not there. He is not where the two Marys left him. But they are surprised, because there is more to relate. Jesus greets them on the way to find the disciples. They are not yet sure of what they have discovered at the empty tomb. They are filled with fear as well as great joy—and probably relief. But we can be sure that they are also a bit confused and unclear about what is happening to and with them. Indeed. Something is happening to them in this unfolding story. But more about that in a moment. On the way to relay their experience to the other disciples, Jesus meets them and greets them. He meets them. Imagine. A simple encounter mediated with only a simple greeting. Jesus, after death, greets them yet one more time and makes them welcome. And they respond by taking hold of him and, I imagine, holding fast, holding tight. Matthew says, "They worshipped him."

Perhaps what happens to them is similar to what happens to us at table, when we remember what happened; when we tell the story, bless the bread and the wine, and then take hold of the bread—his body—and take the cup—his blood—drawing him into us and ourselves toward him. And in our taking hold of him, we worship him. I wonder . . .

Just as we do not remain at the table but are sent out into the world for the sake of others, so also are the two Marys comforted in their fear, and then sent on their way to resume their journey to find the other disciples and to tell them what has happened.

Though Matthew does not tell us, we can only guess what happens to the two women. Surely they are not the same as they were when they set out that morning. Surely their lives are being transformed in the journey they are now taking. Resurrection is happening, transforming their lives as much as it is still transforming Jesus' life. Will the other disciples see what has happened to and with them?

I invite you to hear the greeting of the risen Christ as we gather at our table, tell the story, and then take the bread and wine in thanksgiving that we too may participate in the resurrection that we celebrate on this day. May the great mystery that Christ has died, Christ is risen, Christ will come again, be affirmed once more in our midst. Amen.

OFFERING WITH OFFERTORY   Choir

THE GREAT THANKSGIVING

    Leader: God be with you.

> **People:** **And also with you.**
> Leader: Lift up your hearts.
> **People:** **We lift them up to God.**
> Leader: Let us give thanks to the Eternal One, our God.
> **People:** **It is right to give our thanks and praise . . .**[*]

LORD'S PRAYER

> **Our Father in heaven, hallowed be your name, your kingdom come, your will be done, on earth as in heaven. Give us today our daily bread. Forgive us our sins as we forgive those who sin against us. Save us from the time of trial and deliver us from evil. For the kingdom, the power, and the glory are yours now and forever. Amen.**

SHARING COMMUNION

COMMUNION HYMN   Appropriate Hymn

> **Leader**: Suddenly Jesus met them and said, "Greetings!" And they came to him, took hold of his feet, and worshiped him. Then Jesus said to them, "Do not be afraid; go and tell my brothers to go to Galilee; there they will see me." (Matthew 28:9–10)

PROCESSION TO THE WORLD   Appropriate Hymn

Sharing the Resurrection

> **Leader**: Now the eleven disciples went to Galilee, to the mountain to which Jesus had directed them. When they saw him, they worshiped him; but some doubted. And Jesus came and said to them, "All authority in heaven and on earth has been given to me. Go therefore and make disciples of all nations, baptizing them in the name of the Father and of the Son and of the Holy Spirit, and teaching them to obey everything that I have commanded you. And remember, I am with you always, to the end of the age." (Matthew 28:16–20)

"THE GREAT COMMISSION"   Meditation or Midrash on the Great Commission

Sample Meditation: The other disciples went to Galilee, that is, they went home, but not just home. They were sent to the mountain to which Jesus had

---

[*]The Great Thanksgiving continues. See the text of this prayer on page 73 at the end of chap. 3.

directed them. In Matthew, this designation is significant. Matthew tells his story, over and over, revisiting the view from the mountain—not just any mountain, but Sinai. And in Matthew 17, in a scene that anticipates this one, Jesus is visited by Moses and Elijah. Then, having gone down the mountain, he departs for Jerusalem. Immediately afterwards Jesus heals a boy with epilepsy, a lad whom the disciples have tried to help but cannot. They ask why, and Jesus says their faith was insufficient. Oh, he didn't mean it was not strong enough. Something else was missing. Even faith the size of a mustard seed would do. But it must be able to say to the mountain, "Move." And that was the key. Not just any mountain, but that mountain: Sinai. Sinai was portable, like the ark of old. Sinai was something you carried with you. Surely when Jesus sent the disciples back to Galilee, to the mountain that he had showed them, he meant that mountain. In Matthew, mountains are not throwaway figures. They are symbols of Torah, God's will for neighbor love and love of God.

When Jesus sent the disciples back to Galilee, he sent them to that mountain. In other words, the resurrection brings the disciples back to the mountain, to Sinai. Likewise, if we are going to follow Matthew's guidance in this regard, resurrection, Easter, will take us back to Sinai too. If we are going to bear witness to what has happened to Jesus, then we must include our return to that mountain. Easter, resurrection has something essential to do with Sinai. We carry it with us; and we can find it at home or anywhere else.

Perhaps another way to think about this is to recognize that resurrection, like Jesus' entire ministry, was, is, covenantal. That is, he carried the mountain with him. Covenant life was portable. Consequently, resurrection happens to Jesus; and it happens to the disciples; it happens to us too—all in relation to one another. Resurrection is a relational, covenantal affair. It doesn't happen just to Jesus, but to those in covenantal relationship with him as well. And it is incomplete until it draws us into its life-giving power. Yet even then it remains unfinished.

Whatever else resurrection may be, we may say that the relationships Jesus establishes are not severed by what happens to him. Death has not won in this regard. Rather, the relationships that he established with those who follow him cannot be undone by crucifixion, by betrayal, by denial, by our failures to understand what he was about. His steadfast love endured. Indeed, it still endures.

We may also declare that the relational gestalt that was his life, which we try to capture in the language of Trinity, was manifestly reconfigured even after he died, but it was still recognizably the covenantal gestalt that Jesus embodied with his disciples throughout his ministry. We speak of that gestalt as Father, Son, and Holy Spirit. And with that impetus, in that same relational configuration we call covenant life, the risen Christ extends his presence to the world. And so we are sent. So we are sent. Go. Draw others to this one who embodies the relational gestalt of creation, the relational dance of divine generosity, the relational gift and power of life.

PRAYERS FOR THE WORLD

HYMN   Appropriate Hymn

CHARGE AND BENEDICTION

> **Leader**:   And Jesus came and said to them, "All authority in heaven and on earth has been given to me. Go therefore and make disciples of all nations, baptizing them in the name of the Father and of the Son and of the Holy Spirit, and teaching them to obey everything that I have commanded you. And remember, I am with you always, to the end of the age." (Matthew 28:18–20)

NOTES

1.   Jewish tradition has long identified Mount Moriah with the Temple Mount. Levenson, in his *Resurrection and the Beloved Son*, examines the midrashic and textual possibilities of linking the beloved son traditions of Genesis, particularly as manifest in the near sacrifice of Isaac, with the early Christian community's way of making sense out of what happened in Jesus' crucifixion. Levenson begins with the notion that the followers of Jesus would be trying to make sense out of what happened using their beloved son traditions as an interpretive prism to read their present experience "according to the Scriptures." See Jon D. Levenson, *The Death and Resurrection of the Beloved Son: The Transformation of Child Sacrifice in Judaism and Christianity* (New Haven, CT: Yale University Press, 1993), passim, esp. 200–219.

2.   Franklin H. Littell, *The Crucifixion of the Jews: The Failure of Christians to Understand the Jewish Experience* (New York: Harper & Row, 1975), passim.

3.   See Luise Schottroff's discussion of what the women could know and most probably risked in acting this way: *Lydia's Impatient Sisters: A Feminist Social History of Early Christianity*, trans. Barbara and Martin Rumscheidt (Louisville, KY: Westminster John Knox Press, 1995), 204. According to Schottroff, the women risked their lives in expressing their solidarity with someone who was condemned to crucifixion.

4.   Thorwald Lorenzen, *Resurrection and Discipleship: Interpretive Models, Biblical Reflections, Theological Consequences* (Maryknoll, NY: Orbis Books, 1995), 181.

5.   See Henry Knight, *Confessing Christ in a Post-Holocaust World: A Midrashic Experiment* (Westport, CT: Greenwood Press, 2000), 86–103.

6.   Peter Hodgson, *Winds of the Spirit: A Constructive Christian Theology* (Louisville, KY: Westminster John Knox Press, 1994), 217f.

7.   Ibid., 217.

8.   Kendall Soulen focuses on the relational character of resurrection by describing the resurrection appearances as meetings. However, he differentiates them first as "meetings of recognition, forgiveness, and reconciliation . . . then . . . of fellowship . . . [and eventually] meetings of sending" (*The God of Israel* [Minneapolis: Augsburg Fortress, 1996], 165).

9. "[Rage and outrage] both have determination, passion, and lead to action, but rage is narrow, short-term, and blinded by fury, while outrage is broad, clean, steady, and committed to a sustainable solution." Phillip Moffitt, "Forgiving the Unforgivable," in *Yoga Journal* (January/February 2002), 63.

10. Op. cit.

11. Mary Boys, *Has God Only One Blessing?,* 204.

12. Ibid.

13. Ibid., 208.

14. See the reference to Job in the previous chapter, 111–12, 117–18.

Chapter 7

An Unfinished Journey

Once More to the Garden

The Path of Wounded Return

Having reexamined our steps following Jesus through Jerusalem, we see traces of another way of reading the events of this week and the final outcome at Golgotha. Indeed, those traces are possible because of the vantage point of Easter, but they signal different actions of a God hidden in the plain sight of these events, when we return to them limping. They point beyond triumphalism and contempt. They point beyond the intrinsic valuation of innocent suffering. They point beyond the suffering of any victim having transcendent meaning. They even point beyond the structure of covenantal theism to a covenantal partnership with creation that is representatively christomorphic without being exclusively christocentric. They point beyond conventional piety to a postcritical form of midrashic faithfulness that incorporates the critical in its limping, while never giving up walking the path of faith. They may still point to contending configurations of the holy and to the distinctive identity shaped by encounters with a crucified and risen Christ. But they indicate a different, more responsible confessional path to follow in our return.

Our limping qualifies our approach, especially as it links us to a people and a patriarch who limp as well. We have much to learn from them about how we keep our limping and our walking bound together. Our limping does not remove the conflict between us, however; but it does lead us to reconsider how we shape it and then how we contend with one another as a result. And of course, our limping leads again and again toward further self-examination and growth.

Whatever else we may conclude about our return to Jerusalem, it reminds us that Christian discipleship is a fallible enterprise. Of course, this conclusion is not new. But for most Christians that conclusion is at best a paradox expressive of being loved and embraced by God even though one is a sinner and undeserving of the love God offers us. In its more problematic forms, that paradox becomes a triumphalistic boast used to separate the saved from the lost. In the context of these remarks, however, to describe discipleship as a fallible enterprise is to recognize that the walk of faith limps at its core. And as our return to Jerusalem demonstrates, our fundamental processions of life and faith too often stumble over triumphalistic tendencies; our table fellowships ignore or forget that the pattern in which we gather remembers a night of failure and falling away; our night watches reveal that we fall asleep even in our most intense attempts to remain alert and awake; and our extreme moments of trial and testing are met with betrayal, denial, and even abandonment, when we fall and look on only from a distance. And yet, when we face the truth about ourselves, we discover the promise of joining other limping pilgrims on the way into and through Jerusalem. But now we dare not overlook those walking ahead of us or beside us who have declared their limping all along.

We undertake this journey in the promise of Easter. Indeed, the promise of Easter makes our return possible, but it never takes away the risk of crucifixion. We still live in a Good Friday world even if we have also tasted the firstfruits of an Easter morning. To use the language of Alan Lewis again, we live in the Sabbath between Good Friday and Easter, participating equally in both days' domains.[1] We are able to dwell in this liminal reality because Jesus walked there, choosing covenant life in the face of extreme covenantal crisis. We are able to dwell there because Jesus chose covenant life even when covenant life failed him. But the betrayal he experienced did not undo the covenant fidelity that he embodied in spite of what happened. Nonetheless, when we walk in this mixed domain of promise and peril, we limp. We are wounded by what we know about ourselves, about each other, about our faith, about our world. At the same time we are empowered by what we know about ourselves, about each other, about our faith, about our world. We limp; and yet we are blessed by a limping walk that allows us to keep moving forward, wounded yet whole.

Finally, we move in and out of the life of God—as we participate in discrete gestalts of hospitality, relational moments of generosity, and the abundant graces of sacrificial gifts of life lived for others. In doing so, we discover a way of understanding God's relation to life that from the beginning has provided the framework of creation and a model of God's active care and full embrace of our freedom. Yet, as this week reminds us again and again, the providence of hospitality, like the full embodiment of it we meet in this one we follow, embraces not just our freedom but our rejection of it as well.

The full articulation of this comes in sacred moments with the reconfigurations of Easter as partial glimpses of life in its completed wholeness. For now, we can only anticipate that final fulfillment of creation in the promissory nature of Easter's good news. Easter has, of course, come; and yet Easter has also not yet come. We live, theologically and liturgically, in interim time, the liminal time of in-between. We dwell in the aftermath of crucifixion but with the strong and costly hope of Easter faith. Adopting the language of Irving Greenberg, we may say that we live with "moment faith,"[2] empowered by our so-called Easter moments yet always in tension with our real life encounters with a Good Friday world.

We must learn to confess, at least until the Parousia comes, that Easter morn has not yet fully dawned. To be sure, it has come before—in the story and perhaps in our own experience. But each time we return, we approach its threshold with new concerns, new cautions, new fears, fresh despair. Will the dawn bring good news, as it has in previous visits to this threshold? Will the tomb still be empty? Will the resurrected Christ still greet us as we reassemble in our upper rooms? Any promise of new life, of life not undone by death, must be able to address these new shadows in the valley of post-Shoah reckoning.

In the end, our journey has not been unlike Jacob's return from exile as it took a crucial turn at the threshold of the Jabbok River, our first stop and the source of our guiding metaphor. We have wrestled with the text of the passion story in the shadows of another night. And we have taken hold of that text with a tenacity similar to Jacob's, insisting that the text in its otherness bless us. We have emerged limping, wounded by the encounter. But have we been blessed in the wounding as well?

That remains to be seen. However, I trust we will not let go of the story. Like Jacob with his nocturnal other, we will hold on, insisting that Easter continue to bless us, even as we continue to limp. We will return to its domain, grasping it as we encounter it in its recurring otherness. That is the way of midrashic return.

So we return to the question with which we began the last chapter: Can these bones (read "trees as in an orchard") live? When God asked Ezekiel that question, the survivor priest replied in a humbled, yet still open way, "You know, O LORD." In our time, we ask a similar question of our sacred texts and its orchard of meaning in which we gather and dwell: Can this orchard live? I believe it can and does, but it does depend on how we approach it.

Can These Bones (*Read* Trees/Orchard) Live?

To extend the question, a story: For over a decade I have hosted and participated in a Jewish-Christian dialogue sponsored by the National Conference on Community and Justice (NCCJ). As a mixed gathering of Jews and Christians of various backgrounds, we meet monthly to wrestle with matters central to our shared lives as leaders in our particular communities. When I began this project, we were discussing James Carroll's popular, if somewhat controversial, book *Constantine's Sword*. Each month our conversations were pointed and lively, engaging significant issues in our confessional lives. We are quite a cross-section of folk. Not just Jews and Christians, we embody a mix of political, theological, denominational, and cultural perspectives. As one might expect from such a mix, some in our group resisted Carroll's strong portrait of Christian complicity. Some took exception with his historical reconstructions. Some took umbrage with his portrait of their own tradition. On the other hand, some were relieved to be having the discussions that we were having as a result of our readings. One of our number, a priest, as a Roman Catholic had been particularly troubled by some of Carroll's assertions. With that as background, I would like to share a dream I had, about another priest, not unlike my friend in my dialogue group, who was scrupulous in his responsibilities to represent the larger church, the body of Christ, which he served.

Following an early draft of these reflections, I dreamed that a priest—Father Bill, let us call him—reported that he also had a dream after a recent visit to our dialogue group. In Father Bill's dream, he found himself transported to a deeply cherished orchard he had known and visited since his childhood. The orchard stretched out in every direction and covered the entire landscape before him. In the past, the groves of trees were luscious and filled with fruit; but in his dream they had been cut down. He was overcome by the devastation.

As he took in the landscape, Father Bill saw large and small trunks all around, with lots of broken branches and limbs scattered among them. As my dream unfolded, Father Bill said he walked the orchard in his dream, but not easily, because of the stumps and fallen trees that were strewn about. A few times he actually stumbled over limbs he didn't see; he even fell after tripping over some of them. As he walked the acreage and surveyed the scene, he heard a voice asking, "Father, can this orchard be saved? Can any trees grow here ever again? Will this orchard ever bear any more fruit?" Father Bill held his breath; he did not know what to say or what to do. As far as he knew, he was alone in the orchard. But the mysterious voice suggested otherwise—unless the voice was his own. Before he could determine anything further—where the voice was coming from, or whose voice it was—he awoke and realized that he was dreaming. But as he was waking, he heard himself saying, "You know, dear God! You know," over and over. "You know!"

Now someone may be wondering if my dream really happened. Did I really have a dream like this, about some one else's dream—a priest's, no less? The answer is yes; but not while I was asleep.

NOTES:

1.   Alan E. Lewis, *Between Cross and Resurrection: A Theology of Holy Saturday* (Grand Rapids: Wm. B. Eerdmans Publishing Co., 2001), 33, 43ff.

2.   Irving Greenberg, "Cloud of Smoke, Pillar of Fire: Judaism, Christianity, and Modernity after the Holocaust," in Eva Fleischner, ed., *Auschwitz: Beginning of a New Era?* (New York: KTAV Publishing House, 1977), 27.

Select Bibliography

Bader-Saye, Scott. "Post-Holocaust Hermeneutics: Scripture, Sacrament, and the Jewish Body of Christ." *Cross Currents* 50, no. 4 (Winter 2000/01): 458–73.

Bauman, Zygmunt. *Modernity and the Holocaust.* Ithaca, NY: Cornell University Press, 1989.

Bennett, Victoria J. *Bystanders: Conscience and Complicity during the Holocaust.* Westport, CT: Praeger, 1999, 2000.

Berman, Joshua. *The Temple: Its Symbolism and Meaning Then and Now.* Northvale, NJ: Jason Aronson, 1995.

Borg, Marcus J. *Conflict, Holiness, and Politics in the Teachings of Jesus.* New York and Toronto: Edwin Mellen Press, 1984.

———. *Jesus: A New Vision.* San Francisco: Harper & Row, 1987.

———. *Jesus in Contemporary Scholarship.* Valley Forge, PA: Trinity Press International, 1994.

Boys, Mary. *Has God Only One Blessing? Judaism as a Source of Christian Self-Understanding.* New York: Paulist Press, 2000.

Brown, Raymond. *A Crucified Christ in Holy Week: Essays on the Four Gospel Passion Narratives.* Collegeville, MN: Liturgical Press, 1986.

———. *The Death of the Messiah: From Gethsemane to the Grave.* New York: Doubleday, 1994.

Bruns, Gerald L. "The Hermeneutics of Midrash." In *The Book and the Text: The Bible and Literary Theory,* edited by Regina Schwartz. Oxford: Basil Blackwell, 1990.

Cargas, Harry James. *Reflections of a Post-Holocaust Christian.* Detroit: Wayne State University Press, 1991.

Carroll, James T. *Constantine's Sword: The Church and the Jew.* Boston: Houghton Mifflin Co., 2001.

Chilton, Bruce. *A Feast of Meanings: Eucharistic Theology from Jesus through Johannine Circles.* New York: E. J. Brill, 1994.

———. *Rabbi Jesus: An Intimate Portrait—The Jewish Life and Teaching That Inspired Christianity.* New York: Doubleday, 2000.

———. *The Temple of Jesus: His Sacrificial Program within a Cultural History of Sacrifice.* University Park, PA: Pennsylvania State University Press, 1992.

Cohen, Arthur. "In Our Terrible Age: the *Tremendum* of the Jews." In *The Holocaust as Interruption,* edited by Elisabeth Schüssler Fiorenza and David Tracy. Edinburgh: T. & T. Clark, 1984.

———. *The Tremendum: A Theological Interpretation of the Holocaust.* New York: Continuum, 1981.

Cohen, Norman J. *Self, Struggle, and Change: Family Conflict Stories in Genesis and Their Healing Insights for Our Lives.* Woodstock, VT: Jewish Lights Publishing, 1995.

Cox, Harvey. *Common Prayers: Faith, Family and a Christian's Journey through the Jewish Year.* Boston: Houghton Mifflin Co., 2001.

Crossan, John Dominic. *Who Killed Jesus? Exposing the Roots of Anti-Semitism in the Gospel Story of the Death of Jesus.* San Francisco: Harper, 1991.

Cunningham, Lawrence S. "Elie Wiesel's Anti-Exodus." In *Responses to Elie Wiesel,* edited by Harry J. Cargas. New York: Persea Books, 1978.

Doetzel, Audrey. "Liturgy: 'Walking the Walk' of Dialogue." http://www.cjre.org/Audrey-Docs/LITURGY.htm.

Fackenheim, Emil. *God's Presence in History: Jewish Affirmations and Philosophical Reflections.* New York: Harper Torchbooks, 1970.

———. *The Jewish Bible after the Holocaust: A Re-reading.* Bloomington and Indianapolis: Indiana University Press, 1990.

Fasching, Darrell J. *The Coming of the Millennium: Good News for the Whole Human Race.* Valley Forge, PA: Trinity Press International, 1996.

———. *Narrative Theology after Auschwitz.* Minneapolis: Fortress Press, 1992.

Fishbane, Michael. *Biblical Interpretation in Ancient Israel.* Oxford: Clarendon Press, 1985.

———. *Biblical Text and Texture: A Literary Reading of Selected Texts.* Oxford: Oneworld, 1998.

———. *The Garments of Torah: Essays in Biblical Hermeneutics.* Bloomington: Indiana University Press, 1989.

———, ed. *The Midrashic Imagination: Jewish Exegesis, Thought, and History.* Albany: State University of New York Press, 1993.

Fox, Everett. *Genesis and Exodus: A New English Rendition with Commentary and Notes.* New York: Schocken Books, 1983, 1986, 1990.

Freedman, H., trans. *Midrash Rabbah: Genesis,* vol. 2, LXXVII: III. London: Soncino Press, 1939.

Garber, Zev. *SHOAH: The Paradigmatic Genocide–Essays in Exegesis and Eisegesis.* Lanham, MD: University Press of America, 1994.

Goldberg, Michael. *Jews and Christians: Getting Our Stories Straight.* Nashville, Abingdon Press, 1985.

Greeley, Andrew and Jacob Neusner. *Common Ground: A Priest and a Rabbi Read Scripture Together.* Cleveland: Pilgrim Press, 1996.

Greenberg, Irving. "Cloud of Smoke, Pillar of Fire: Judaism, Christianity, and Modernity after the Holocaust." In *Auschwitz: Beginning of a New Era?* edited by Eva Fleischner. New York: KTAV Publishing House, 1977.

———. "History, Holocaust, and Covenant." In *Remembering for the Future: The Impact of the Holocaust and Genocide on Jews and Christians,* Proceedings of an International Conference, Oxford and London, July 10-17, 1988. Oxford: Pergamon Press, 1989.

———. "Religious Values after the Holocaust: A Jewish View." In *Jews and Christians after the Holocaust,* edited by Abraham J. Peck. Philadelphia: Fortress Press, 1982.

———. "Voluntary Covenant." In *Contemporary Jewish Religious Responses to the Shoah,* edited by Steven L. Jacobs. Lanham, MD: University Press of America, 1993.

Hall, Douglas John. *Professing the Faith: Christian Theology in a North American Context.* Minneapolis: Fortress Press, 1993.

Hartman, Geoffrey H., and Sanford Budick, ed. *Midrash and Literature.* New Haven, CT: Yale University Press, 1986.

Hickman, Hoyt L., Don E. Saliers, Laurence Hull Stookey, James F. White. *The New Handbook of the Christian Year.* Nashville: Abingdon Press, 1986, 1992.

Hodgson, Peter C. *Christian Faith: A Brief Introduction.* Louisville, KY: Westminster John Knox Press, 2001.

———. *Winds of the Spirit.* Louisville, KY: Westminster John Knox Press, 1994.

Huneke, Douglas K. *The Stones Will Cry Out: Pastoral Reflections on the Shoah (with Liturgical Resources).* Westport, CT: Greenwood Press, 1995.

Jacobs, Steven J. *Contemporary Christian Responses to the Shoah.* Lanham, MD: University Press of America, 1993.

———. *Contemporary Jewish Responses to the Shoah.* Lanham, Md.: University Press of America, 1993.

Knight, Henry F. "Choosing Life between the Fires: Toward an Intentionalist Voice of Faith." In *Remembering for the Future: The Impact of the Holocaust and Genocide on Jews and Christians,* Proceedings of an International Conference. Oxford and London, July 10-17, 1988. Oxford: Pergamon Press, 1989.

———. *Confessing Christ in a Post-Holocaust World: A Midrashic Experiment.* Westport, CT: Greenwood Press, 2000.

———. "The Face of Forgiveness in a Post-Holocaust World." In *AFTER-WORDS: Post-Holocaust Struggles with Forgiveness, Reconciliation, and Justice,* edited by David Patterson and John K. Roth. Seattle: University of Washington Press, 2004.

———. "From Shame to Responsibility and Christian Identity: The Dynamics of Shame and Christian Confession Regarding the Shoah." *Journal of Ecumenical Studies* 35, no. 1 (Winter 1998): 41–62.

———. "The Holy Ground of Hospitality: Good News for a Post-Shoah World?" In Roth and Rittner, *"Good News" after Auschwitz?* Macon, GA: Mercer University Press, 2001.

———. "The Inclusive Call of Covenant Life." *New Conversations: Confronting and Combatting Christian Anti-Judaism* 15, no. 3 (Autumn 1993): 32-36.

Laytner, Anson. *Arguing with God: A Jewish Tradition.* Northvale, NJ: Jason Aronson, 1990.

Levenson, Jon. *The Death and Resurrection of the Beloved Son.* New Haven, CT: Yale University Press, 1993.

Levinas, Emmanuel. *Beyond the Verse: Talmudic Readings and Lectures.* Translated by Gary D. Mole. Bloomington and Indianapolis: Indiana University Press, 1994.

Littell, Franklin. *The Crucifixion of the Jews: The Failure of Christians to Understand the Jewish Experience.* New York: Harper & Row, 1975.

Metz, J. B. *The Emergent Church: The Future of Christianity in a Postbourgeois World.* New York: Crossroad, 1987.

Moore, James F. *Christian Theology after the Shoah: A Re-Interpretation of the Passion Narratives.* Lanham, MD: University Press of America, 1993.

———, special edition ed. *Shofar: Jewish-Christian Dialogue after the Shoah* 15, no. 1 (Fall 1996).

Neusner, Jacob. *The Midrash: An Introduction.* Northvale, NJ: Jason Aronson, 1990.

———. *What Is Midrash?* Philadelphia: Fortress Press, 1987.

Nicholls, William. *Christian Antisemitism: A History of Hate.* Northvale, NJ: Jason Aronson, 1993.

Nicholson, Ernest. *God and His People: Covenant and Theology in the Old Testament.* Oxford: Clarendon Press, 1986.

Novak, David. *Jewish-Christian Dialogue: A Jewish Justification.* New York and Oxford: Oxford University Press, 1989.

Ochs, Peter. *The Return to Scripture in Judaism and Christianity: Essays in Postcritical Scriptural Interpretation.* New York : Paulist Press, 1993.
———. "Returning to Scripture: Trends in Postcritical Scriptural Interpretation." *Cross Currents* 44, no. 4 (Winter 1994/95): 437-51.
Ogeltree, Thomas W. *Hospitality to the Stranger: Dimensions of Moral Understanding.* Philadelphia: Fortress Press, 1985.
Patte, Daniel. *The Gospel according to Matthew: A Structural Commentary on Matthew's Faith.* Philadelphia: Fortress Press, 1987.
Patterson, David, and John K. Roth, eds. *AFTER-WORDS: Post Holocaust Struggles with Forgiveness, Reconciliation, and Justice.* Seattle: University of Washington Press, 2004.
Pawlikowski, John T. "Liturgy and the Holocaust: How Do We Worship in an Age of Genocide?" In *Christian Responses to the Holocaust: Moral and Ethical Issues,* edited by Donald J. Dietrich, 69–176. Syracuse: Syracuse University Press, 2003.
Plaskow, Judith. *Standing Again at Sinai: Judaism from a Feminist Perspective.* San Francisco: Harper & Row, 1990.
Polanyi, Michael and Harry Prosch. *Meaning.* Chicago: University of Chicago Press, 1975.
Ricoeur, Paul. *Figuring the Sacred: Religion, Narrative and Imagination.* Translated by David Pellauer. Edited by Mark I. Wallace. Minneapolis: Fortress Press, 1995.
Ricoeur, Paul, and Andre LeCoque. *Thinking Biblically.* Chicago: University of Chicago Press, 1998.
Rittner, Carol, Steven D. Smith, and Irena Steinfeldt, eds. *The Holocaust and the Christian World: Reflections on the Past, Challenges for the Future.* New York: Continuum, 2000.
Robbins, Jill. *Prodigal Son/Elder Brother: Interpretation and Alterity in Augustine, Petrarch, Kafka, Levinas.* Chicago: University of Chicago Press, 1991.
Roth, John K. and Carol Rittner. *"Good News" after Auschwitz?* Macon, GA: Mercer University Press, 2001.
Rubenstein, Richard L. *After Auschwitz: Radical Theology and Contemporary Judaism.* New York: Bobbs-Merrill, 1966.
Rubenstein, Richard L., and John K. Roth. *Approaches to Auschwitz: The Holocaust and Its Legacy.* Atlanta: John Knox Press, 1987. Rev. and exp., Louisville, KY: Westminster John Knox Press, 2003.
Ruether, Rosemary Radford. *Faith and Fratricide: The Theological Roots of Anti-Semitism,* with an introduction by Gregory Baum. New York: Seabury Press, 1974.
Schottroff, Luise. *Lydia's Impatient Sisters: A Feminist Social History of Early Christianity.* Translated by Barbara and Martin Rumscheidt. Louisville, KY: Westminster John Knox Press, 1995.
Schwartz, Regina. *The Book and the Text: The Bible and Literary Theory.* Oxford: Basil Blackwell, 1990.
———. *The Curse of Cain: The Violent Legacy of Monotheism.* Chicago: University of Chicago Press, 1997.
Scott, Bernard Brandon. *Hear Then the Parables.* Minneapolis: Fortress Press, 1989.
Segal, Alan. *Rebecca's Children: Judaism and Christianity in the Roman World.* Cambridge, MA: Harvard University Press, 1986.
Senior, Donald. *The Passion of Jesus in the Gospel of Matthew.* Wilmington, DE: Michael Glazier, 1985.
Soulen, R. Kendall. *The God of Israel and Christian Theology.* Minneapolis: Augsburg Fortress, 1996.

Spong, John Shelby. *Liberating the Gospels: Reading the Bible with Jewish Eyes.* San Francisco: Harper, 1996.

Steinsaltz, Adin. "The Downfall of Rabbi Eliezer." In *The Strife of the Spirit,* edited by Arthur Kurzweil. Northvale, NJ: Jason Aronson, 1988.

——— . *The Essential Talmud.* Translated by Chaya Galai. New York: Basic Books, 1976.

Stemberger, Günter. *Introduction to the Talmud and Midrash.* Translated and edited by Markus Bockmuehl. Edinburgh: T. & T. Clark, 1991.

van Buren, Paul. *According to the Scriptures: Origins of the Gospel and of the Church's Old Testament.* Grand Rapids: Wm. B. Eerdmans Publishing Co., 1998.

——— . *The Change in the Church's Understanding of the Jewish People*, Westminster Tanner-Mcmurrin Lectures on the History and Philosophy of Religion. Salt Lake City: Westminster College of Salt Lake City, 1990.

van Buren, Paul, Otfried Hofius, J. Christian Beker, et al. *The Church and Israel: Romans 9–11. Princeton Seminary Bulletin* supplementary issue, no. 1, 1990.

Visotzky, Burton. *The Genesis of Ethics: How the Tormented Family of Genesis Leads Us to Moral Development.* New York: Crown Publishers, 1996.

——— . *Reading the Book: Making the Bible a Timeless Text.* New York: Schocken Books, 1996.

Volf, Miroslav. *Exclusion and Embrace: A Theological Exploration of Identity, Otherness, and Reconciliation.* Nashville: Abingdon Press, 1996.

Wallace, Mark I. *Fragments of the Spirit: Nature, Violence, and the Renewal of Creation.* New York: Continuum, 1996.

Waskow, Arthur. *Godwrestling.* New York: Schocken Books, 1978.

Westermann, Claus. *Genesis 12–36: A Commentary.* Translated by John J. Scullion. London: SPCK, 1985.

Wiesel, Elie. *Against Silence: The Voice and Vision of Elie Wiesel.* Edited by Irving Abrahamson. New York: Holocaust Library, 1985.

——— . *All Rivers Run to the Sea.* New York: Alfred A. Knopf, 1995.

——— . *Messengers of God.* New York: Random House, 1976.

——— . *Night.* Translated by Stella Rodway. New York: Bantam Books, 1960.

Williams, Rowan. *Christ on Trial: How the Gospel Unsettles Our Judgment.* Grand Rapids: Wm. B. Eerdmans Publishing Co., 2003.

——— . *Resurrection: Interpreting the Easter Gospel.* Harrisburg, PA: Morehouse Publishing, 1982.

Williamson, Clark M. *A Guest in the House of Israel: Post-Holocaust Church Theology.* Louisville, KY: Westminster/John Knox Press, 1993.

——— . *Way of Blessing, Way of Life: A Christian Theology.* St. Louis: Chalice Press, 1999.

Williamson, Clark M., and Ronald J. Allen. *Interpreting Difficult Texts: Anti-Judaism and Christian Preaching.* Philadelphia: Trinity Press, 1989.

Scripture Index

Subject and Author Index